Level 2

BRICKWORK

NVQ/SVQ and CAA Diploma

3rd Edition

carillion

LRC Stoke Park
GUILDFORD COLLEGE

www.pearsonschoolsandfecolleges.co.uk

✓ Free online support
✓ Useful weblinks
✓ 24 hour online ordering

0845 630 44 44

Heinemann

Part of Pearson

Heinemann is an imprint of Pearson Education Limited, a company incorporated in England and Wales, having its registered office at Edinburgh Gate, Harlow, Essex, CM20 2JE. Registered company number: 872828

www.pearsonschoolsandfecolleges.co.uk

Heinemann is a registered trademark of Pearson Education Limited

Text © Carillion Construction Ltd 2010

First published 2006
Second edition published 2008
Third edition published 2010

14 13 12 11 10
10 9 8 7 6 5 4 3 2 1

British Library Cataloguing in Publication Data is available from the British Library on request.

ISBN 978 0 435027 09 4

Copyright notice

Designed by Wooden Ark
Typeset by Tek-Art
Original illustrations © Pearson Education 2010
Illustrated by Oxford Designers & Illustrators Ltd
Cover design by Wooden Ark
Cover photo/illustration © Construction Photography/ Phil Starling
Printed in the UK by Scotprint, Haddington

Acknowledgements

Every effort has been made to contact copyright holders of material reproduced in this book. Any omissions will be rectified in subsequent printings if notice is given to the publishers.

Websites

The websites used in this book were correct and up-to-date at the time of publication. It is essential for tutors to preview each website before using it in class so as to ensure that the URL is still accurate, relevant and appropriate. We suggest that tutors bookmark useful websites and consider enabling students to access them through the school/college intranet.

The information and activities in this book have been prepared according to the standards reasonably to be expected of a competent trainer in the relevant subject matter. However, you should be aware that errors and omissions can be made and that different employers may adopt different standards and practices over time. Before doing any practical activity, you should always carry out your own Risk Assessment and make your own enquires and investigations into appropriate standards and practices to be observed.

Acknowledgements

Photo acknowledgements
The publisher would like to thank the following for their kind permission to reproduce their photographs:

(Key: b-bottom; c-centre; l-left; r-right; t-top)

Alamy Images: David J. Green 34, Eric Nathan 93/3.7, Geoff du Feu 51, Image Source Pink 14, ImageBroker 89/3.5, 147/4.16, Kirsty Pargeter 135/4.2, Mark Boulton 217, Nikreates 219, Paul Glendell 136, Peter Noyce 99, Pintail Pictures 93/3.8, Travelshots.com 137; **Construction Photography:** Buildpix 121, Damian Gillie 107/3.25, David Stewart-Smith 120, DIY Photolibrary 119/3.47, ImageBroker 131, Ken Price 27/1.10, Make Stock 45, Mark St Maur Sheil 135/4.1, Paul McMullin 107/3.22; **Corbis:** Creasource 53, Natalie Fobes 220/6.46; **CSCS:** 9; **Getty Images:** PhotoDisc 15, Stone / Ralf Gerard 159; **Image Source Ltd:** 85, 214/6.33, 237; **iStockphoto:** Suljo 205; **Jupiterimages:** Photos.com 108; **Martyn F. Chillmaid:** 161; **Masterfile UK Ltd:** Rick Gomez 193; **Pearson Education Ltd:** Chris Honeywell 37/1.17, David Sanderson 38/1.23, 39, 40, Ian Wedgewood 163, 164, 165, 218, Jules Selmes 13, 119/3.48, 148/4.19; **Rex Features:** OJO Images 243; **Robert Down Photography:** 167; **Science Photo Library Ltd:** Garry Watson 17tl; **Shutterstock:** Alex Kosev 37/1.16, Andrey Bayda 17tc, Colour 89/3.6, Diego Cervo 1, Ed Westmacott 37/1.21, Frances A. Miller 27/1.9, IOFoto 37/1.19, Michael Shake 37/1.18, Rob Byron 37/1.20, StillFX 38/1.22, Yobidaba 17tr, Yuri Arcurs 9/INSET

Cover image: Construction Photography: Phil Starling

All other images © Pearson Education Ltd / Gareth Boden

Picture Research by: Chrissie Martin

Every effort has been made to trace the copyright holders and we apologise in advance for any unintentional omissions. We would be pleased to insert the appropriate acknowledgement in any subsequent edition of this publication.

Contents

Introduction

Welcome to NVQ/SVQ CAA Diploma Level 2 Brickwork!

Brickwork combines many different practical and visual skills with a knowledge of specialised materials and techniques. This book will introduce you to the construction trade and in particular the knowledge and skills needed for carrying out thin joint masonry, building solid walling, isolated and attached piers and constructing cavity walling.

About this book

This book has been produced to help you build a sound knowledge and understanding of all aspects of the Diploma and NVQ requirements associated with brickwork.

The information in this book covers the information you will need to attain your Level 2 qualification in Brickwork. Each unit of the book relates to a particular unit of the CAA Diploma and provides the information needed to form the required knowledge and understanding of that area. The book is also designed to support those undertaking the NVQ at Level 2.

This book has been written based on a concept used by Carillion Training Centres for many years. The concept is about providing learners with the necessary information they need to support their studies and at the same time ensuring it is presented in a style which is both manageable and relevant.

This book will also be a useful reference tool for you in your professional life once you have gained your qualifications and are a practising builder.

Qualifications for the construction industry

There are many ways of entering the construction industry, but the most common method is as an apprentice.

Apprenticeships

You can become an apprentice by being employed:

* directly by a construction company who will send you to college
* by a training provider, such as Carillion, which combines construction training with practical work experience.

Construction Skills is the national training organisation for construction in the UK and is responsible for setting training standards.

The framework of an apprenticeship is based around an NVQ (or SVQ in Scotland). These qualifications are developed and approved by industry experts and will measure your practical skills and job knowledge on site.

You will also need to achieve:

- a technical certificate
- the Construction Skills health and safety test
- the appropriate level of functional skills assessment
- an Employers' Rights and Responsibilities briefing.

You will also need to achieve the right qualifications to get on a construction site, including qualifying for the CSCS card scheme.

CAA Diploma

The Construction Awards Alliance (CAA) Diploma was launched on 1 August 2008 to replace Construction Awards. The CAA Diploma is a common testing strategy with knowledge tests for each unit, a practical assignment and the GOLA (Global Online Assessment) test.

The CAA Diploma meets the requirements of the new Qualifications and Credit Framework (QCF) which bases a qualification on the number of credits (with ten learning hours gaining one credit):

- Award (1 to 12 credits)
- Certificate (13 to 36 credits)
- Diploma (37+ credits)

As part of the CAA Diploma you will gain the skills needed for the NVQ, as well as the functional skills knowledge you will need to complete your qualification.

National Vocational Qualifications (NVQs)

NVQs are available to anyone, with no restrictions on age or length or type of training, although learners below a certain age can only perform certain tasks. There are different levels of NVQ which are broken down into units of competence. An NVQ is a 'doing' qualification, which means it lets the industry know that you have the knowledge, skills and ability to actually 'do' something.

NVQs are made up of both mandatory and optional units and the number of units that you need to complete for an NVQ depends on the level and the occupation.

Carillion would like to thank the following people for their contribution to this book: Ralph Need, Kevin Jarvis, David Whitten and John Harvie McLaughlin.

Pearson Education Limited would like to thank the following for providing technical feedback: Rob Harrison from Stoke College and Jim Neil from North Glasgow College.

Features of this book

This book has been fully illustrated with artworks and photographs. These will help to give you more information about a concept or a procedure, as well as helping you to follow a step-by-step procedure, or identify a particular tool or material.

This book also contains a number of different features to help your learning and development.

Functional skills

Functional skills are the skills needed to work independently in everyday life. The references are headed FM for mathematics and FE for English.

Key term

These are new or difficult words. They are picked out in **bold** in the text and then defined in the margin.

Did you know?

This feature gives you interesting facts about the building trade.

Safety tip

This feature gives you guidance for working safely on the tasks in this book.

Find out

These are short activities and research opportunities, designed to help you gain further information about, and understanding of, a topic area.

Working life

This feature gives you a chance to read about and debate a real life work scenario or problem. Why has the situation occurred? What would you do?

Remember

This highlights key facts or concepts, sometimes from earlier in the text, to remind you of important things you will need to think about.

FAQ

These are frequently asked questions appearing at the end of each unit to answer your questions with informative answers from the experts.

Check it out

A series of questions at the end of each unit to check your understanding. Some of these questions may support the collecting of evidence for the NVQ.

Getting ready for assessment

This feature provides guidance for preparing for the practical assessment. It will give you advice on using the theory you have learnt about in a practical way.

Knowledge check

This is a series of multiple choice questions at the end of each unit, in the style of the GOLA end of unit tests.

UNIT 2001

Safe working practices in construction

Health and safety is a vital part of all construction work. All work should be completed in a way that is safe not only for the individual worker, but also for the other workers on the site, people near by and the final users of the building.

Every year in the construction industry many people are killed and many more are seriously injured as a result of the work that they do. Therefore, learning as much as you can about health and safety is very important. This unit also supports NVQ Unit VR01 Conform to General Workplace Safety and VR03 Move and Handle Resources.

This unit contains material that supports TAP Unit 1: Erect and Dismantle Working Platforms. It also contains material that supports the delivery of the five generic units.

This unit will cover the following learning outcomes:

- Health and safety regulations – roles and responsibilities
- Accident/first aid/emergency procedures and reporting
- Hazards on construction sites
- Health and hygiene
- Safe handling of materials and equipment
- Basic working platforms
- Working with electricity
- Use of appropriate personal protective equipment (PPE)
- Fire and emergency procedures
- Safety signs and notices.

K1. Health and safety regulations

While at work, whatever your location or the type of work you are doing, there is important **legislation** you must comply with. Health and safety legislation is there not just to protect you – it also states what you must, and must not do, to ensure that no workers are placed in a situation **hazardous** to themselves or others.

There are hundreds of Acts covering all manner of work from hairdressing to construction. Each Act states the duties of the **employer** and **employee** and you should be aware of both. If an employer or employee does something they shouldn't – or doesn't do something they should – they can end up in court and be fined or even imprisoned.

Approved code of practice, guidance notes and safety policies

As well as Acts, there are two sorts of codes of practice and guidance notes: those produced by the Health and Safety Executive (HSE; see page 4), and those created by companies themselves. Most large construction companies – and many smaller ones – have their own guidance notes, which go further than health and safety law. For example, the law states that everyone must wear safety boots in a hazardous area, but a company's code may state that everyone must wear safety boots at all times. This is called taking a **proactive** approach, rather than a **reactive** one.

Health and safety legislation you need to be aware of

One phrase that often comes up in the legislation is 'so far as is reasonably practicable'. This means that health and safety must be adhered to at all times, but must take a common sense, practical approach.

The Health and Safety at Work Act 1974 (HASAW)

The HASAW applies to all types and places of work and to employers, employees, self-employed people, **subcontractors** and even **suppliers**. The Act is there to protect not only the people at work but also the general public, who may be affected in some way by the work that has been or will be carried out.

The main objectives of the HASAW are to:

- ensure the health, safety and welfare of all persons at work
- protect the general public from all work activities

Key terms

Subcontractor – workers who have been hired by the main contractor to carry out works, usually specialist works, e.g. a general builder may hire a plumber as a subcontractor as none of their staff can do plumbing work

Supplier – a company that supplies goods, materials or services

- control the use, handling, storage and transportation of explosives and highly **flammable** substances
- control the release of noxious or offensive substances into the atmosphere.

To ensure that these objectives are met there are duties for all employers, employees and suppliers.

The employer's duties

Employers must:

- provide safe **access** and **egress** to and within the work area
- provide a safe place to work
- provide and maintain plant and machinery that is safe and without risks to health
- provide information, instruction, training and supervision to ensure the health and safety at work of all employees
- ensure safety and the absence of risks to health in connection with the handling, storage and transportation of articles and substances
- have a written safety policy that must be revised and updated regularly and ensure all employees are aware of it
- involve trade union safety representatives, where appointed, in all matters relating to health and safety
- carry out risk assessments (see page 14) and provide supervision where necessary
- provide and not charge for personal protective equipment (**PPE**).

The employee's duties

Employees must:

- take reasonable care for their own health and safety
- take reasonable care for the health and safety of anyone who may be affected by their acts or **omissions**
- co-operate with their employer or any other person to ensure the legal **obligations** are met
- not misuse or interfere with anything provided for their health and safety
- report hazards and accidents (see page 10)
- use any equipment and safeguards provided by their employer.

The supplier's duties

Persons designing, manufacturing, importing or supplying articles or substances for use at work must ensure that:

Key terms

Flammable – something that is easily lit and burns rapidly

Access – entrance, a way in

Egress – exit, a way out

PPE – personal protective equipment, such as gloves, a safety harness or goggles

Remember

Employers can't charge their employees for anything that has been done or provided for them to ensure that legal requirements on health and safety are met. Self-employed people and subcontractors have the same duties as employees. If they have employees of their own, they must also obey the duties set down for employers

Key terms

Omission – something that has not been done or has been missed out

Obligation –something you have a duty or a responsibility to do

- articles are designed and constructed so that they will be safe and without risk to health at all times while they are being used or constructed
- substances will be safe and without risk to health at all times when being used, handled, transported and stored
- tests on articles and substances are carried out as necessary
- adequate information is provided about the use, handling, transporting and storing of articles or substances.

Health and Safety Executive (HSE)

The HASAW, like most of the other Acts mentioned, is enforced by the Health and Safety Executive (HSE).

The HSE is the government body responsible for the encouragement, regulation and enforcement of health, safety and welfare in the workplace in the UK. It also has responsibility for research into occupational risks in England, Wales and Scotland. In Northern Ireland the responsibility lies with the Health and Safety Executive for Northern Ireland.

The HSE's duties are to:

- assist and encourage anyone who has any dealings with the objectives of the HASAW
- produce and encourage research, publication, training and information on health and safety at work
- ensure that employers, employees, suppliers and other people are provided with an information and advisory service and are kept informed and advised on any health and safety matters
- propose regulations
- enforce the HASAW.

To aid in theses duties the HSE has several resources, including a laboratory used for, among other things, research, development and **forensic investigation** into the causes of accidents. The enforcement of the HASAW is usually delegated to local government bodies such as county or district councils.

An enforcing authority may appoint **inspectors**, who, under the authority, have the power to:

- enter any premises which she or he has reason to believe it is necessary to enter to enforce the Act, at any reasonable time, or in a dangerous situation
- bring a police constable if there is reasonable cause to fear any serious obstruction in carrying out their duty

Did you know?

The HSE now also includes the Health and Safety Commission (HSC) which was merged with it in 2008

Did you know?

Local government bodies can be **enforcing authorities** for several workplaces, including offices, shops, retail and wholesale distribution, hotel and catering establishments, petrol filling stations, residential care homes and the leisure industry

Key terms

Enforcing authorities – an organisation or people who have the authority to enforce certain laws or Acts, as well as providing guidance or advice

Forensic investigation – a branch of science that looks at how things happen

Inspectors – someone who is appointed or employed to inspect/ examine something in order to judge its quality or compliance with any laws

- bring any other person authorised by the enforcing authority and any equipment or materials required
- examine and investigate any circumstance that is necessary for the purpose of enforcing the Act
- give orders that the premises, any part of them or anything therein, shall be left undisturbed for so long as is needed for the purpose of any examination or investigation
- take measurements, photographs and make any recordings considered necessary for the purpose of examination or investigation
- take samples of any articles or substances found and of the atmosphere in or in the vicinity of the premises
- have an article or substance which appears to be a danger to health or safety, dismantled, tested or even destroyed if necessary
- take possession of such an article and detain it for so long as is necessary in order to examine it and ensure that it is not tampered with and that it is available for use as evidence in any **prosecution**
- interview any person believed to have information, ask any questions the inspector thinks fit to ask and ensure all statements are signed as a declaration of the truth of the answers
- require the production of, inspect and take copies of, any entry in any book or document which is necessary for the purposes of any examination or investigation
- utilise any other power which is necessary to enforce the Act.

> **Key term**
>
> **Prosecution** – accusing someone of committing a crime, which usually results in the accused being taken to court and, if found guilty, being punished

Contacting the HSE

Employers, self-employed people or someone in control of work premises have legal duties to record and report to the HSE some work-related accidents. The incidents that must be reported are:

- death, major injury or disease
- dangerous occurrence – an event that may not have caused injury, but could have done so
- over three day injury – an injury at work that results in the worker being away from work for more than three consecutive days.

Construction (Design and Management) Regulations 2007

The Construction (Design and Management) Regulations 2007, often referred to as CDM, are important regulations in the construction industry. They were introduced by the HSE's

Construction Division. The regulations deal mainly with the construction industry and aim to improve safety.

The duties for employers under the regulations are to:

- plan, manage and monitor their own work and that of employees
- check the competence of all their appointees and employees
- train their employees
- provide information to their employees
- comply with the specific requirements in Part 4 of the Regulations, which deals with lighting, excavations, traffic routes, etc.
- ensure there are adequate welfare facilities for their employees.

The duties for employees are to:

- check their own competence
- co-operate with others and co-ordinate work so as to ensure the health and safety of construction workers and others who may be affected by the work
- report obvious risks.

Provision and Use of Work Equipment Regulations 1998 (PUWER)

These regulations cover all new or existing work equipment – leased, hired or second-hand. They apply in most working environments where the HASAW applies, including all industrial, offshore and service operations. PUWER covers starting, stopping, regular use, transport, repair, modification, servicing and cleaning of equipment.

'Work equipment' includes any machinery, appliance, apparatus or tool and any assembly of components that are used in non-domestic premises.

The general duties of the Act require equipment to be:

- suitable for its intended purpose and only to be used in suitable conditions
- maintained in an efficient state and maintenance records kept
- used, repaired and maintained only by a suitably trained person, when that equipment poses a particular risk
- able to be isolated from all its sources of energy
- constructed or adapted to ensure that maintenance can be carried out without risks to health and safety
- fitted with warnings or warning devices as appropriate.

Did you know?

On large projects, a person is appointed as the CDM co-ordinator. This person has overall responsibility for compliance with CDM. There is a general expectation by the HSE that all parties involved in a project will co-operate and co-ordinate with each other

Did you know?

Dumper trucks, circular saws, ladders, overhead projectors and chisels are all covered by PUWER, but substances, private cars and structural items are not

In addition, the Act requires:

- all those who use, supervise or manage work equipment to be suitably trained
- access to any dangerous parts of the machinery to be prevented or controlled
- injury to be prevented from any work equipment that may have a very high or low temperature
- suitable controls to be provided for starting and stopping the work equipment
- suitable emergency stopping systems and braking systems to be fitted to ensure the work equipment is brought to a safe condition as soon as reasonably practicable
- suitable and sufficient lighting to be provided for operating the work equipment.

Functional skills

When reading and understanding Government legislation, you are practising several functional skills:
FE 1.2.1 – Identifying how the main points and ideas are organised in different texts.
FE 1.2.2 – Understanding different texts in detail.
FE 1.2.3 – Read different texts and take appropriate action, e.g. respond to advice/instructions.
If there are any words or phrases you do not understand, use a dictionary, look them up using the Internet or discuss with your tutor.

Other pieces of legislation

Legislation	Content
The Reporting of Injuries, Diseases and Dangerous Occurrences Regulations 1995 (RIDDOR)	Employers have a duty to report accidents, diseases or dangerous occurrences. The HSE uses this information to identify where and how risk arises and to investigate serious accidents.
Control of Substances Hazardous to Health Regulations 2002 (COSHH)	States how employees and employers should work with, handle, store, transport and dispose of potentially hazardous substances. This includes substances used and generated during work (e.g. paints or dust), naturally occurring substances (e.g. sand) and biological elements (e.g. bacteria).
The Control of Noise at Work Regulations 2005	Protects employees from consequences of exposure to noise. These state employers must: • assess the risks to the employee and make sure legal limits are not exceeded • take action to reduce noise exposure and provide hearing protection • provide information, instruction and training.
The Electricity at Work Regulations 1989	Covers any work involving electricity or electrical equipment. Employers must keep electrical systems safe and regularly maintained and do everything to reduce the risk of employers coming into contact with live electrical currents.
The Manual Handling Operations Regulations 1992	Covers all work activities involving a person lifting. Where possible, manual handling should be avoided, but where unavoidable a risk assessment must be carried out, focusing on the load, the individual, the task and the environment.

Legislation	Content
The Personal Protective Equipment at Work Regulations 1992 and 2002 (PPER)	Covers all types of personal protective equipment (PPE) which must be checked prior to use by a trained and competent person, in line with manufacturer's instructions. PPE must be provided by the employer free of charge with a suitable and secure storage place. Employers must ensure employees know the risks PPE will avoid, its purpose, how to maintain it and its limitations. Employees must ensure they are trained to use PPE, they use it in line with instructions, return it to storage after use and report any loss or defect.
The Work at Height Regulations 2005	Ensures employers do all they can to reduce the risk of injury or death from working at height. Employers must avoid working at height where possible and use equipment/safeguards that prevent or minimise the danger of falls. Employees must follow any training, report hazards and use any safety equipment provided.

Remember

Legislation can change or be updated. New legislation can be created as well – this could even supersede all pieces of legislation

Health and safety is a large and varied subject that changes regularly. The introduction of new regulations or updates to current legislation means it is often hard to remember or keep up-to-date. Your tutor will be able to give you information on current legislation.

Any future employers should also keep you updated on any changes to legislation that will affect you. There are also other sources of information that can be accessed to keep you informed. The main sources of Health and Safety Information are shown in the table below.

The Health and Safety Executive	Wide range of information ranging from actual legislation to helpful guides. The website has videos, leaflets and documents available for free download, with specific sections dedicated to different industries. The construction website is www.hse.gov.uk/construction.
Construction Skills	As well as advice on qualifications, they also offer advice on health and safety matters and on sitting the CSCS health and safety test. The website address is www.cskills.org.
Royal Society for the Prevention of Accidents (RoSPA)	Provides information, advice, resources and training and are actively involved in the promotion of safety and accident prevention. The website address is www.rospa.com.
Royal Society for the Promotion of Health (RSPH)	An independent organisation with the goal of promoting and protection of health. Uses advocacy, mediation, knowledge and practice to advise on policy development. Also provides education, training, research, communicates information and provides certification for products, training centres and processes. The website address is www.rsph.org/en/health-promotion.

Site inductions

Site inductions are the process that an individual undergoes in order to accelerate their awareness of the potential health and safety hazards and risks they may face in their working environment but excludes job related skills training.

Different site inductions will include different topics depending on the work that is being carried out. The basic information inductions should contain is:

- the scope of operations carried out at the site, project etc.
- the activities that have health and safety hazards and risks
- the control measures, emergency arrangements and welfare arrangements in place
- the local organisation and management structure
- the consultation procedures and resources for health and safety advice
- the process for reporting near misses.

Inductions are also vital for informing all people working on the site of amenities, restricted areas, dress code (PPE) and even evacuation procedures. Inductions must be carried out by a competent person. Records of all inductions must be kept to ensure that all workers have received an induction. Some sites will even hand out cards to those who have been inducted and people without cards will not be admitted to the site.

Toolbox talks

Toolbox talks are a vital tool used by management, supervisors and employees to deliver basic training and/or to inform all workers of any updates to policy, hazardous activities/areas or other information. They should be delivered by a competent person and a record of all attendees should be kept.

Toolbox talks should be relevant to the people they are being delivered to. The topics can vary from being informative, such as letting everyone know a reclassification of a PPE area, to basic training on the use of a certain tool.

Construction Skills Certification Scheme (CSCS)

The Construction Skills Certification Scheme (CSCS) was introduced to help improve the quality of work and to reduce accidents. It requires all workers to obtain a CSCS card before they are allowed to carry out work on a building site. There

> **Remember**
> A site induction must take place *before* you start work on that site

> **Remember**
> Visitors to the site who may not be actually doing any work should still receive an induction of sorts as they also need to be aware of amenities, restricted areas and procedures etc.

> **Did you know?**
> Toolbox talks don't need to be formal meetings but can be held in a canteen at break time. However a list of all attendees must be kept to ensure that everyone who needs to receive the talk does so

Figure 1.1 CSCS card

Safety tip

You should also be aware of any sirens or warning noises that accompany each and every type of emergency such as bomb scares or fire alarms. Some sites may have different variations of sirens or emergency procedures, so it is vital that you pay attention and listen to all instructions. If you are unsure always ask

Remember

Most accidents are caused by human error, which means someone has done something they shouldn't have done or, just as importantly, not done something they should have done. Accidents often happen when someone is hurrying, not paying enough attention to what they are doing or they have not received the correct training

Remember

An accident that falls under RIDDOR should be reported by the safety officer or site manager and can be reported to the HSE by telephone (0845 300 99 23) or via the RIDDOR website (www.riddor.gov.uk)

are various levels of cards which indicate competence and skill background. This ensures that only skilled and competent tradespeople can carry out the required work on site.

To get a CSCS card all applicants must sit a health and safety test. The aim of the test is to examine knowledge across a wide range of topics in order to improve safety and productivity on site. It is usually taken as a PC-based touch screen test, either at a mobile testing unit or an accredited test centre. The type of card being applied for will determine the level of test that needs to be taken.

As a trainee once you pass the health and safety test you will qualify for a trainee card and once you have achieved a Level 2 qualification you can then upgrade your card to an experienced worker card. Achieving a Level 3 qualification allows you to apply for a gold card. People who make regular visits to site can apply for a visitor card.

K2. Accident, first aid and emergency procedures and reporting

Major types of emergency

There are several major types of emergencies that could occur on site. These include not only accidents but also fires, security alerts and bomb alerts. At your site induction, it should be made perfectly clear to you what you should do in the event of an emergency.

Reporting accidents

All accidents need to be reported and recorded in the accident book and the injured person must report to a trained first aider in order to receive treatment. Serious accidents must be reported under the Reporting of Injuries, Diseases and Dangerous Occurrences Regulations 1995 (RIDDOR).

The nature and seriousness of the accident will decide who it needs to be reported to. There are several types of documentation used to record accidents and emergencies.

Relevant authorised person	What to do
First aiders	All accidents must be reported to a first aider. If you are unsure who they are or cannot contact them, report it to your supervisor.
Supervisors	Must be informed so they can inform the first aider and their manager, and stop the work if necessary to prevent further accidents.
Safety officers	Will be alerted by your supervisor or site manager and will assess the area to check it is safe, investigate the cause of the accident and prepare a report for HSE (if needed).
HSE	Must be reported to immediately if the accident results in death or major injury and followed up by a written report within ten days. This is done on form F2508.
Managers	Should be informed by the supervisor or safety officer as they may need to report to head office. They will also be tasked with contacting the HSE.
Emergency services	Should be contacted as soon as possible. Usually first aiders contact ambulances and supervisors contact the fire brigade. If in doubt call the emergency services yourself.

The accident book

The accident book is completed by the person who had the accident or, if this is not possible, someone who is representing the injured person.

The accident book will ask for some basic details, including:

* who was involved
* what happened and where
* the date and time of the accident
* any witnesses to the accident
* the address of the injured person
* what PPE was being worn
* what first aid treatment was given.

Major and minor accidents

Often an accident will result in an injury which may be minor (e.g. a cut or a bruise) or possibly major (e.g. loss of a limb). Accidents can also be fatal.

Near misses

As well as reporting accidents, 'near misses' must also be reported. A 'near miss' is when an accident nearly happened, but did not actually occur. Reporting near misses might identify a problem and can prevent accidents from happening in the future. This allows a company to be proactive rather than reactive.

Work related injuries in the construction industry

Construction has the largest number of fatal injuries of all the main industry groups. In 2007–2008 there were 72 fatal injuries. This gave a rate of 3.4 people injured per 100,000 workers. The rate of fatal injuries in construction over the past decade has shown a downward trend, although the rate has shown little change in the most recent years.

- From 1999–2000 to 2006–2007 the rate of reported major injuries in construction fell. It is unclear whether the rise in 2007–2008 means an end to this trend. Despite this falling trend, the rate of major injury in construction is the highest of any main industry group (599.2 per 100 000 employees in 2007–2008).

- Compared to other industries, a higher proportion of reported injuries were caused by falls from height, falling objects and contact with moving machinery.

- The THOR-GP surveillance scheme data (2006–2007), indicates a higher rate of work-related illness in construction than across all industries. The rate of self-reported work-related ill health in construction is similar to other industries.

The cost of accidents

As well as the tragedy, pain and suffering that accidents cause they can also have a negative financial and business impact.

> **Remember**
>
> Companies that have a lot of accidents will have a poor company image for health and safety and will find it increasingly difficult to gain future contracts. Unsafe companies with lots of accidents will also see injured people claiming against their insurance which will see their premiums rise. This will eventually make them uninsurable meaning they will not get any work

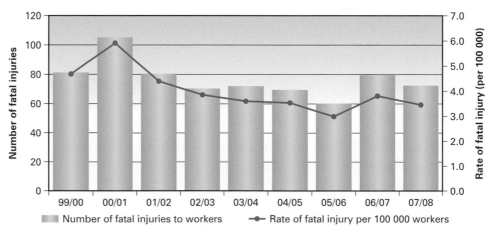

Figure 1.2 Number and rate of fatal injury to workers, 1999–2000 to 2007–2008

Small accidents will affect profits as sick pay may need to be paid. Production may also slow down or stop if the injured person is a specialist. Replacement or temporary workers may need to be used to keep the job going. More serious accidents will see the financial loss rise as the injured person will be off work for longer. This can cause jobs to fall seriously behind and, in extreme cases, may even cause the contractor to lose the job and possibly have to close the site.

First aid

If there are more than five people on a site, then a qualified first aider must be present at all times. On large building sites there must be several first-aiders. A good first aid box should have plasters, bandages, antiseptic wipes, latex gloves, eye patches, slings, wound dressings and safety pins. Other equipment, such as eye wash stations, must also be available if the work being carried out requires it.

Actions for an unsafe area

On discovering an accident the first thing to do is to ensure that the victim is in no further danger. This will require you to do tasks such as switching off the electricity supply. Tasks like this must only be done if there is no danger to yourself. You should then contact the first-aider or emergency services for help.

K3. Hazards on construction sites

A major part of health and safety at work is being able to identify hazards and to help prevent them in the first place, therefore avoiding the risk of injury.

Hazards on the building site

The building industry can be a very dangerous place to work and there are certain hazards that all workers need to be aware of. Some of these common hazards are covered later in this unit: falling from height (page 27), electrical (page 34) and fires (page 39).

Tripping

The main cause of tripping is poor housekeeping. Whether working on scaffolding or on ground level, an untidy workplace is an accident waiting to happen. All workplaces should be kept tidy and free of debris. Not only will this prevent trip hazards, but it

Remember

Health and safety is everyone's duty. If you receive first aid treatment and notice that there are only two plasters left, you should report it to your line manager

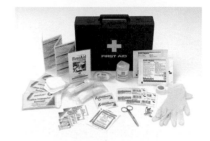

Figure 1.3 A first aid box provides the supplies to deal with minor injuries

Safety tip

Turning off the electricity is just one possible example. There will be specific safety issues for individual jobs the injured individual may have been working on. However, you should always make sure the area is safe before you continue – otherwise you could become a casualty as well

Did you know?

Housekeeping is the simple term used for cleaning up after you and ensuring your work area is clear and tidy. Good housekeeping is vital on a construction site as an unclean work area is dangerous. Correct storage is a big part of housekeeping and is covered on pages 23–26

Figure 1.4 An untidy work site can present many trip hazards

Remember

When a hazardous substance is being used a COSHH or risk assessment will have been made, and it should include a plan for dealing with a spillage

Key term

Carry out a risk assessment – measure the dangers of an activity against the likelihood of accidents taking place

Functional skills

When completing risk assessments you will be practising the following functional skills: FE 1.3.1 – 1.3.5: Write clearly with a level of detail to suit the purpose.

will also prevent costly clean-up operations at the end of the job and will promote a good professional image.

Chemical spills

Chemical spillages can range from minor inconvenience to major disaster. Most spillages are small and create minimal or no risk. If the material involved is not hazardous, it can simply be cleaned up. However, some spills may involve a hazardous material, so it is important to know what to do before the spillage happens so that remedial action can be prompt and harmful effects minimised.

Burns

Burns can occur not only from the obvious source of fire and heat but also from materials containing chemicals such as cement or painter's solvents. Even electricity can cause burns. It is vital when working with materials that you are aware of the hazards they may present and take the necessary precautions.

Risk assessments

You will have noticed that most of the legislation we have looked at requires risk assessments to be carried out. The Management of Health and Safety at Work Regulations 1999 require every employer to make suitable and sufficient assessment of:

- the risks to the health and safety of their employees to which the employees are exposed while at work
- the risks to the health and safety of persons not in their employment arising out of or in connection with their work activities.

It is vital that you know how to **carry out a risk assessment**. Often you may be in a position where you are given direct responsibility for this and the care and attention you take over it may have a direct impact on the safety of others. You must be aware of the dangers or hazards of any task, and know what can be done to prevent or reduce the risk.

There are five steps in a risk assessment:

- **Step 1** – identify the hazards.
- **Step 2** – identify who is at risk.
- **Step 3** – calculate the risk from the hazard against the likelihood of it taking place.
- **Step 4** – introduce measures to reduce the risk.
- **Step 5** – monitor the risk.

Method statements

Method statements are a key safety document that takes the information about significant risks from your risk assessment, and combines them with the job specification, to produce a practical and safe working method for the workers to follow for tasks on site.

Hazard books

The hazard book is a tool used on some sites that identifies hazards within certain tasks and can help to produce risk assessments. The book will list tasks and what hazards are associated with those tasks.

K4. Health and hygiene

As well as keeping an eye out for hazards, you must also make sure that you look after yourself and stay healthy. This is a responsibility that lies with both the employer and the employee.

Staying healthy

One of the easiest ways to stay healthy is to wash your hands on a regular basis. By washing your hands you are preventing hazardous substances from entering your body through ingestion (swallowing). You should always wash your hands after going to the toilet and before eating or drinking. Personal hygiene is vital to ensure good health.

Remember that some health problems do not show symptoms straight away and what you do now can affect you much later in life.

Welfare facilities

Welfare facilities are things such as toilets, which must be provided by your employer to ensure a safe and healthy workplace. There are several things that your employer must provide to meet welfare standards and these are:

- toilets
- washing facilities
- drinking water
- storage room for clothes and personal belongings
- lunch areas.

Remember

There may be different hazards that are associated with tasks. Different working environments can create different types of hazard so risk assessments must always look at the specific task and not a generic one

Figure 1.5 Always wash your hands to prevent ingesting hazardous substances

Safety tip

When placing clothes in a drying room, do not place them directly on to heaters as this can lead to fire

Unit 2001

Safe working pratices in construction

Substance abuse

Substance abuse is a general term and mainly covers things such as drinking alcohol and taking drugs. Taking drugs or inhaling solvents at work is not only illegal, but is also highly dangerous to the person taking them and everyone around them as reduced concentration problems can lead to accidents. Drinking alcohol is also dangerous at work. Going to the pub for lunch and having just one drink can lead to slower reflexes and reduced concentration.

Health effects of noise

Damage to hearing has a range of causes, from ear infections to loud noises. Hearing loss can result from one very loud noise lasting only a few seconds, or from relatively loud noise lasting for hours, such as a drill.

The damage to hearing can be caused by one of two things:

- **Intensity** – you can be hurt in an instant from an explosive or very loud noise which can burst your ear drum.
- **Duration** – noise doesn't have to be deafening to harm you, it can be a quieter noise over a long period e.g. a 12 hour shift.

Hazardous substances

Hazardous substances are a major health and safety risk on a construction site. To this end, they need to be handled, stored, transported and disposed of in very specific ways.

- **Step 1** – assess the risks to health from hazardous substances used or created by employees' activities.
- **Step 2** – decide what precautions are needed.
- **Step 3** – prevent employees from being exposed to any hazardous substances. If prevention is impossible, the risk must be adequately controlled.
- **Step 4** – ensure control methods are used and maintained properly.
- **Step 5** – monitor the exposure of employees to hazardous substances.
- **Step 6** – carry out health surveillance to ascertain if any health problems are occurring.
- **Step 7** – prepare plans and procedures to deal with accidents such as spillages.
- **Step 8** – ensure all employees are properly informed, trained and supervised.

Figure 1.6 Common safety signs for corrosive, toxic and explosive materials

Identifying a substance that may fall under the COSHH regulations is not always easy, but you can ask the supplier or manufacturer for a COSHH data sheet, outlining the risks involved with a substance. Most substance containers carry a warning sign stating whether the contents are corrosive, harmful, toxic or bad for the environment.

Waste

Many different types of waste material are produced in construction work. It is your responsibility to identify the type of waste you have created and the best way of disposing it.

There are several pieces of legislation that dictate the disposal of waste materials. They include:

- Environmental Protection Act 1990
- Controlled Waste Regulations 1992
- Waste Management Licensing Regulations 1994.

Several different types of waste are defined by these regulations:

- **household waste** – normal household rubbish
- **commercial waste** – for example, from shops or offices
- **industrial waste** – from factories and industrial sites.

All waste must be handled properly and disposed of safely. The Controlled Waste Regulations state that only those authorised to do so may dispose of waste and that a record should be kept of all waste disposal.

Hazardous waste

Some types of waste, such as chemicals or material that is toxic or explosive, are too dangerous for normal disposal and must be disposed of with special care. The Hazardous Waste (England and Wales) Regulations cover this disposal. If hazardous material is inside a container the container must be clearly marked and a consignment note completed for its disposal.

Unit 2001

Safe working pratices in construction

Key terms

Symptoms – signs of illness or disease (e.g. difficulty breathing, a sore hand or a lump under the skin)

Leptospirosis – an infectious disease that affects humans and animals. The human form is commonly called Weil's disease. The disease can cause fever, muscle pain and jaundice. In severe cases it can affect the liver and kidneys. Leptospirosis is a germ that is spread by the urine of the infected person. It can often be caught from contaminated soil or water that has been urinated in

Dermatitis – a skin condition where the affected area is red, itchy and sore

Vibration white finger – a condition that can be caused by using vibrating machinery (usually for very long periods of time). The blood supply to the fingers is reduced which causes pain, tingling and sometimes spasms (shaking)

Remember

Activities on site can also damage your body. You could have eye damage, head injury and burns along with other physical wounds

Health risks in the workplace

While working in the construction industry, you will be exposed to substances or situations that may be harmful to your health. Some of these health risks may not be noticeable straight away. It may take years for **symptoms** to be noticed and recognised.

Ill-health can result from:

- exposure to dust (such as asbestos), which can cause eye injuries, breathing problems and cancer
- exposure to solvents or chemicals, which can cause **leptospirosis**, **dermatitis** and other skin problems
- lifting heavy or difficult loads, which can cause back injury and pulled muscles
- exposure to loud noise, which can cause hearing problems and deafness
- exposure to sunlight, which can cause skin cancer
- using vibrating tools, which can cause **vibration white finger** and other problems with the hands
- head injuries, which can lead to blackouts and epilepsy
- cuts, which if infected can lead to disease.

Everyone has a responsibility for health and safety in the construction industry but accidents and health problems still happen too often. Make sure you do what you can to prevent them.

K5. Safe handling of materials and equipment

Manual handling

Manual handling means lifting and moving a piece of equipment or material from one place to another without using machinery. Lifting and moving loads by hand is one of the most common causes of injury at work.

Poor manual handling can cause injuries such as muscle strain, pulled ligaments and hernias. The most common injury by far is spinal injury. Spinal injuries are very serious because there is very little that doctors can do to correct them and, in extreme cases, workers have been left paralysed.

Lifting correctly (kinetic lifting)

When lifting any load it is important to keep the correct posture and to use the correct technique.

The correct posture before lifting:

- feet shoulder width apart with one foot slightly in front of the other
- knees should be bent
- back must be straight
- arms should be as close to the body as possible
- grip must be firm using the whole hand and not just the finger tips.

The correct technique when lifting:

- approach the load squarely facing the direction of travel
- adopt the correct posture
- place hands under the load and pull the load close to your body
- lift the load using your legs and not your back.

When lowering a load you must also adopt the correct posture and technique:

- bend at the knees, not the back
- adjust the load to avoid trapping fingers
- release the load.

Remember

The Manual Handling Operations Regulations 1992 is the key piece of legislation related to manual handling

Safety tip

Most injuries caused by manual handling result from years of lifting items that are too heavy, are awkward shapes or sizes, or from using the wrong technique. However, it is also possible to cause a lifetime of back pain with just one single lift

Remember

Even light loads can cause back problems so when lifting anything, always take care to avoid twisting or stretching

Think before lifting

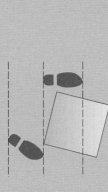

Adopt the correct posture before lifting

Get a good grip on the load

Adopt the correct posture when lifting

Move smoothly with the load

Adopt the correct posture and technique when lowering

Safe handling

Safe manual handling methods are discussed in detail on pages 18–19. When handling any materials or equipment, always think about the health and safety issues involved and remember the manual handling practices explained to you during your induction.

You aren't expected to remember everything but basic common sense will help you to work safely.

- Always wear your safety helmet and boots at work.
- Wear gloves and ear defenders when necessary.
- Keep your work areas free from debris and materials, tools and equipment not being used.
- Wash your hands before eating.
- Use barrier cream before starting work.
- Always use correct lifting techniques.

Ensure you follow instructions given to you at all times when moving any materials or equipment. The main points to remember are:

- Always try to avoid manual handling (or use mechanical means to aid the process).
- Always assess the situation first to decide on the best method of handling the load.
- Always reduce any risks as much as possible (e.g. split a very heavy load, move obstacles from your path before lifting).
- Tell others around you what you are doing.
- If you need help with a load, get it. Don't try to lift something beyond what you can manage.

Did you know?

In 2004/2005 there were over 50 000 injuries while handling, lifting or carrying in the UK (Source: HSE)

Basic health and safety for power tools

Always treat power tools with respect – they have the potential to cause harm either to the person using them or to others around. All power tools used on site should be regularly tested (PAT tested) by a qualified person. There are several health and safety regulations governing the use of power tools. Make sure that you wear suitable PPE at all times and that power tools are operated safely. In some cases, you must be qualified to use them. Refer to PUWER (Provision and Use of Work Equipment Regulations) 1998 if needed.

On-site transformers are used to reduce the mains voltage from 230 volts to 110 volts. All power tools used should be designed for 110 volts.

As well as the traditional powered tools there are also tools powered by gas or compressed air. Gas powered tools, such as nail guns, also require batteries to operate them. They must be handled carefully similar to other power tools.

Special care should be taken with electrical tools.

Always:

- check plugs and connections (make sure you have the correct fuse rating in the plug)
- inspect all leads to ensure there is no damage
- check that the power is off when connecting leads
- unwind extension leads completed from the reel to prevent the cable from overheating.

Never:

- use a tool in a way not recommended by the manufacturer
- use a tool with loose, damaged or makeshift parts
- lay a driver down while it is still switched on
- use a drill unless the chuck (the part in which the drill bit is held) is tight
- throw the tool onto the ground
- pass the tool down by its lead
- use a drill where it is difficult to see what you are doing or to hold the tool tightly
- allow leads to trail in water.

Remember

PAT stands for 'portable appliance testing'

Safety tip

When using power tools, always read the manufacturer's instructions and safety guidelines before use. This will ensure that they are being operated correctly and for the correct purpose

Safe storage and handling of tools and equipment

Tools

All tools need to be stored safely and securely in suitable bags or boxes to protect them from weather and rust. When not in use they should be safely locked away.

Bricks and blocks

Type	Storage and handling issues
Bricks	• Now largely pre-packed and banded using either plastic or metal bands to stop bricks separating until ready for use. Edges are protected by plastic strips to prevent damage during moving. Usually covered in shrink-wrapped plastic to protect from the elements. • Store on level ground close to where they are required and stack no more than two packs high. • Once banding is cut bricks can collapse, so great care must be taken • Bricks should be taken from a minimum of three packs and mixed to stop changes in colour. If bricks are not mixed different colour shades will appear in brickwork – this is called banding. • If unloaded by hand the bricks should be stacked on edge in rows with the ends of stacks bonded and no higher than 1.8 m. All stacks should be covered with tarpaulin or polythene sheets.
Blocks	Made from concrete and may be dense or lightweight. Storage is the same as bricks.
Paving slabs	• Made from concrete or stone in a variety of shapes and sizes. • Normally delivered by lorry in wooden crates, covered in shrink-wrapped plastic, or banded and covered on pallets. Do not stack higher than two packs, to help prevent accidents and weight pressure on slabs which can cause damage. • Store outside and stack on edge to prevent lower slabs being damaged by the weight of the stack. Smaller numbers can be stored flat. Store on firm, level ground with timber bearers below to prevent damage to edges.

Safety tips

• Hand tools with sharp edges should be covered to prevent cuts
• Power tools should be carried by the handle
• Power tools that have gas powered cartridges must be stored in an area that is safe and away from sources of ignition to prevent explosion. Used cartridges must be disposed of safely

Remember

Guidance for the storage of power tools will be provided in the manufacturer's manual. Most power tools come with a plastic carry case that can be used for storage

Functional skills

To store materials safely and correctly, you will need to be familiar with manufacturers' instructions. In doing this you will be practising the following FE 1.2.3: Reading different texts and taking appropriate action.

Safety tip

It is good practice to put an intermediate flat stack in long rows to prevent rows from toppling

Remember

Aggregates can be supplied as bagged materials, as can cement and plaster

Did you know?

On larger sites some companies use a machine spray system to cover large areas with plaster quickly, using many plasterers to complete the work

Aggregates

Aggregates are granules or particles that are mixed with cement and water to make mortar and concrete. Aggregates should be hard, durable and should not contain any form of plant life, or anything that can be dissolved in water.

Aggregates are normally delivered in tipper lorries, although nowadays one tonne bags are available and may be crane handled. The aggregates should be stored on a concrete base, with a fall to allow for any water to drain away. In order to protect aggregates from becoming contaminated with leaves and litter, it is a good idea to situate stores away from trees and cover aggregates with a tarpaulin or plastic sheets.

Cement and plaster

Plaster is made from gypsum, water and cement or lime. Aggregates can also be added depending on the finish desired. Plaster provides a joint-less, smooth, easily decorated surface for internal walls and ceilings. Cement is made from limestone or chalk and is used in the creation of mortar and concrete.

Both cement and plaster are usually available in 25 kg bags. The bags are made from multi-wall layers of paper with a polythene liner. Care must be taken not to puncture the bags before use. Each bag, if offloaded manually, should be stored in a ventilated, waterproof shed, on a dry floor on pallets. If offloaded by crane they should be transferred to the shed and the same storage method used.

The bags should be kept clear of the walls and piled no higher than five bags.

Wood and sheet materials

There are various types of wood and sheet materials available, but the most common are as follows:

Type	Storage and handling issues
Carcassing timber	Store outside under a covered framework, on timber bearers clear of ground, which should be vegetation free, to reduce the risk of ground moisture absorption. Use piling sticks between each layer of timber to provide support and allow air circulation.
Joinery grade and Hardwoods	Store under full cover, preferably in a storage shed. Good ventilation is needed to prevent a build-up of moisture. Store on bearers on a well-prepared base.

Type	Storage and handling issues
Plywood and sheet materials	Store in a dry, well-ventilated environment. Specialised covers are available to give added protection, helping to prevent condensation from other types of sheeting. Stack flat on timber cross-bearers, spaced close together to prevent sagging. Where space is short, store on edge in purpose-made racks. There should be sufficient space for easy loading and removal. Do not lean against walls as this makes the wood bow. For sheet materials with faces, these should be placed against each other to minimise the risk of damage. Keep different sizes, grades and qualities of sheet materials separate. Sheet materials are heavy and easy to damage so extra care is needed when moving them.
Joinery components	These can be doors, kitchen units etc. and must be stored safely and securely. Doors, frames etc. should ideally be stored flat on timber bearers under cover to protect from the weather. In limited space they can be stored upright in a rack, but do not lean against a wall. Wall and floor units must be stacked on a flat surface no more than two units high. Store inside, preferably in the room they are to be fitted in. Use protective sheeting to prevent damage and staining.
Plasterboard	Larger sheets can be very awkward to carry, particularly in strong wind. Store in a flat waterproof area and do not lean against a wall.

Adhesives

Adhesives are substances used to bond (stick) surfaces together. Because of their chemical nature, there are a number of potentially serious risks connected with adhesives if they are not stored, used and handled correctly.

All adhesives should be stored and used in line with the manufacturer's instructions. This usually involves storing them on shelving, with labels facing outward, in a safe, secure area (preferably a lockable store room). It is important to keep the labels facing outwards so that the correct adhesive can be selected.

Figure 1.7 Adhesives should be stored according to the manufacturer's instructions

Remember

Heavy materials should be stored at low levels to aid manual handling and should never be stacked more than two levels high

Paint and decorating equipment

Type	Storage issues
Oil-based	Store on clearly marked shelves with the labels turned to the front. Always order in date order, with new stock at the back. They should be regularly **inverted** to prevent settlement or separation of ingredients and kept tightly sealed to prevent **skinning**. Store at a constant temperature to maintain consistency.
Water based	Store on clearly marked shelves with the labels turned to the front and in date order. Store at a constant temperature and protect from frost to prevent freezing. Use before the use-by-date expires.
Powdered materials	Heavy bags should be stored at ground or platform level. Smaller items can be stored on shelves with loose materials in sealed containers. Protect from frost and moisture and from high humidity. Do not store in the open air.

Figure 1.8 Correct storage of paints

Substances hazardous to health

Some substances a decorator will work with are potentially hazardous to health, with **volatile** and highly flammable characteristics. The COSHH Regulations apply to such materials and detail how they must be stored and handled.

Decorating materials that might be hazardous to health include spirits (i.e. methylated and white), turpentine (turps), paint thinners and varnish removers. These should be stored out of the way on shelves, preferably in a suitable locker or similar room that meets the requirements of COSHH. The temperatures must be kept below 15°C as a warmer environment may cause storage containers to expand and blow up.

K6. Basic working platforms

Fall protection

With any task that involves working at height, the main danger to workers is falling. Although scaffolding, etc. should have edge protection to prevent falls, there are certain tasks where edge protection or scaffolding simply cannot be used.

In these instances some form of fall protection must be in place to prevent the worker falling, keep the fall distance to a minimum or ensure the landing point is cushioned.

Harnesses and lanyards

Harnesses and lanyards are a type of fall-arrest system, which means that, in the event of a slip or fall, the worker will only fall a few feet at most.

The system works with a harness that is attached to the worker and a lanyard attached to a secure beam/eyebolt. If the worker slips, then they will only fall as far as the length of cord/lanyard and will be left hanging, rather than falling to the ground.

Safety netting

Safety netting is also a type of fall-arrest system, but is used mainly on the top floor where there is no higher point to attach a lanyard. The nets are attached to the joists/beams and are used to catch any worker who may slip or fall.

Air bags

An airbag safety system is a form of soft fall-arrest and is comprised of interlinked modular air mattresses that expand together to form a continuous protective safety surface, giving a cushioned soft fall and preventing serious injury.

The system must be kept inflated and should be checked regularly to ensure that it is still functioning. This system is ideal for short fall jobs, but should not be used where a large fall could occur.

Figure 1.9 A harness and lanyard can prevent a worker from falling to the ground

Figure 1.10 Safety netting is used when working at the highest point

Unit 2001 Safe working practices in construction

Stepladders and ladders

Stepladders

A stepladder has a prop, which when folded out allows the ladder to be used without having to lean it against something. Stepladders are one of the most frequently used pieces of access equipment in the construction industry and are often used every day. This means that they are not always treated with the respect they demand.

Stepladders are often misused. They should only be used for work that will take a few minutes to complete. When work is likely to take longer, use a sturdier alternative.

When stepladders are used, the following safety points should be observed:

- Ensure the ground on which the stepladder is to be placed is firm and level. If the ladder rocks or sinks into the ground it should not be used for the work.
- Always open the steps fully.
- Never work off the top tread of the stepladder.
- Always keep your knees below the top tread.
- Never use stepladders to gain additional height on another working platform.
- Always look for the BSI kite mark (Figure 1.11), which shows that the ladder has been made to BSI standards.

A number of other safety points need to be observed depending on the type of stepladder being used.

Figure 1.11 British Standards Institution kitemark

Wooden stepladder

Before using a wooden stepladder, you should check:

- for loose screws, nuts, bolts and hinges
- that the tie ropes between the two sets of **stiles** are in good condition and not frayed
- for splits or cracks in the stiles
- that the treads are not loose or split.

Never paint any part of a wooden stepladder as this can hide defects, which may cause the ladder to fail during use, causing injury.

Aluminium stepladder

Before using an aluminium stepladder:

- check for damage to stiles and treads to see whether they are twisted, badly dented or loose
- ensure you are not working close to live electricity supplies as aluminium will conduct electricity.

Key term

Stiles – the side pieces of a stepladder into which the steps are set

Fibreglass stepladder

Before using a fibreglass stepladder, check for damage to stiles and treads. Once damaged, fibreglass stepladders cannot be repaired and must be disposed of.

Ladders

A ladder, unlike a stepladder, does not have a prop and so has to be leant against something in order for it to be used. Together with stepladders, ladders are one of the most common pieces of equipment used to carry out work at height and to gain access to the work area.

Ladders are also made of timber, aluminium or fibreglass and require similar checks to stepladders before use.

Erecting and using a ladder

The following points should be noted when considering the use of a ladder:

- As with stepladders, ladders are not designed for work of long duration. Alternative working platforms (see pages 31–33) should be considered if the work will take longer than a few minutes.
- The work should not require the use of both hands. One hand should be free to hold the ladder.
- You should be able to do the work without stretching.
- You should make sure that the ladder can be adequately secured to prevent it slipping on the surface it is leaning against.

Pre-use checks

Before using a ladder check its general condition. Make sure that:

- no rungs are damaged or missing
- the stiles are not damaged
- no **tie-rods** are missing
- no repairs have been made to the ladder.

In addition, for wooden ladders ensure that:

- they have not been painted, which may hide defects or damage
- there is no decay or rot
- the ladder is not twisted or warped.

Safety tip

If any faults are revealed when checking a stepladder, it should be taken out of use, reported to the person in charge and a warning notice attached to it to stop anyone using it

Find out

What are the advantages and disadvantages of each type of stepladder?

Did you know?

Ladders and stepladders should be stored under cover to protect them from damage such as rust or rotting

Key term

Tie-rods – metal rods underneath the rungs of a ladder that give extra support to the rungs

Did you know?

On average in the UK, every year 14 people die at work falling from ladders, and nearly 1200 suffer major injuries (source: HSE)

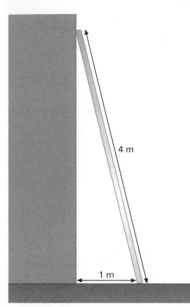

Figure 1.12 Correct angle for a ladder

4 m

1 m

Remember

You must carry out a thorough risk assessment before working from a ladder. Ask yourself, 'Would I be safer using an alternative method?'

Safety tip

A-frame trestles should never be used as a stepladder as they are not designed for this purpose

Erecting a ladder

Observe the following guidelines when erecting a ladder:

- Ensure you have a solid, level base.
- Do not pack anything under either (or both) of the stiles to level it.
- If the ladder is too heavy to put it in position on your own, get someone to help.
- Ensure that there is at least a four rung overlap on each extension section.
- Never rest the ladder on plastic guttering as it may break, causing the ladder to slip and the user to fall.
- Where the base of the ladder is in an exposed position, ensure it is adequately guarded so that no one knocks it or walks into it.
- The ladder should be secured at both the top and bottom. The bottom of the ladder can be secured by a second person. However, this person must not leave the base of the ladder while it is in use.
- The angle of the ladder should be a ratio of 1: 4 (or 75°). This means that the bottom of the ladder is 1 m away from the wall for every 4 m in height (see Figure 1.12).
- The top of the ladder must extend at least 1 m, or five rungs, above its landing point.

Trestle platforms

Frames

A-frames

These are most commonly used by carpenters and painters. As the name suggests, the frame is in the shape of a capital A and can be made from timber, aluminium or fibreglass. Two are used together to support a platform (a scaffold or staging board).

When using A-frames:

- they should always be opened fully and, in the same way as stepladders, must be placed on firm, level ground
- the platform width should be no less than 450 mm
- the overhang of the board at each end of the platform should be not more than four times its thickness.

Steel trestles

These are sturdier than A-frame trestles and are adjustable in height. They are also capable of providing a wider platform than timber trestles. As with the A-frame type, they must be used only on firm and level ground but the trestle itself should be placed on a flat scaffold board on top of the ground. Trestles should not be placed more than 1.2 m apart.

Platforms

Scaffold boards

To ensure that scaffold boards provide a safe working platform, before using them check that they:

- are not split
- are not twisted or warped
- have no large knots, which cause weakness.

Care should be taken when handling scaffold boards as they can be long and unwieldy. Ideally two people should be used when carrying them. It is important to store scaffold boards correctly, that is flat and level, otherwise they will twist or bow. They also need to be kept covered to prevent damage from rain, which could lead to rot.

Staging boards

These are designed to span a greater distance than scaffold boards and can offer a 600 mm wide working platform. They are ideal for use with trestles.

Hop-ups

Also known as step-ups, hop-ups are ideal for reaching low-level work that can be carried out in a relatively short period of time. A hop-up needs to be of sturdy construction and have a base of not less than 600 mm by 500 mm. Hop-ups have the disadvantage that they are heavy and awkward to move around.

Scaffolding

Tubular scaffold is the most commonly used type of scaffolding within the construction industry. There are two types of tubular scaffold:

- **Independent scaffold** – free-standing scaffold that does not rely on any part of the building to support it (although it must be tied to the building to provide additional stability).
- **Putlog scaffold** – scaffolding that is attached to the building via the entry of some of the poles into holes left in the brickwork by the bricklayer. The poles stay in position until the construction is complete and give the scaffold extra support.

No one other than a qualified **carded scaffolder** is allowed to erect or alter scaffolding. Although you are not allowed to erect or alter this type of scaffold, you must be sure it is safe before you work on it.

Safety tip

Do not use items as hop-ups that are not designed for the purpose (e.g. milk crates, stools or chairs). They are usually not very sturdy and can't take the weight of someone standing on them. This may result in falls and injury

Key term

Carded scaffolder
– someone who holds a recognised certificate showing competence in scaffold erection

Figure 1.13 Mobile tower scaffold

Mobile tower scaffolds

Mobile tower scaffolds are so called because they can be moved around without being dismantled. Lockable wheels make this possible and they are used extensively throughout the construction industry by many different trades. A tower can be made from either traditional steel tubes and fittings or aluminium, which is lightweight and easy to move. The aluminium type of tower is normally specially designed and is referred to as a 'proprietary tower'.

A different type of tower scaffold is a 'low tower'. These are designed to be used by one person and have a recommended working height of 2.5 m and a working load of 150 kg. They need no assembly beyond locking in place the platform and handrails, but make sure you follow the manufacturer's instructions to do this.

Erecting a tower scaffold

It is essential that tower scaffolds are situated on a firm and level base. The stability of any tower depends on the height in relation the size of the base:

- for use inside a building, the height should be no more than three-and-a-half times the smallest base length
- for outside use, the height should be no more than three times the smallest base length.

The height of a tower can be increased provided the area of the base is increased **proportionately**. The base area can be increased by fitting outriggers to each corner of the tower.

For mobile towers, the wheels must be in the locked position whilst they are in use and unlocked only when they are being repositioned.

There are several important points you should observe when working from a scaffold tower:

- any working platform above 2 m high must be fitted with guardrails and toe boards; guard rails may also be required at heights of less than 2 m if there is a risk of falling onto potential hazards below, for example reinforcing rods; guardrails must be fitted at a minimum height of 950 mm
- if guardrails and toe boards are needed, they must be positioned on all four sides of the platform
- any tower higher than 9 m must be secured to the structure

- towers must not exceed 12 m in height unless they have been specifically designed for that purpose
- the working platform of any tower must be fully boarded and be at least 600 mm wide
- if the working platform is to be used for materials then the minimum width must be 800 mm
- all towers must have their own access and this should be by an internal ladder.

The dangers of working at height

As well as falling from the height there are additional dangers in working at height that are not present when working at ground level.

Although good housekeeping is important while working at ground level to prevent slips and trips, it is *vital* when working at height. Not only are you at added risk, but materials and tools that are left on a working platform can be knocked off the platform onto people working below. There is a risk of causing serious head injuries to those below – and not just the workforce, as in some instances the working platform may be in an area that involves the general public.

When working in a public area the public must be protected from hazards by way of barriers around the work area. You must also ensure that the sides of the working platform are sealed off to prevent any materials or other objects from falling.

Working life

Ralph and Vijay are working on the second level of some scaffolding, clearing some debris. Ralph suggests that, to speed up the task, they should throw the debris over the edge of the scaffolding into the skip below. The building Ralph and Vijay are working on is on a main road and the skip is not in a closed off area.

What do you think about Ralph's idea? Ralph seems to have forgotten that working at height poses a risk not only to himself and Vijay, but also to the people below them. What might be the effects of following Ralph's plan? The scaffold should be set up to prevent materials from going over the edge, so to follow the plan will already mean having to make the scaffold less safe for Ralph and Vijay.

What should Ralph and Vijay be doing to clear the debris from the scaffold?

K7. Working with electricity

Electricity is a killer. One of the main problems with electricity is that it is invisible. You don't even have to be working with an electric tool to be electrocuted. You can get an electric shock:

- working too close to live overhead cables
- plastering a wall with electric sockets
- carrying out maintenance work on a floor
- drilling into a wall.

Voltages

There are two main types of voltage in use in the UK. These are 230 V and 110 V. The standard UK power supply is 230 V and this is what all the sockets in your house are.

On construction sites 230 V has been deemed as unsafe so 110 V must be used. The 110 V is identified by a yellow casement and different style plug. It works from a transformer which converts the 230 V to 110 V.

When working within domestic dwellings where 230V is the standard power source ideally a portable transformer should be used. If this is not possible then residual current devices (RCD) should be used.

Contained within the wiring there should be three wires: the live and neutral, which carry the alternating current, and the earth wire, which acts as a safety device. The three wires are colour-coded as follows to make them easy to recognise:

Live – Brown
Neutral – Blue
Earth – Yellow and green

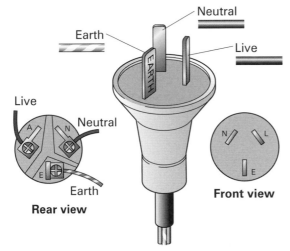

Figure 1.14 Colour coding of the wires in a 230 V plug

Figure 1.15 A 110 V plug

Precautions to take to prevent electric shocks

Never:

- carry electrical equipment by the cable
- remove plugs by pulling on the lead
- allow tools to get wet – if they do, get them checked before use.

Always:

- check equipment, leads and plugs before use – if you find a fault don't use the equipment and tell your supervisor immediately
- keep cables off the ground where possible to avoid damage/ trips
- avoid damage to the cable by keeping it away from sharp edges
- keep the equipment locked away and labelled to prevent it being used by accident
- use cordless tools where possible
- follow instructions on extension leads.

Dealing with electric shocks

In helping the victim of an electric shock, the first thing you must do is disconnect the power supply – if it is safe to do and will not take long to find. Touching the power source may put you in danger.

- If the victim is in contact with something portable, such as a drill, attempt to move it away using a non-conductive object such as a wooden broom.
- Time is precious and separating the victim from the source can prove an effective way to speed the process.
- Don't attempt to touch the affected person until they are free and clear of the supplied power. Be especially careful in wet areas, such as bathrooms – most water will conduct electricity and electrocuting yourself is also possible.

People 'hung up' in a live current flow may think they are calling out for help but most likely no sound will be heard from them. When the muscles contract under household current (most electrocutions happen from house current at home), the person affected will appear in a 'locked-up' state, unable to move or react to you.

- Using a wooden object, swiftly and strongly knock the person free, trying not to injure them, and land them clear of the source.
- The source may also be lifted or removed, if possible, with the same wooden item. This is not recommended on voltages that exceed 500 V.

Safety tip

Don't attempt going near a victim of an electric shock without wearing rubber or some form of insulated sole shoes; bare or socked feet will allow the current to flow to ground through your body as well

K8. Using appropriate PPE

Personal protective equipment (PPE) is the name for clothes and other wearable items that form a line of defence against accidents or injury. PPE is not the only way of preventing accidents or injury. It should be used with all the other methods of staying healthy and safe in the workplace (equipment, training, regulations and laws etc.).

Maintaining and storing PPE

It is important that PPE is regularly well maintained. The effectiveness of the protection it offers will be affected if the PPE is damaged in any way. Maintenance may include:

* cleaning
* examination
* replacement
* repair and testing.

The wearer may be able to carry out simple maintenance (such as cleaning), but more intricate repairs must only be carried out by a competent person. The costs associated with the maintenance of PPE are the responsibility of the employer.

Where PPE is provided, adequate storage facilities for PPE must also be provided for when it is not in use, unless the employee may take PPE away from the workplace (e.g. footwear or clothing).

Accommodation may be simple (e.g. pegs for waterproof clothing or safety helmets) and it need not be fixed (e.g. a case for safety glasses or a container in a vehicle). Storage should be adequate to protect the PPE from contamination, loss, damage, damp or sunlight. Where PPE may become contaminated during use, storage should be separate from any storage provided for ordinary clothing.

All PPE should be 'CE' marked. This will indicate that it complies with the requirements of the Personal Protective Equipment at Work Regulations 2002 (see page 8). The CE marking shows that the PPE satisfies safety requirements. In some cases it may have been tested and certified by an independent body.

The possible consequences of not using PPE can be serious and cause long-term health problems. The health problems and their consequences are described on pages 37–38.

Remember

PPE only works properly if it is being used and used correctly!

The main pieces of legislation that govern the use of PPE are:

* Control of Substances Hazardous to Health 2002
* Provision and Use of Work Equipment Regulations (1992 and 1998)
* Personal Protective Equipment at Work Regulations 1992 and 2002

Types of PPE

Head protection

The most common piece of head protection used in construction is the safety helmet (or hard hat). This protects the head from falling objects and knocks and has an adjustable strap to ensure a snug fit.

Figure 1.16 A safety helmet

Eye protection

Eye protection is used to protect the eyes from dust and flying debris. The three main types are:

- **Safety goggles** – made of a durable plastic and used when there is a danger of dust getting into the eyes or a chance of impact injury.
- **Safety spectacles** – these are also made from a durable plastic but give less protection than goggles. This is because they don't fully enclose the eyes and so only protect from flying debris.
- **Facemasks** – again made of durable plastic, facemasks protect the entire face from flying debris. They do not, however, protect the eyes from dust.

Figure 1.17 Safety goggles

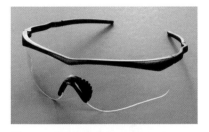

Figure 1.18 Safety spectacles

Foot protection

Safety boots or shoes are used to protect the feet from falling objects and to prevent sharp objects such as nails from injuring the foot. Safety boots should have a steel toe-cap and steel mid-sole.

Hearing protection

Hearing protection is used to prevent damage to the ears caused by a very loud noise. The two most common types are ear-plugs and ear defenders.

- **Ear-plugs** – these are small fibre plugs that are inserted into the ear and used when the noise is not too severe.
- **Ear defenders** – these are worn to cover the entire ear to protect from excessive noise and are connected to a band that fits over the top of the head.

Figure 1.19 Safety boots

Figure 1.20 Ear-plugs

Figure 1.21 Ear defenders

Safety tip

Dust masks only offer protection from non-toxic dust, so if the worker is to be exposed to toxic dust or fumes, a full respiratory system should be used

Respiratory protection

Respiratory protection is used to prevent the worker from breathing in any dust or fumes that may be hazardous. The main type of respiratory protection is the dust mask.

Dust masks are used when working in a dusty environment and are lightweight, comfortable and easy to fit.

Figure 1.22 A respiratory system

Hand protection

There are several types of hand protection and the correct type should be used for each task. For example, wearing lightweight rubber gloves to move glass will not offer much protection, so leather gauntlets must be used. Plastic–coated gloves will protect you from certain chemicals and Kevlar® gloves offer cut resistance.

Figure 1.23 Safety gloves

Skin and sun protection

Another precaution you can take is ensuring that you wear barrier cream. This is a cream used to protect the skin from damage and infection. Don't forget to ensure that your skin is protected from the sun with a good sunscreen, and make sure your back, arms and legs are covered by suitable clothing.

Whole body protection

The rest of the body also needs protecting when working on site. This will usually involve either overalls which protect from dirt and minor cuts, or high-visibility jackets which make the wearer visible at all times.

K9. Fire and emergency procedures

Fires can start almost anywhere and at any time, but a fire needs all the ingredients of 'the triangle of fire' to burn. Remove one side of the triangle and the fire will be extinguished. Fire moves by consuming all these ingredients and burns fuel as it moves.

Figure 1.24 The triangle of fire

Fires can be classified according to the type of material that is involved:

- **Class A** – wood, paper, textiles, etc.
- **Class B** – flammable liquids, petrol, oil, etc.
- **Class C** – flammable gases, liquefied petroleum gas (LPG), propane, etc.
- **Class D** – metal, metal powder, etc.
- **Class E** – electrical equipment.

Fire-fighting equipment

There are several types of fire-fighting equipment, such as fire blankets and fire extinguishers. Each type is designed to be the most effective at putting out a particular class of fire and some should never be used in certain types of fire.

Fire extinguishers

A fire extinguisher is a metal canister containing a substance that can put out a fire. There are several different types and it is important that you learn which type should be used on specific classes of fires.

Fire blankets

Fire blankets are made of a fireproof material and work by smothering the fire and stopping any more oxygen from getting to it, thus putting it out. A fire blanket can also be used if a person is on fire.

What to do in the event of a fire

During your induction to any workplace, you will be made aware of the fire procedure as well as where the fire assembly points (also known as muster points) are and what the alarm sounds like. All muster points should be clearly indicated by signs and a

Find out

What fire risks are there in the construction industry? Think about some of the materials (fuel) and heat sources that could make up two sides of 'the triangle of fire'

Remember

- Remove the fuel – without anything to burn, the fire will go out
- Remove the heat and the fire will go out
- Remove the oxygen and the fire will go out – without oxygen, a fire won't even ignite

Safety tip

It is important to remember that when you put out a fire with a fire blanket, you must take extra care as you will have to get quite close to the fire

Figure 1.25 A fire blanket

Remember

Fire and smoke can kill in seconds, so think and act clearly, quickly and sensibly

map of their location clearly displayed in the building. On hearing the alarm you must stop what you are doing and make your way calmly to the nearest muster point. This is so that everyone can be accounted for. If you do not go to the muster point or if you leave before someone has taken your name, someone may risk their life to go back into the fire to get you.

Fire extinguisher	Colour Band	Main use	Details
Water fire extinguisher	Red	Class A fires	Never use it for an electrical or burning fat/oil fire, as water can conduct the electricity back to the person using the extinguisher. Putting water on oil or fat fires will 'explode' the fire, making it worse.
Foam fire extinguisher	Cream	Class A fires	This can also be used on Class B if no liquid is flowing and on Class C if gas is in liquid form.
Carbon dioxide (CO_2) extinguisher	Black	Class E	Primarily used on electrical fires can also be used in Class A, B and C.
Dry powder extinguisher	Blue	All classes	Most commonly used on electrical and liquid fires. The powder puts out the fire by smothering the flames.

K10. Safety signs and notices

There are many different safety signs but each will usually fit into one of four categories:

1. **Prohibition signs** – these tell you that something *must not* be done. They always have a white background and a red circle with a red line through it.

Figure 1.26 A prohibition sign

2. **Mandatory signs** – these tell you that something *must* be done. They are also circular, but have a white symbol on a blue background.

Figure 1.27 A mandatory sign

3. **Warning signs** – these signs are there to alert you to a specific hazard. They are triangular and have a yellow background and a black border.

Figure 1.28 A warning sign

4. **Safe condition signs** (often called information signs) – these give you useful information like the location of things (e.g. a first aid point). They can be square or rectangular and are green with a white symbol.

Figure 1.29 An information sign

FAQ

Am I protected from electrocution if I am working on a wooden stepladder?

No. If you are working near a live current on a wooden stepladder or if any metal parts of the ladder, such as the tie rods, come into contact with the current, they will conduct the flow of electricity and you may be electrocuted. Take every precaution possible in order to avoid the risk of electrocution – the simplest precaution is turning off the electricity supply.

What determines the type of scaffolding used on a job?

As you will have read in this unit, only a carded scaffolder is allowed to erect or alter scaffolding. They will select the scaffolding to be used according to the ground condition at the site, whether or not people will be working on the scaffolding, the types of materials and equipment that will be used on the scaffolding and the height to which access will be needed.

What happens if there is a delivery of timber but there is no room in the wood store?

It is probably best to remove some of the old stock from the wood store and either store it flat on timber cross-bearers or on edge in racks. This timber should be used first, and as soon as possible. The new timber can now be stored in the wood store.

What should I do if I notice a leakage in the LPG store?

Leaking LPG should be treated as a very dangerous situation. Don't turn on any lights or ignite any naked flames, for example a cigarette lighter. Any kind of spark could ignite the LPG. Report the situation immediately and don't attempt to clear up the spillage yourself.

Check it out

1. What do COSHH and RIDDOR stand for?
2. Describe what might happen to you or your employer if a health and safety law is broken.
3. Write a method statement stating the actions you can take to avoid injury when lifting and carrying loads using manual handling techniques.
4. Describe the class(es) of fire that can be put out with a carbon dioxide (CO_2) extinguisher.
5. Describe why it is important to report 'near misses'.
6. State two sources of health and safety information and give a small explanation of what services they provide.
7. Prepare a method statement, describing what should be covered during a site induction.
8. State why the CSCS scheme was introduced.
9. What are the three key health and safety duties when working at height?
10. Explain the 1:4 (or 75°) ratio rule which should be observed when erecting a ladder.

Getting ready for assessment

The information contained in this unit, as well as continued health and safety good practice throughout your training, will help you with preparing for both your end of unit test and the diploma multiple-choice test. It will also help you to understand the dangers of working in the construction industry. Wherever you work in the construction industry, you will need to understand the dangers of this occupation. You will also need to know the safe working practices for the work required for your synoptic practical assignments.

Your college or training centre should provide you with the opportunity to practise these skills, as part of preparing for the test.

You will need to know about and understand the dangers that could arise, and precautions that can be taken, for:

- the safety rules and regulations
- knowing accident and emergency procedures
- identifying hazards on site
- health and hygiene
- safe handling of materials and equipment
- working at height
- working with electricity
- using personal protective equipment (PPE)
- fire and emergency procedures
- safety signs.

You will need to apply the things you have learnt in this unit to the actual work you will be carrying out in the synoptic test, and in your professional life. For example, with learning outcome six you have seen why basic working platforms are used and the good practice you should use when working on these platforms. You have also seen the different parts of ladders and scaffolding and identified the dangers of working at height. You will now need to use this knowledge yourself when you are working, by using access equipment to the correct legislation and safeguarding your health, through using the correct PPE. You will also need to use your understanding of how PPE should be stored to maintain it in perfect condition.

Before you start work you should always think of a plan of action. You will need to know the clear sequences that materials for the practical are to be constructed to be sure you are not making mistakes as you work and that you are working safely at all times.

Your speed in carrying out these tasks in a practise setting will also help to prepare you for the time set for the test. However you must never rush the test! This is particularly important with health and safety, as you must always make sure you are working safely. Make sure throughout the test that you are wearing appropriate and correct PPE and using tools correctly.

This unit has explained the dangers you may face when working. Understanding these dangers and the precautions that can be taken to help prevent them, will not only aid you in your training but will help you remain safe and healthy throughout your working life.

Good luck!

Knowledge check

1 A risk assessment should be done:

a) when the job involves more than 50 people

b) for every job

c) never

d) only when working on a scaffold

2 Leptospirosis is also know as

a) Weil's disease

b) dermatitis

c) vibration white finger

d) none of the above

3 The most common injury from incorrect manual handling is:

a) broken fingernails

b) spinal injury

c) crushing fingers under item

d) dropping item on toes

4 Who is authorised to alter a scaffold?

a) anyone

b) the site agent

c) a health and safety inspector

d) a qualified, carded scaffolder

5 What is the first thing to do if you suspect a co-worker is having an electric shock?

a) move them away from the power source

b) switch off the power

c) dial 999

d) start first aid procedure

6 With regards to PPE, the employee must:

a) not misuse it

b) wear it when needed

c) report any damage to it

d) do all of the above

7 A fire extinguisher with a red coloured band can be used on:

a) class A fires

b) class B fires

c) class C fires

d) class D fires

8 Under RIDDOR your employer must report:

a) near misses

b) any accident that results in three consecutive work days lost

c) cut fingers

d) all of the above

9 When lifting manually you should:

a) have feet shoulder-width apart

b) have back slightly bent

c) keep load away from body

d) lift using your back muscles

10 Which of the following can be the cause of an electric shock?

a) working too close to electric power lines

b) drilling into an internal brick/block wall

c) plastering walls with electric sockets

d) all of the above

UNIT 2002

Knowledge of information, quantities and communicating with others 2

One of the key skills in all workplaces is the ability to share knowledge and communicate effectively with the people you work with. On any one construction project there will be a whole range of different information sources that you will need to be familiar with. These documents will affect every stage of the construction process, so any changes to them need to be communicated to everyone involved.

Communicating clearly will have a large impact on making sure a team works effectively. This unit also supports NVQ Unit VR02 Conform to Efficient Work Practices. This unit contains material that supports the five generic units. It will also support your completion of scaled drawings throughout all TAP units.

This unit will cover the following learning outcomes:

- How to interpret and produce building information
- How to estimate quantities of resources
- How to communicate workplace requirements effectively.

K1. Interpret and produce building information

There are a number of types of information available. You will be familiar with these from Level 1. The most commonly used are below.

Drawings

Drawings are done by the architect and are used to pass on the client's wishes to the building contractor. Drawings are usually done to scale because it would be impossible to draw a full-sized version of the project. A common scale is 1:10, which means that a line 10 mm long on the drawing represents 100 mm in real life. Drawings often contain symbols instead of written words to get the maximum amount of information across without cluttering the page.

These are covered in more detail on page 54 and include the following types of drawing:

- location drawings
- component range drawings
- assembly or detail drawings.

Work programmes

A method of showing very easily what work is being carried out when. The most common form of work programme is a bar chart, listing tasks down the left side and a timeline across the top.

Procedures

Procedures are the ways in which a company will go about doing things, such as certain tasks. Larger companies will have procedures for most things, such as a procedure for ordering materials, a procedure for making payments, etc.

Hierarchical charts

This chart shows the level of authority and reporting lines for all people working on site, from the top (most authority) to the bottom (least authority).

Mediation

Mediation occurs after a conflict arises between two or more groups who can't agree on an outcome. A mediator is installed to listen to all sides of the debate and try to resolve the conflict by making compromises and changes so that all parties agree.

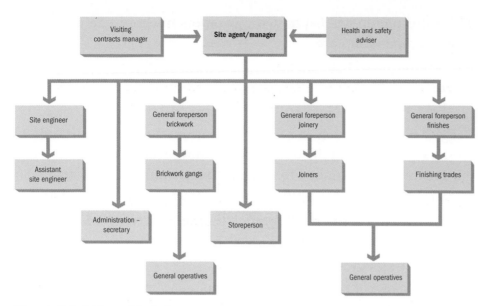

Figure 2.1 A hierarchical chart

Mediators can come from outside organisations. It is important that mediators are not seen to have any stake in the outcome of the solution. If they did, then it could influence the decision that they reach.

Before a mediation, both sides often agree to abide with the final decision of the mediator.

Disciplinary

A disciplinary is what employees receive for breaches in company rules. A disciplinary can either be verbal or written, with serious offences leading to sacking.

The type of disciplinary procedure used will depend on the offence. Most companies will run a three strike system, wherein you will receive three warnings before you are sacked.

Serious breaches such as theft or violence may result in the employee being suspended until an investigation has been carried out. If the findings state the employee has done what they are accused of then it will lead to instant dismissal

Specifications

These accompany a drawing and give you the sizes that are not available on the drawing as well as telling you the type of material to be used and the quality that the work has to be finished to.

Manufacturer's technical information

Everything you buy, whether it is a power tool or a bag of cement, will always come with the manufacturer's technical information.

Did you know?

Organisations are required by law to give at least one written warning before dismissing an employee. However, most employees have clauses in their contract stating that they can be dismissed instantly for a serious breach

Remember

Reading the technical information from the manufacturers will not only give you useful information about how to use the product, it will also allow you to confirm that it is right for the job

This information will list how the component should be used and what its capabilities are.

Power tools often have their technical information provided in a booklet which will give you detailed instructions on how the machine is set up, etc.

Bagged materials, such as cement, will normally have information on the bag. Even lengths of timber will have technical information, but for this you may need to contact the manufacturer. With lengths of timber this is important as timber is stress graded and you need to be sure that the materials you are planning to use are up for the job.

Organisation documentation

No building site functions without paperwork. Some of the key documents include:

- **Timesheet** – these record hours worked and are completed by every employee individually. They can be used to work out how many hours the client will be charged for.
- **Day worksheets** – often confused with timesheets, but different as they are used when there is no price or estimate for the work, to enable the contractor to charge. They record work done, hours worked and sometimes materials used.
- **Job sheet** – this is used when the work has already been priced and enable the worker to see what needs to be done and the site agent to see what has been completed.
- **Variation orders** – used by the architect to make any changes to the original plans, including omissions, alterations and extra works.
- **Confirmation notice –** given to the contractor to confirm any changes made in the variation order, so that the contractor can go ahead.

P. Gresford Building Contractors

Time sheet

Employee ______ Project/site ______

Date	Job no.	Start time	Finish time	Total time	Travel time	Expenses
M						
Tu						
W						
Th						
F						
Sa						
Su						
Totals						

Employee's signature ______

Supervisor's signature ______

Date ______

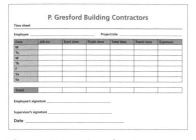

Figure 2.2 A timesheet

P. Gresford Building Contractors

Day worksheet

Customer Chris MacFarlane Date ______

Description of work being carried out ______

Hang internal door in kitchen

Labour	Craft	Hours	Gross rate	TOTALS
Materials	**Quantity**	**Rate**	**% addition**	
Plant	**Hours**	**Rate**	**% addition**	

Comments

Signed ______ Date ______

Site manager/foreman signature ______

Figure 2.3 A day worksheet

P. Gresford Building Contractors

Job sheet

Customer Chris MacFarlane

Address 1 High Street
Any Town
Any County

Work to be carried out

Hang internal door in kitchen

Special conditions/Instructions

Fit with door closer

3 x 75 mm butt hinges

Figure 2.4 A job sheet

VARIATION TO PROPOSED WORKS AT 123 A STREET

REFERENCE NO:

DATE ______

FROM ______

TO ______

POSSIBLE VARIATIONS TO WORK AT 123 A STREET

ADDITIONS

OMISSIONS

SIGNED ....

Figure 2.5 A variation order

CONFIRMATION FOR VARIATION TO PROPOSED WORKS AT 123 A STREET

REFERENCE NO:

DATE ______

FROM ______

TO ______

I CONFIRM THAT I HAVE RECEIVED WRITTEN INSTRUCTIONS
FROM ______
POSITION ______
TO CARRY OUT THE FOLLOWING POSSIBLE VARIATIONS TO THE ABOVE NAMED CONTRACT

ADDITIONS

OMISSIONS

SIGNED ....

Figure 2.6 A confirmation notice

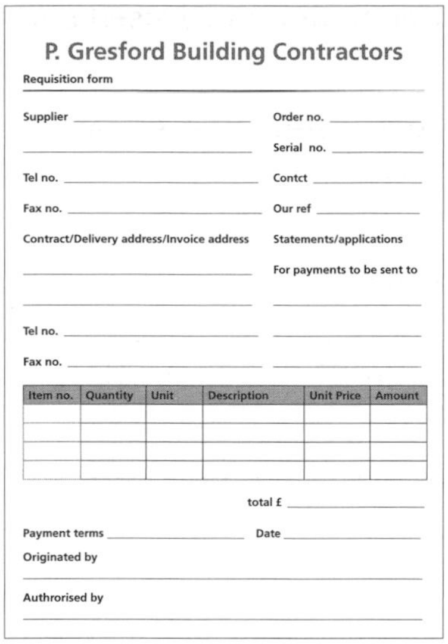

P. Gresford Building Contractors

Requisition form

Supplier ______ Order no. ______

______ Serial no. ______

Tel no. ______ Contct ______

Fax no. ______ Our ref ______

Contract/Delivery address/Invoice address Statements/applications

______ For payments to be sent to

Tel no. ______

Fax no. ______

Item no.	Quantity	Unit	Description	Unit Price	Amount

total £ ______

Payment terms ______ Date ______

Originated by

Authorised by

Figure 2.7 A requisition form

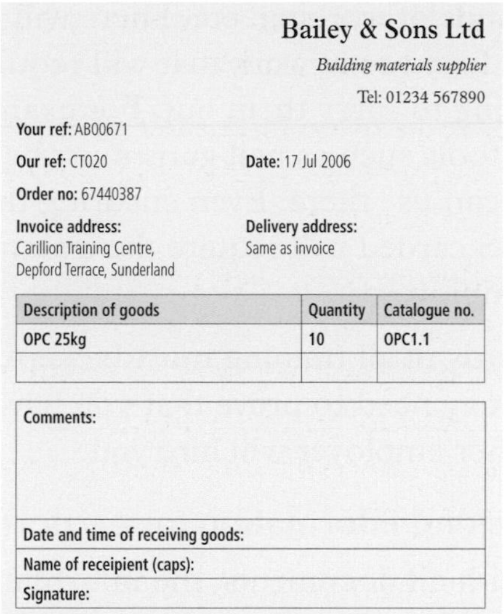

Bailey & Sons Ltd

Building materials supplier

Tel: 01234 567890

Your ref: AB00671

Our ref: CT020 **Date:** 17 Jul 2006

Order no: 67440387

Invoice address: Carillion Training Centre, Depford Terrace, Sunderland

Delivery address: Same as invoice

Description of goods	Quantity	Catalogue no.
OPC 25kg	10	OPC1.1

Comments:

Date and time of receiving goods:

Name of receipient (caps):

Signature:

Figure 2.8 A delivery note

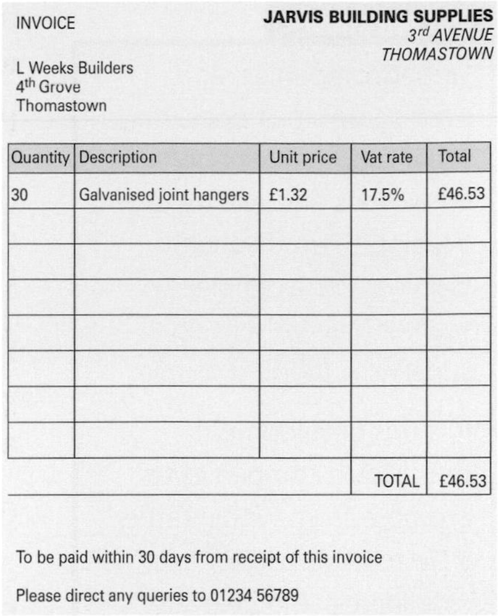

INVOICE

JARVIS BUILDING SUPPLIES
3rd AVENUE
THOMASTOWN

L Weeks Builders
4th Grove
Thomastown

Quantity	Description	Unit price	Vat rate	Total
30	Galvanised joint hangers	£1.32	17.5%	£46.53
			TOTAL	£46.53

To be paid within 30 days from receipt of this invoice

Please direct any queries to 01234 56789

Figure 2.9 An invoice

- **Orders/requisitions** – used to order materials from a supplier.
- **Delivery notes** – given to the contractor by the supplier, listing all the materials and components being delivered. Each should be checked for accuracy against the order and the delivery (to ensure what is delivered is correct and matches the note).
- **Invoices** – these come from a variety of sources and state what services or goods have been provided and the charge for it.
- **Delivery records** – these list all deliveries over a certain period (usually a month) and are sent to the contractor's Head Office so that payment can be made.
- **Daily report** – used to pass general information on to a company's Head Office.
- **Accidents and near miss reports** – a legal requirement that a company has an accident book in which all reports must be made. Reports must also be made when an accident nearly happened, but did not occur – a 'near miss'.

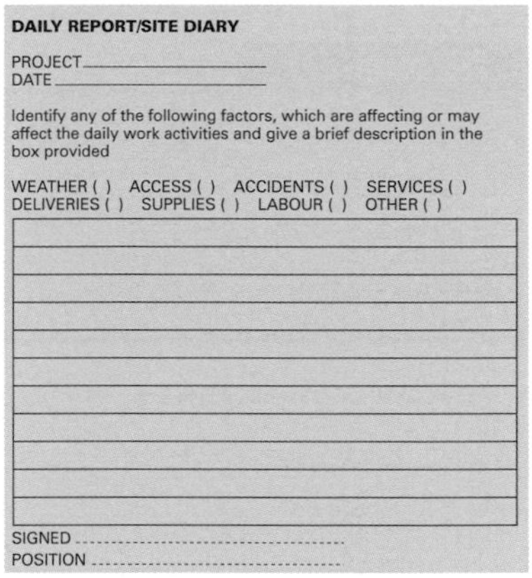

DAILY REPORT/SITE DIARY

PROJECT______

DATE______

Identify any of the following factors, which are affecting or may affect the daily work activities and give a brief description in the box provided

WEATHER ( ) ACCESS ( ) ACCIDENTS ( ) SERVICES ( )
DELIVERIES ( ) SUPPLIES ( ) LABOUR ( ) OTHER ( )

SIGNED ......

POSITION ......

Figure 2.10 A daily report

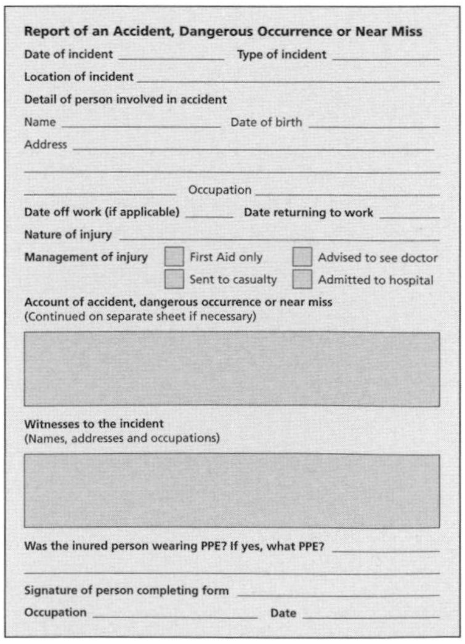

Report of an Accident, Dangerous Occurrence or Near Miss

Date of incident ______ Type of incident ______

Location of incident ______

Detail of person involved in accident

Name ______ Date of birth ______

Address ______

______ Occupation ______

Date off work (if applicable) ______ Date returning to work ______

Nature of injury ______

Management of injury [ ] First Aid only [ ] Advised to see doctor [ ] Sent to casualty [ ] Admitted to hospital

Account of accident, dangerous occurrence or near miss (Continued on separate sheet if necessary)

Witnesses to the incident (Names, addresses and occupations)

Was the inured person wearing PPE? If yes, what PPE? ______

Signature of person completing form ______

Occupation ______ Date ______

Figure 2.11 An accident/near miss report

Training and development records

As learners in the construction industry you are currently undertaking training that will develop your skills. During your training there will be records of what you have been trained in. These are used at the end as evidence so that you can achieve your qualification.

However, training doesn't stop as soon as you qualify! Further training and development is important in the construction industry, especially with technological advances in tools,

Did you know?

Larger companies, and even some small ones, may see the potential of certain employees and will try to develop them through training. For example, a worker may be sent on a supervisor training course.

It is this development that allows companies to promote from within rather than to advertise for external candidates. The next site managers need to come from somewhere!

Key term

Conformity – a document that follows a fixed standard, regulation or requirement

methods of working, etc. There will be certain tasks you are introduced to at work that will require you to receive some training to carry them out. For example, any employee who uses tools such as nail guns must be trained in their uses before they can use them. Even ensuring that all employees are CSCS carded will require the training and development of all employees.

Records of all training must be kept, as if you leave one employer you may need to prove that you have received training before another employer will hire you.

Checking information for conformity

As with all documents, the information above needs to be checked for **conformity.** Using documents that don't conform to, or meet, the companies standards could cause problems, delays or confusion in the building process. For example, faxing a blank piece of paper with a few materials on it to a supplier may be rejected by suppliers which will lead to materials not being ordered and delays to the build.

Only documents that have been approved must be used. If in doubt ask your supervisor.

Contract documents and interpreting specifications

Contract documents are also vital to a construction project. They are created by a team of specialists – the architect, structural engineer, services engineer and quantity surveyor – who first look at the draft of drawings from the architect and client. Just which contract documents this team goes on to produce will vary depending on the size and type of work being done, but will usually include:

- plans and drawings
- specification
- schedules
- bill of quantities
- conditions of contract.

Plans and drawings have already been covered, so here we will start with the specification.

Specification

The specification or 'spec' is a document produced alongside the plans and drawings and is used to show information that cannot be shown on the drawings. Specifications are almost always used, for things such as:

- foundations
- walls
- materials
- surface finish
- floors
- roofs
- components.

The only exceptions might be in the case of very small contracts. A specification should contain:

- **Site description** – a brief description of the site including the address.
- **Restrictions** – what restrictions apply, such as working hours or limited access.
- **Services** – what services are available, what services need to be connected and what type of connection should be used.
- **Materials description** – including type, sizes, quality, moisture content etc.
- **Workmanship** – including methods of fixing, quality of work and finish.

The specification may also name subcontractors or suppliers, or give details such as how the site should be cleared, and so on.

Figure 2.12 A good 'spec' helps avoid confusion when dealing with subcontractors or suppliers

Schedules

A schedule is used to record repeated design information that applies to a range of components or fittings. Schedules are mainly used on bigger sites where there are multiples of several types of house (4-bedroom, 3-bedroom, 3-bedroom with dormers, etc.), each type having different components and fittings. The schedule avoids the wrong component or fitting being put in the wrong house. Schedules can also be used on smaller jobs such as a block of flats with 200 windows, where there are six different types of window.

Bill of quantities

The bill of quantities is produced by the quantity surveyor. It gives a complete description of everything that is required to do the job, including labour, materials and any items or components, based on information from the drawings, specification and schedule. The same bill of quantities is sent out to all prospective contractors so they can submit a tender based on the same information – this helps the client select the best contractor for the job.

All bills of quantities contain the following information:

- **Preliminaries** – general information such as the names of the client and architect, details of the work and descriptions of the site.
- **Preambles** – similar to the specification, outlining the quality and description of materials and workmanship, etc.
- **Measured quantities** – a description of how each task or material is measured with measurements in metres (linear and square), hours, litres, kilograms or simply the number of components required.
- **Provisional quantities** – approximate amounts where items or components cannot be measured accurately.
- **Cost** – the amount of money that will be charged per unit of quantity.

The bill of quantities may also contain:

- any costs that may result from using subcontractors or specialists
- a sum of money for work that has not been finally detailed
- a sum of money to cover contingencies for unforeseen work.

This is an extract from a bill of quantities that might be sent to prospective contractors, who would then complete the cost section and return it as their tender.

To ensure that all contractors interpret and understand the bill of quantities consistently, the Royal Institution of Chartered Surveyors (RICS) and the Building Employers' Confederation produce a document called the *Standard Method of Measurement of Building Works (SMM)*. This provides a uniform basis for

Item ref No	Description	Quantity	Unit	Rate £	Cost £
A1	Treated 50 × 225mm sawn carcass	200	M		
A2	Treated 75 × 225mm sawn carcass	50	M		
B1	50mm galvanised steel joist hangers	20	N/A		
B2	75mm galvanised steel joist hangers	7	N/A		
C1	Supply and fit the above floor joists as described in the preambles				

Figure 2.13 Extract from a bill of quantities

measuring building work, for example stating that carcassing timber is measured by the metre whereas plasterboard is measured in square metres.

Conditions of contract

Almost all building work is carried out under a contract. A small job with a single client (e.g. a loft conversion) will have a basic contract stating that the contractor will do the work to the client's satisfaction, and that the client will pay the contractor the agreed sum of money once the work is finished. Larger contracts with clients such as the Government will have additional clauses, terms or stipulations, which may include any of the following.

Variations

A variation is a modification of the original drawing or specification. The architect, or client, must give the contractor written confirmation of the variation, then the contractor submits a price for the variation to the quantity surveyor (or client, on a small job). Once the price is accepted, the variation work can be completed.

Interim payment

An interim payment schedule may be written into the contract, meaning that the client pays for the work in instalments. The client may pay an amount each month, linked to how far the job has progressed, or may make regular payments regardless of how far the job has progressed.

Final payment

Here the client makes a one-off full payment once the job has been completed to the specification. A final payment scheme may also have additional clauses included, such as:

- **Retention** – this is when the client holds a small percentage of the full payment back for a specified period (usually six months). It may take some time for any defects to show, such as cracks in plaster. If the contractor fixes the defects, they will receive the retention payment; if they don't fix them, the retention payment can be used to hire another contractor to do so.
- **Penalty clause** – this is usually introduced in contracts with a tight deadline, where the building must be finished and ready to operate on time. If the project overruns, the client will be unable to trade in the premises and will lose money, so the contractor will have to compensate the client for lost revenue.

Did you know?

On a poorly run contract, a penalty clause can be very costly and could incur a substantial payment. In an extreme case, the contractor may end up making a loss instead of a profit on the project

Figure 2.14 Maintaining a good relationship will keep the job running smoothly

Types of drawing

Working drawings

Working drawings are scale drawings showing plans, elevations, sections, details and location of a proposed construction. They can be classified as:

- location drawings
- component range drawings
- assembly or detail drawings.

Component range drawings

Component range drawings show the basic sizes and reference system of a standard range of components produced by a manufacturer. This helps in selecting components suitable for a task and available off-the-shelf. An example is shown in Figure 2.15.

Location drawings

Location drawings include block plans and site plans.

Block plans identify the proposed site by giving a bird's eye view of the site in relation to the surrounding area. An example is shown in Figure 2.16.

Site plans give the position of the proposed building and the general layout of the roads, services, drainage etc. on site. An example is shown in Figure 2.17.

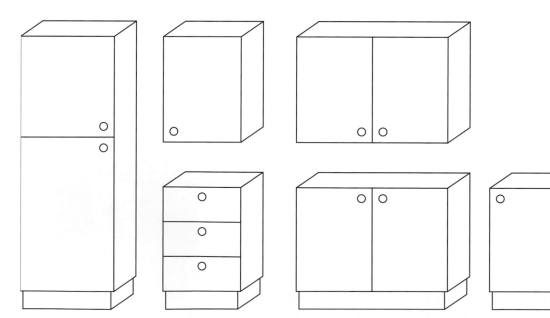

Figure 2.15 Component range drawing

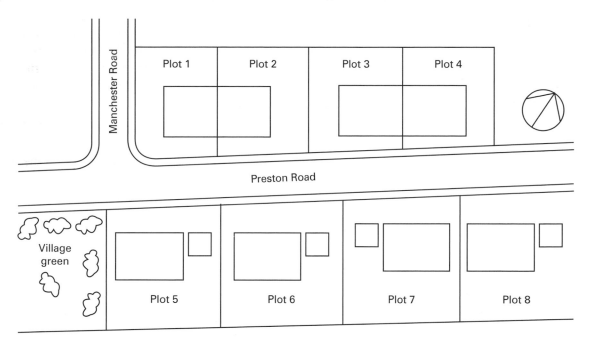

Figure 2.16 Block plan showing location

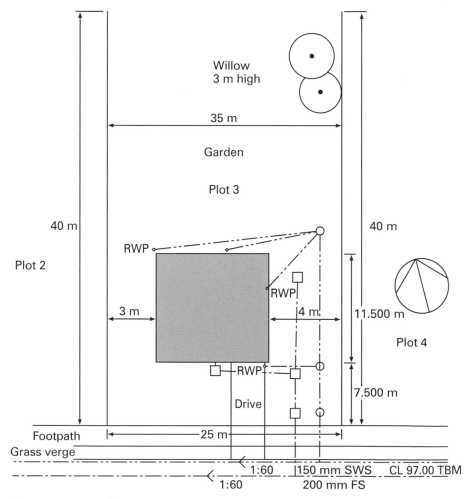

Figure 2.17 Site plan

Unit 2002 Knowledge of information, quantities and communicating with others 2

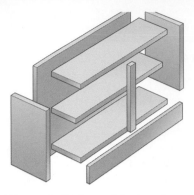

Figure 2.18 Assembly drawing

Assembly or detail drawings

Assembly or detail drawings give all the information required to manufacture a given component. They show how things are put together and what the finished item will look like. An example is shown in Figure 2.18.

Types of projection

Building, engineering and similar drawings aim to give as much information as possible in a way that is easy to understand. They frequently combine several views on a single drawing.

These may be elevations (the view we would see if we stood in front or to the side of the finished building) or plan (the view we would have if we were looking down on it). The view we see depends on where we are looking from. There are then different ways of 'projecting' what we would see onto the drawings.

The two main methods of projection, used on standard building drawings, are orthographic and isometric.

Orthographic projection

Orthographic projection works as if parallel lines were drawn from every point on a model of the building on to a sheet of paper held up behind it (an elevation view), or laid out underneath it (plan view).

There are then different ways that we can display the views on a drawing. The method most commonly used in the building industry for detailed construction drawings, is called 'third angle projection'. In this the front elevation is roughly central. The plan view is drawn directly below the front elevation and all other elevations are drawn in line with the front elevation. An example is shown in Figure 2.19.

Front Elevation

Side Elevation

Figure 2.19 Orthographic projection

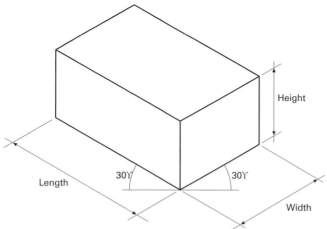

Figure 2.20 Isometric projection of rectangular box

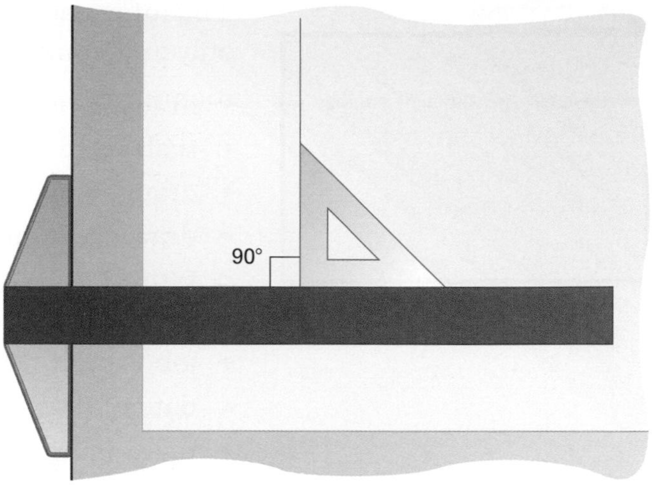

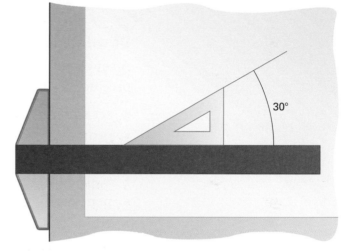

Figure 2.21 Drawing vertical lines

Isometric projection

In isometric views, the object is drawn at an angle where one corner of the object is closest to the viewer. Vertical lines remain vertical, but horizontal lines are drawn at an angle of 30° to the horizontal. This can be seen in Figure 2.20, which shows a simple rectangular box.

Figures 2.21 and 2.22 show the method of drawing these using a T-square and set square.

Datum points

The need to apply levels is required at the beginning of the construction process and continues right up to the completion of building. The whole country is mapped in detail and the Ordnance Survey place datum points (bench marks) at suitable locations from which all levels can be taken.

Figure 2.22 Drawing horizontal lines

The site datum gives a reference point on site from which all levels can be related.

Title panels

Every drawing must have a title panel, which is normally located in the bottom right-hand corner of each drawing sheet. See Figure 2.23 (on page 58) for an example.

Remember

It is important to check the date of a drawing to make sure the most up-to-date version is being used, as revisions to drawings can be frequent

The information contained in the panel is relevant to that drawing only and contains such information as:

- drawing title
- scale used
- draughtsman's name
- drawing number/ project number
- company name
- job/project title
- date of drawing
- revision notes
- projection type.

ARCHITECTS	CLIENT
Peterson, Thompson Associates	Carillion Development
237 Cumberland Way	
Ipswich	**JOB TITLE**
IP3 7FT	Appleford Drive
Tel: 01234 567891	Felixstowe
Fax: 09876 543210	4 bed detached
Email: enquiries@pta.co.uk	

	SCALE 1:50
DRAWING TITLE	
Plan – garage	**DRAWING NO:** 2205-06
DATE: 27.08.2008	**DRAWN BY:** RW

Figure 2.23 Typical title panel

Drawing equipment

A set of good quality drawing equipment is required when producing drawings. It should include:

- set squares (A)
- protractors (B)
- compasses (C)
- scale rule (D)
- pencils (E)
- eraser (F)
- drawing board (G)
- T-square (H)
- dividers.

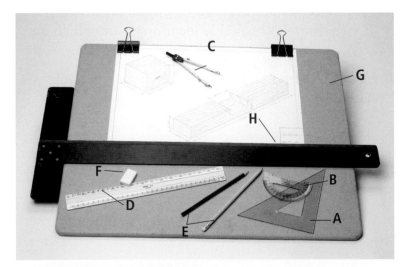

Figure 2.24 Drawing equipment

Set squares

Two set squares are required, one a 45° set square and the other a 60°/30° set square. These are used to draw vertical and inclined lines. A 45° set square (A) is shown in Figure 2.24.

Protractors

Protractors (B) are used for setting out and measuring angles.

Compass and dividers

Compasses (C) are used to draw circles and arcs. Dividers (not shown) are used for transferring measurements and dividing lines.

Scale rule

A scale rule that contains the following scales is to be recommended:

1:5/1:50   1:10/1:100   1:20/1:200   1:250/1:2500

An example (D) is shown in the photo.

The main scales that may be used on location drawings are:

- 1:1
- 1:2
- 1:5
- 1:10
- 1:20
- 1:50

Pencils

Two pencils (E) are required:

- HB for printing and sketching
- 2H or 3H for drawing.

Eraser

A vinyl or rubber eraser (F) is required for alterations or corrections to pencil lines.

Drawing board

A drawing board (G) is made from a smooth flat surface material, with edges truly square and parallel.

T-square

The T-square (H) is used mainly for drawing horizontal lines.

K2. Estimate quantities of resources

To complete estimates of calculations, you will need to be familiar with the mathematical principles behind these calculations.

Calculations

Throughout your career in the construction industry you will have to make use of numbers and calculations in order to plan and carry out work. You will therefore need to make sure you are confident dealing with numbers, which may mean that you have to develop and improve your maths and numeracy skills.

To make estimates, you will need to be familiar with some calculation techniques used in the industry. These methods will help you to make calculate the amounts of materials you will need to use on a project.

Decimal numbers

Most of the time, the numbers we use are whole numbers. For example, we might buy six apples, or two loaves of bread or one car. However, sometimes we need to use numbers that are less than whole numbers, for example, we might eat one and a quarter sandwiches, two and a half cakes and drink three-quarters of a

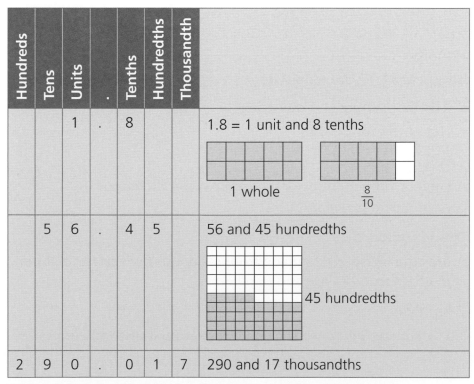

Hundreds	Tens	Units	.	Tenths	Hundredths	Thousandth	
		1	.	8			1.8 = 1 unit and 8 tenths — 1 whole — $\frac{8}{10}$
	5	6	.	4	5		56 and 45 hundredths — 45 hundredths
2	9	0	.	0	1	7	290 and 17 thousandths

Table 2.1 A place value table for digits to the right of a decimal point

cup of tea. You can use decimals to show fractions or parts of quantities. Table 2.1 shows the value of the digits to the right of a decimal point.

Rounding to a number of decimal places

To round a number to a given number of decimal places, look at the digit in the place value position after the one you want.

- If it is 5 or more, round up.
- If it is less than 5, round down.

For example, say we wanted to round 4.634 to two decimal places, the digit in the third decimal place is 4, so we round down. Therefore, 4.634 rounded to 2 decimal places (d.p.) is 4.63.

If we look at the number 16.127, the digit in the third decimal place is 7, so we round up. Therefore, 16.127 rounded to 2 d.p. is 16.13.

Rounding to a number of significant figures

The most significant figure in a number is the digit with the highest place value. To round a number to a given number of significant figures, look at the digit in the place value position after the one you want.

- If it is 5 or more round up.
- If it is less than 5 round down.

For example, say we wanted to write 80,597 to one significant figure, the most significant figure is 8. The second significant figure is 0, so we round down. Therefore, 80,597 to 1 significant figure (s.f.) is 80,000.

If we wanted to write 80,597 to two significant figures, the first two significant figures are 8 and 0. The third significant figure is 5, so we round up. Therefore, 80,597 to 2 s.f. is 81,000.

Multiplying and dividing by 10, 100, 1000...

- To multiply a number by 10, move the digits one place value to the left.
- To multiply a number by 100, move the digits two place values to the left.
- To multiply a number by 1000, move the digits three place values to the left.

For example:

	5		3.25
5 × 10 =	50	3.25 × 10 =	32.5
5 × 100 =	500	3.25 × 100 =	325
5 × 1000 =	5000	3.25 × 1000 =	3250

Did you know?

Knowing about place value helps you to read numbers and to put numbers and quantities in order of size

Remember

If a calculation results in an answer with a lot of decimal places, such as 34.568923, you can round to 1 or 2 decimal places to make it simpler

- To divide a number by 10, move the digits one place value to the right.
- To divide a number by 100, move the digits two place values to the right.
- To divide a number by 1000, move the digits three place values to the right.

For example:

$80\ 000 \div 10 = 8000$	$473.6 \div 10 = 47.36$
$80\ 000 \div 100 = 800$	$473.6 \div 100 = 4.736$
$80\ 000 \div 1000 = 80$	$473.6 \div 1000 = 0.4736$

Converting decimals to fractions

You can use place value to convert a decimal to a fraction. For example:

0.3 is 3 tenths which is $\frac{3}{10}$

0.25 is 25 hundredths which is $\frac{25}{100}$

$\frac{25}{100}$ simplifies to $\frac{1}{4}$ (by dividing the top and bottom numbers by 25)

Table 2.1 (on page 60) shows some useful fraction/decimal equivalents.

See page 64 for more on simplifying fractions.

Multiples

Multiples are the numbers you get when you multiply any number by other numbers. For example:

- the multiples of 3 are 3, 6, 9, 12, 15, 18, 21, 24, 27, 30 and so on
- the multiples of 4 are 4, 8, 12, 16, 20, 24, 28, 32, 36, 40 and so on
- the multiples of 5 are 5, 10, 15, 20, 25, 30, 35, 40, 45, 50 and so on.

Common multiples

Here are the multiples of 3 and 5:

- Multiples of 3: 3, 6, 9, 12, 15, 18, 21, 24, 27, 30, 33, 36…
- Multiples of 5: 5, 10, 15, 20, 25, 30, 35…

3 and 5 have the multiples 15 and 30 in common. 15 and 30 are common multiples of 3 and 5. The lowest common multiple of 3 and 5 is 15.

Did you know?

Knowing how to multiply and divide by 10, 100, 1000 etc. is useful for converting metric units of measurement and finding percentages (see page 66)

Did you know?

Knowing how to convert between fractions and decimals helps with working out parts of quantities and calculating percentages (see page 67)

Remember

The multiples of a number are the numbers in its 'times' table (multiplication table)

Did you know?

Knowing how to find the lowest common multiple of two numbers helps in adding and subtracting fractions (see pages 65–66)

Factors

The factors of a number are the whole numbers that divide into it exactly. For example:

- The factors of 18 are 1, 2, 3, 6, 9 and 18
- The factors of 30 are 1, 2, 3, 5, 6, 10, 15 and 30
- 5 is a factor of 5, 10, 15, 20…
- 7 is a factor of 7, 14, 21, 28…

Common factors

Here are the factors of 28 and 36:

- The factors of 28 are 1, 2, 4, 7, 14, 28
- The factors of 36 are 1, 2, 3, 4, 6, 9, 12, 18, 36

From these lists you can see that 28 and 36 have the factors 1, 2 and 4 in common. 1, 2 and 4 are the common factors of 28 and 36. 4 is the highest common factor of 28 and 36.

Fractions

Fractions describe parts of a whole, for example a half of a pie, a third of a can of cola or a quarter of a cake.

In a fraction:

$\frac{3}{4}$ – the top number is called the numerator
– the bottom number is called the denominator

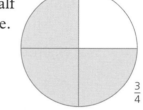

$\frac{3}{4}$

The denominator shows how many *equal parts* the whole is divided into. The numerator shows how many of those parts you have.

Finding a fraction of a quantity

To find a fraction of a quantity you divide by the denominator and multiply by the numerator. For example:

- to find $\frac{1}{2}$ of 500 m, divide by 2 (500 m ÷ 2 = 250 m)
- to find $\frac{2}{5}$ of £40, divide by 5 (£40 ÷ 5 = £8) and multiply by 2 (£8 × 2 = £16)

Equivalent fractions

Two fractions are equivalent if they have the same value. For example:

$\frac{1}{2} = \frac{2}{4} = \frac{3}{6} = \frac{4}{8}$ $\frac{1}{2}$ $\frac{2}{4}$ $\frac{3}{6}$ $\frac{4}{8}$

$\frac{2}{3} = \frac{4}{6} = \frac{6}{9} = \frac{8}{12}$ $\frac{2}{3}$ $\frac{4}{6}$ $\frac{6}{9}$ $\frac{8}{12}$

Did you know?

Knowing multiplication tables will help you to work out factors

Did you know?

Knowing how to find common factors of numbers helps with simplifying fractions (see page 64)

Did you know?

To find equivalent fractions you can:

- multiply the numerator and denominator by the same number
- divide the numerator and denominator by the same number.

Did you know?

To simplify a fraction, divide the numerator and denominator by a common factor of both

Simplifying fractions

To simplify a fraction, write it as an equivalent fraction with smaller numbers in the numerator and denominator.

For example, $\frac{8}{12}$ simplifies to $\frac{2}{3}$

When a fraction cannot be simplified any more, it is in its simplest form, or its lowest terms.

For example:

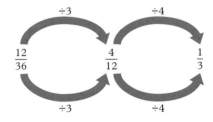

$\frac{12}{36} = \frac{1}{3}$ in its simplest form.

Multiplying fractions

To multiply a fraction by a whole number, multiply the numerator by the whole number.

For example:

$\frac{2}{9} \times 4 = \frac{8}{9}$

To multiply a fraction by another fraction, multiply the numerators and the denominators. For example:

$\frac{2}{3} \times \frac{5}{8} \times \frac{2 \times 5}{3 \times 8} = \frac{10}{24}$

Give the answer in its simplest form:

$\frac{10}{24} = \frac{5}{12}$ (dividing numerator and denominator by 2)

Dividing fractions

To divide one fraction by another, you invert (turn upside down) the fraction you are dividing by and multiply.

For example:

$\frac{3}{4} \div \frac{2}{3} = \frac{3}{4} \times \frac{3}{2} = \frac{9}{8} = 1\frac{1}{8}$

To divide a fraction by a whole number, or to divide a whole number by a fraction, write the whole number as a fraction with denominator 1, and use the same method.

$\frac{4}{5} \div 3 = \frac{4}{5} \div \frac{3}{1} = \frac{4}{5} \times \frac{1}{3} = \frac{4}{15}$

$6 \div \frac{3}{4} = \frac{6}{1} \div \frac{3}{4} = \frac{6}{1} \times \frac{4}{3} = \frac{24}{3} = 8$

Adding fractions

To add fractions with the same denominator, add the numerators.

For example:

$\frac{1}{3} + \frac{1}{3} = \frac{2}{3}$ $\square$ $+$ $\square$ $=$ $\square$

$\frac{1}{3}$ $\frac{1}{3}$ $\frac{2}{3}$

$\frac{1}{5} + \frac{3}{5} = \frac{4}{5}$ $\square$ $+$ $\square$ $=$ $\square$

$\frac{1}{5}$ $\frac{3}{5}$ $\frac{4}{5}$

To add fractions with different denominators, first write the fractions as equivalent fractions with the same denominator. Use the lowest common multiple of the two denominators. You can use any common multiple as the denominator, but using the lowest common multiple keeps the numbers smaller and the calculations simpler.

For example:

$\frac{1}{2} + \frac{1}{3}$

- The denominators are not the same. The lowest common multiple of 2 and 3 is 6.
- To write $\frac{1}{2}$ as an equivalent fraction with denominator 6, multiply numerator and denominator by 3, to give $\frac{3}{6}$
- To write $\frac{1}{3}$ as an equivalent fraction with denominator 6, multiply numerator and denominator by 2, to give $\frac{2}{6}$
- The calculation is now $\frac{3}{6} + \frac{2}{6} = \frac{5}{6}$

A mixed number has a whole number and a fraction part, for example $3\frac{1}{4}$

To add mixed numbers, add together the whole number parts and then the fractions.

For example, if we wanted to add together $1\frac{1}{2}$ and $2\frac{1}{3}$:

- Add the whole numbers: $1 + 2 = 3$
- Now add the fractions: $\frac{1}{2} + \frac{1}{3} = \frac{3}{6} + \frac{2}{6} = \frac{5}{6}$
- Combine the two answers: $1\frac{1}{2} + 2\frac{1}{3} = 3\frac{5}{6}$

Subtracting fractions

To subtract fractions with the same denominator, subtract the numerators.

For example:

$$\frac{7}{8} - \frac{3}{8} = \frac{4}{8} = \frac{1}{2}$$

$$\frac{7}{8} \qquad \frac{3}{8} \qquad \frac{4}{8}$$

To subtract mixed numbers, first write them as improper (top heavy) fractions with a common denominator.

For example: $2\frac{1}{3} - \frac{1}{2} = \frac{7}{3} - \frac{1}{2} = \frac{14}{6} - \frac{3}{6} = 1\frac{5}{6}$

Percentages

Percentages are another way of showing parts of a quantity. Percentage means 'number of parts per hundred'. The symbol % means per cent. For example:

- 1% means 1 out of a hundred or $\frac{1}{100}$
- 10% means 10 out of a hundred or $\frac{10}{100}$
- 84% means 84 out of a hundred or $\frac{84}{100}$
- 100% means the whole quantity.

10%

84%

Finding a percentage of a quantity

To find a percentage of a quantity, find 1% first, by dividing by 100, then multiply by the number you need. For example:

- 20% of £45
- 1% of £45 = $\frac{£45}{100}$ = £45 ÷ 100 = £0.45
- So 20% of £45 = 20 × £0.45 = £9

Did you know?

Percentages are also used for:

- paying deposits – a deposit is a percentage of the whole price (e.g. 20% deposit)
- paying interest – interest is a percentage of money. It is repaid on top of the money (e.g. a loan from a bank of £1000 at 15% interest)
- profit – when charging a client for work you have carried out, you will need to add on to your costs a percentage for your profit
- Value Added Tax (VAT) – VAT is a government tax added to many items or goods that we buy (the standard VAT rate is 17.5%)

Example

A set of paintbrushes costs £12.99. In the sale there is 15% off.

1. How much money do you save by buying the paintbrushes in the sale?
2. What is the sale price of the paintbrushes? Work out 15% of £12.99
   1% of £12.99 = £0.1299
   So 15% of £12.99 = 15 × £0.1299 = £1.9485 = £1.95 to the nearest penny

   You save £1.95
3. The sale price is
   £12.99 – £1.95 = £11.04

Percentage change

A number can be increased or decreased by a percentage. Wages are often increased by a percentage (e.g. a 4% rise in wages). Items are often reduced by a percentage in sales (e.g. 10% off, 20% reduction, etc.).

Ratio

A ratio describes a relationship between quantities. You can read a ratio as a 'for every' statement. For example:

Green paint is made by mixing blue and yellow in the ratio 1 : 2. This means, *for every* 1 litre of blue paint you need 2 litres of yellow paint.

A labourer and a bricklayer agree to share their bonus in the ratio 2 : 5. The bonus is £42. The ratio 2:5 means that for every 2 parts the labourer receives, the bricklayer receives 5 parts. So the bonus needs to be split into 2 + 5 = 7 parts. One part can be calculated: £42 ÷ 7 = £6. Therefore, the labourer receives two parts = 2 × £6 = £12 and the bricklayer receives five parts = 5 × £6 = £30.

Volume

Volume is the amount of space taken up by a 3-D or solid shape. It is measured in cube units, such as cubic centimetres (cm³) and cubic metres (m³).

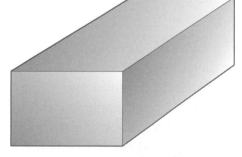

A cuboid is a 3-D shape whose faces are all rectangles.

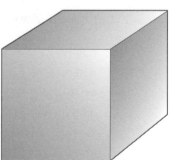

A cube is a 3-D shape whose faces are all squares.

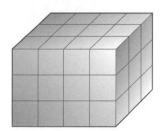

This cuboid is made of 1cm³ cubes.

You can find the volume by counting the cubes. Volume = number of cubes = 36 cm³.

Functional skills

Working with volumes and ratios allows you to practise FM 1.2.1d: Calculate perimeters and areas of 2D and 3D shapes, FM1.2.1i: Use simple formula for one and two-step operations and FM1.2.2: Check accuracy of results.

Did you know?

Scales for scale drawings can also be given as ratios

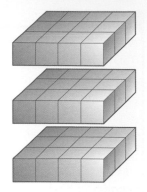

You can also calculate the volume by splitting the solid into equal rectangular layers.

Each layer has 4 × 3 cubes.

There are three layers, so the total number of cubes is 3 × 4 × 3 = 36 cm³.

The volume of a cuboid with length l, width w and height h is:

$$V = l \times w \times h$$

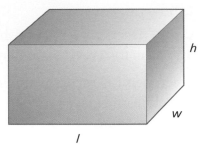

For a cube, length = width = height, so the volume of a cube with side l is:

$$V = l^3$$

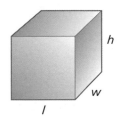

You can find the volume of concrete needed for a rectangular floor by measuring the length and width of the floor, and the depth of the concrete required and using the formula for the volume of a cuboid. For example, we can work out the volume of concrete needed for the floor of a rectangular room with length 3.7 m and width 2.9 m, if the depth of the concrete is to be 0.15 m.

Visualise the floor as a cuboid, like this:

The depth of the concrete (0.15 m) is the height of the cuboid.

$$V = l \times w \times h$$
$$= 3.7 \times 2.9 \times 0.15$$
$$= 1.6095 \text{ m}^3$$
$$= 1.61 \text{ m}^3 \text{ (to 2 d.p.)}$$

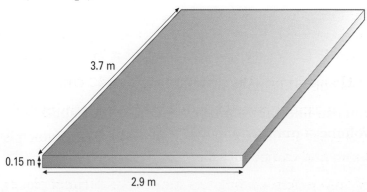

Units of volume

Volume is measured in cube units such as mm^3, cm^3, m^3. The volume of this cube is $1\ cm^3$ or $10 \times 10 \times 10 = 1000\ mm^3$.

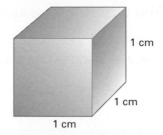

The volume of this cube is $1\ m^3$ or $100 \times 100 \times 100 = 1\ 000\ 000\ cm^3$.

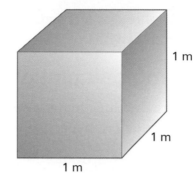

Remember

$1\ cm^3 = 1000\ mm^3$

$1\ m^3 = 1\ 000\ 000\ cm^3$

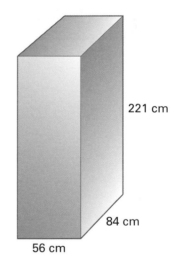

A cuboid is a 3-D shape with rectangular faces (like a box). The formula for the volume of a cuboid is $V = l \times w \times h$. For example, we can calculate the volume of this cuboid:

- in cm^3
- in m^3
- $V = l \times w \times h = 56 \times 84 \times 221 = 1\ 039\ 584\ cm^3$
- $1\ 039\ 584 \div 1\ 000\ 000 = 1.039584\ m^3 = 1.04\ m^3$ (to 2 d.p.)

Rounding to a sensible degree of accuracy

Sometimes measurement calculations give an answer to a large number of decimal places. It is sensible to round the answer to a measurement that is practical. For example, Ahmed has a piece of wood 190 cm long. He wants to cut it into 7 equal lengths.

- He works out $190 \div 7 = 14.28578142$ cm.
- You cannot measure 0.28578142 of a centimetre!

It is sensible to round to 14.3 cm (to 1 d.p.), which is 14 cm and 3 mm and can be measured.

For more on rounding to a number of decimal places, see page 61.

Example

A plasterer calculates the total area of walls in a room as 36 m².

Plasterboard sheets have area 2.88 m².

The number of plasterboard sheets needed is $36 \div 2.88 = 12.5$

If the plasterer buys 12 sheets he will not have enough.

If he buys 13 sheets he will have half a sheet left over.

In this case it is sensible to round up and buy 13 sheets.

You may find there are times when you need to round down.

In some situations it is most sensible to round down. How many 2 metre lengths can be cut from 7 metres of pipe?

$$7 \div 2 = 3.5$$

You can cut three 2 metre lengths. The rest (0.5 of a 2 metre length) is wasted.

So in this case it is sensible to round down: you can only cut three 2 metre lengths.

Using calculations

There are three main areas where you will need to use these types of calculation in a construction setting.

The tender process

Tendering is a competitive process where the contractor works with a specification and drawings from the client and submits a cost estimate for the work (including materials, labour and equipment). Tenders are often invited for large contracts, such as Government contracts, with strict fixed deadlines for the tenders to be received.

An estimator will calculate the total cost in the tender. Using the information in the specification the estimator calculates the amount of materials and labour needed to complete the work. The final tender is based on this estimation.

All the tenders for a contract will then present their case and costs to the client, who will then decide on one business to be offered the contract.

Quoting

A quote is basically part of the tender process but it will only contain pricing information on materials, labour, etc. The quote will state how much the job will cost without any additional information that may appear on a tender, such as using a percentage of the local work force or recycling a certain amount of materials.

The quote is then used as part of the tender to give an idea of the potential cost of a job. Companies submitting tenders will look to make this quote as attractive as possible to the client.

Estimated pricing

Estimated pricing is used to create the quote. An estimator will look at what is required and provide an estimated price for it.

Tenders for jobs may take many months for the successful tender to be selected so an estimator who prices everything up exactly as it is now may be wrong in six months time as the price of labour or materials may have changed. This means they will instead give an estimated price, based on a calculation of how much the materials or labour may cost in the future.

The resources used for making an estimated price and then a final price include:

- materials
- purchase orders
- invoices
- basic time study sheets
- labour schedules
- information technology
- job sheets
- site diaries
- equipment availability lead times
- building supplier's price lists
- book systems used for pricing.

Predicting waste

When working out what materials you require to complete a job it is advisable to add on a certain amount to your calculations for material waste.

This is necessary as if you order the exact amount you require you are not considering any off cuts or damages to the material. Even when cementing or plastering, not all the plaster will go on the wall. Some will fall on the floor and some may go off too quickly if you mix up too much to use in one day. It is generally accepted that between 5% and 10% is added on to the total to allow for waste.

For adding on a percentage you simply need to divide the amount by 100 and then multiply by 100 + whatever the percent is.

Deciding what materials to use

The materials used for the job will depend solely on what the architect agrees with the client. Larger companies will have an agreement with suppliers so that they can order all their materials with them at a discounted rate.

Remember

You also need to make allowance for mistakes, such as cutting materials wrong, as well as more natural waste

Example

300 metres of timber is the required amount and you want to add on 7% for waste so:

$$\frac{300}{100} = 3$$

$$3 \times 107 = 321$$

So with 7% waste you would order 321 metres.

Any specialist materials will be resourced by a buyer. They will look at which companies provide the materials, what the cost is and what attributes the company has, such as do they work with fair trade, etc.

A small company on a smaller job will again discuss this with the client. The client may themselves wish to order the materials so that they are sure they are getting exactly what they want. If not, the company will get the materials from suppliers, such as a local builder's merchant.

Estimating labour rates

The way that labour is paid can be split into two different ways.

Day work/hourly rate

This rate is used when the tradesperson will be paid a specific amount for every hour that they work. The amount will depend on where the work is being carried out, as the cost of living is different in each area.

Places where the cost of living is low may receive £10–£20 per hour. In areas with a high cost of living (such as London) the rate may be £20–£30 per hour. The experience of a worker will also affect the day work rate. Newly qualified Level 2 apprentices will not be paid the same as someone with 30 years of experience.

Price work

This rate is used when the tradesperson will be paid for the work they carry out. Examples of this include a carpenter who receives £20 for every door they hang or a painter who gets £300 for every flat they decorate. This method is often preferred, though it means that you may have to work harder. However, the more work you do the more you will earn.

Again, the prices for these will vary not only from area to area but even within trades. A carpenter may get paid £2000 to fit a truss roof, but only £250 to fit a small kitchen in a flat. A painter may get paid £15 to paint the inside of a window compared with £20 to paint the outside. These differences in price are worked out prior to the job starting and take into account things such as weather or hazards. The roof may look like the best job at £2000, but if it is raining heavily for a week, or alterations to the scaffold are required, then you may not get much work done. You may be able to fit seven kitchens in a week no matter what the weather.

Did you know?

When estimating the labour costs for a job it is easier to use the day work rate method as you can calculate how many hours the job will take

The price work method is calculated by working out how many hours it will take to complete the task and then giving a certain price to that task, based on the day work rate.

For example, the day work rate may be £20 per hour and a roof should take 100 hours. This means a price of £2000 will be put forward.

Remember

The £2000 price is for the whole roof. If four people work on it they will get paid £500 each, not the full £2000

K3. Communicate workplace requirements effectively

Within the construction industry there is a range of different job and career types that you could choose from. What all these job roles have in common, however, is that clear communication with co-workers is always vital.

Job and careers

Jobs and careers in the construction industry fall mainly into one of four categories:

- building
- civil engineering
- electrical engineering
- mechanical engineering.

- **building** – involves the physical construction (making) of a structure. It also involves the maintenance, restoration and refurbishment of structures.

- **civil engineering** – involves the construction and maintenance of work such as roads, railways, bridges etc.

- **electrical engineering** – involves the installation and maintenance of electrical systems and devices such as lights, power sockets and electrical appliances etc.

- **mechanical engineering** – involves the installation and maintenance of things such as heating, ventilation and lifts.

The category that is the most relevant to your course is building.

Job types

The construction industry employs people in four specific areas:

- professionals
- technicians
- building craft workers
- building operatives.

Professionals

Professionals are generally of graduate level (i.e. people who have a degree from a university) and may have one of the following types of job in the construction industry:

- **architect** – someone who designs and draws the building or structure
- **structural engineer** – someone who oversees the strength and structure of the building
- **land surveyor** – someone who checks the land for suitability to build on
- **building surveyor** – someone who provides advice on construction projects
- **service engineer** – someone who plans the services needed within the building, for example gas, electricity and water supplies.

Technicians

Technicians link professional workers with craft workers and are made up of the following people:

- **architectural technician** – someone who looks at the architect's information and makes drawings that can be used by the builder
- **building technician** – someone who is responsible for estimating the cost of the work and materials and general site management
- **quantity surveyor** – someone who calculates ongoing costs and payment for work done.

Building craft workers

Building craft workers are the skilled people who work with materials to physically construct the building. The following jobs fall into this category:

- **carpenter or joiner** – someone who works with wood, but also other construction materials such as plastic and iron;

a carpenter primarily works on site, while a joiner usually works off site, producing components such as windows, stairs, doors, kitchens, and **trusses**, which the carpenter then fits into the building

- **bricklayer** – someone who works with bricks, blocks and cement to build the structure of the building
- **plasterer** – someone who adds finish to the internal walls and ceilings by applying a **plaster skim**; they also make and fix plaster **covings** and plaster decorations
- **painter and decorator** – someone who uses paint and paper to decorate the internal plaster and timberwork such as walls, ceilings, windows and doors, as well as **architraves** and **skirting**
- **electrician** – someone who fits all electrical systems and fittings within a building, including power supplies, lights and power sockets
- **plumber** – someone who fits all water services within a building, including sinks, boilers, water tanks, radiators, toilets and baths; the plumber also deals with lead work and rainwater fittings such as guttering
- **slater and tiler** – someone who fits tiles on to the roof of a building, ensuring that the building is watertight
- **woodworking machinist** – someone who works in a machine shop, converting timber into joinery components such as window sections, spindles for stairs, architraves and skirting boards, amongst other things; they use a variety of machines such as lathes, bench saws, planers and sanders.

Building operatives

There are two different building operatives working on a construction site:

- **Specialist building operative** – someone who carries out specialist operations such as dry wall lining, asphalting, scaffolding, floor and wall tiling and glazing.
- **General building operative** – someone who carries out non-specialist operations such as kerb laying, concreting, path laying and drainage. These operatives also support other craft workers and do general labouring. They use a variety of hand tools and power tools as well as plant, such as dumper trucks and JCBs.

Key terms

Trusses – prefabricated components of a roof which spread the load of a roof over the outer walls and form its shape

Plaster skim – a thin layer of plaster that is put on to walls to give a smooth and even finish

Covings – decorative mouldings that are fitted to the top of a wall where it meets the ceiling

Architrave – a decorative moulding, usually made from timber, that is fitted around door and window frames to hide the gap between the frame and the wall

Skirting – a decorative moulding that is fitted at the bottom of a wall to hide the gap between the wall and the floor

The building team

Constructing a building or structure is a huge task that needs to be done by a team of people who all need to work together towards the same goal. The team of people is often known as the building team and is made up of the following people.

Client

The client is the person who requires the building or refurbishment. This person is the most important person in the building team because they finance the project fully and without the client there is no work. The client can be a single person or a large organisation.

Architect

The architect works closely with the client, interpreting their requirements to produce contract documents that enable the client's wishes to be realised.

Clerk of works

Selected by the architect or client to oversee the actual building process, the clerk of works ensures that construction sticks to agreed deadlines. They also monitor the quality of workmanship.

Local Authority

The Local Authority is responsible for ensuring that construction projects meet relevant planning and building legislation. Planning and building control officers approve and inspect building work.

Quantity surveyor

The quantity surveyor works closely with the architect and client, acting as an accountant for the job. They are responsible for the ongoing evaluation of cost and interim payments from the client, establishing whether or not the contract is on budget. The quantity surveyor will prepare and sign off final accounts when the contract is complete.

Specialist engineers

Specialist engineers assist the architect in specialist areas, such as civil engineering, structural engineering and service engineering.

Health and safety inspectors

Employed by the Health and Safety Executive (HSE), health and safety inspectors ensure that the building contractor fully implements and complies with government health and safety legislation. For more information on health and safety in the construction industry, see Unit 2001 (page 4).

Building contractors

The building contractors agree to carry out building work for the client. Contractors will employ the required workforce based on the size of the contract.

Estimator

The estimator works with the contractor on the cost of carrying out the building contract, listing each item in the bill of quantities (e.g. materials, labour and plant). They calculate the overall cost for the contractor to complete the contract, including further costs as overheads, such as site offices, management administration and pay, not forgetting profit.

Site agent

The site agent works for the building contractor and is responsible for the day-to-day running of the site such as organising deliveries, etc.

Suppliers

The suppliers work with the contractor and estimator to arrange the materials that are needed on site and ensure that they are delivered on time and in good condition.

General foreman

The general foreman works for the site manager and is responsible for coordinating the work of the ganger (see below), craft foreman and subcontractors. They may also be responsible for the hiring and firing of site operatives. The general foreman also liaises with the clerk of works.

Craft foreman

The craft foreman works for the general foreman organising and supervising the work of particular crafts. For example, the carpentry craft foreman will be responsible for all carpenters on site.

Ganger

The ganger supervises general building operatives.

Chargehand

The chargehand is normally employed only on large building projects, being responsible for various craftsmen and working with joiners, bricklayers, and plasterers.

Operatives

Operatives are the workers who carry out the building work, and are divided into three subsections:

1. Craft operatives are skilled tradesman such as joiners, plasterers and bricklayers.
2. Building operatives include general building operatives who are responsible for drain laying, mixing concrete, unloading materials and keeping the site clean.
3. Specialist operatives include tilers, pavers, glaziers, scaffolders and plant operators.

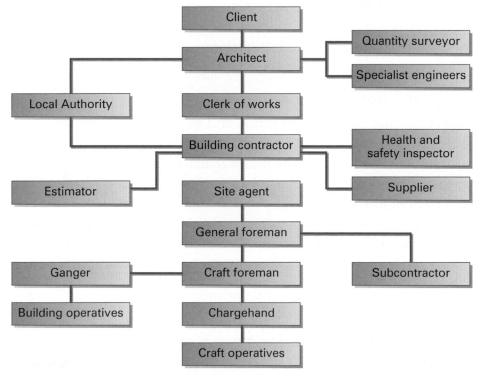

Figure 2.25 The building team

Communicating effectively is an essential skill in every day work. You may be expected to take part in discussions about your work and be asked for your opinions and suggestions. When you do this you will be practising FE 1.1.1 and FE 1.1.3 – 4 which relate to your speaking and listening skills.

Methods of communication

There are many different ways of communicating with others and they all generally fit into one of these four categories:

- **speaking** – (verbal communication) for example talking face-to-face or over the telephone
- **writing** – for example sending a letter or taking a message
- **body language** – for example the way we stand or our facial expressions
- **electronic** – for example email, fax and text messages.

Verbal communication

Verbal communication is instant, easy and can be repeated or rephrased if the message is not understood. However, it can be easily forgotten, or changed if it is passed onto to other people. Accent and slang can make it harder to understand.

Written communication

This provides physical evidence of the message and can be passed on without being changed. It can also be read again if it is not understood. However, it takes longer to arrive and can be misunderstood or lost. Handwritten messages can sometimes be hard to read.

Body language

This can add extra meaning to a communication – if your body language is negative, then this will have an impact on how a positive message is received. Body language can be quick and effective – for example, waving and hand signals.

Electronic communication

This takes the best parts of verbal and written communication, being instant and leaving a record of the message. E-mail can also inform the sender if the message has been sent and received. E-mail attachments also mean larger messages and documents can be sent immediately. However, no signal or flat battery on a mobile phone or wi-fi can stop messages from being sent. Some people are uncomfortable with electronic messages, and e-mail needs the person receiving the message to be at a computer and have access to their account.

Other types of communication

Meetings and performance reviews

Meetings are used to pass on information face-to-face. Meetings can be very useful as they allow information on things such as

Meetings can be an informal 30 minute gathering over a cup of tea or last a full day

safety or job progress to be passed both ways – from the person leading the meeting and from those attending the meeting. The main downside to meetings is that for the duration of the meeting no actual work is getting done.

Performance reviews are done usually as a one to one and allows a line manager to inform the worker of how they are performing in their job. The performance review will record both areas where the worker has done well and areas where they may need to improve. The review should also suggest methods for informing – for example the worker may need more training or might want to have opportunities to progress their career.

The good thing about reviews is that they can be used to stop future problems from occurring, by discussing any failings that the worker may have. They also allow the manager to praise the individual which may have a positive effect. The main negative side of reviews is that the worker may react badly to criticism which may affect their work in the future.

Media and posters/signs

Using media such as posters or signs is a good way of communicating specific information without the need for face-to-face or verbal communication. Safety signs are a good example of this, and a correctly displayed safety sign will inform all who pass it of a particular issue. The downside to media is that not everyone will see the information if it is poorly positioned or poorly designed. A poster or sign that is too cluttered or unclear will often just cause confusion.

Which type of communication should I use?

Of the many different types of communication, the type you should use will depend upon the situation. If someone needs to be told something formally, then written communication is generally the best way. If the message is informal, then verbal communication is usually acceptable.

The way that you communicate will also be affected by who it is you are communicating with. You should of course always communicate in a polite and respectful manner with anyone you have contact with, but you must also be aware of the need to sometimes alter the style of your communication. For example, when talking to a friend, it may be fine to talk in a very informal way and use slang language, but in a work situation with a client or a colleague, it is best to alter your communication to a more formal style in order to show professionalism. In the same way, it may be fine to leave a message or send a text to a friend that says 'C U @ 8 4 wk', but if you wrote this down for a work colleague or a client to read, it would not look very professional and they may not understand it.

Communication and teamwork

When working in a team communication is extremely important as you must be aware of what other members of the team are doing. This is because what you do will not only affect your working but theirs as well, and vice versa. Even simple things like lifting in a group can lead to injuries if there is no communication between the people involved – for example, one person may begin lifting when the others are not ready.

Communicating what has been done or needs to be done is also important. Duplication of labour is a big problem in teams that do not communicate well – you don't want to go and get all the materials and tools ready for a task only to discover when you get there that another member of the team has already done it. Effective communication can prevent this from happening and also help your team to work together more efficiently.

Communicating with other trades

Figure 2.26 You will work with people from other trades

Communicating with other trades is vital because they need to know what you are doing and when, and you need to know the same information from them. Poor communication can lead to delays and mistakes, and both can be costly. It is all too easy for poor communication to lead to work having to be stopped or redone. Imagine you are decorating a room in a new building. You are just about to finish when you find out that the electrician, plumber and carpenter all have work to finish in the room. This information didn't reach you and now the decorating will have to be redone once the other work has been finished. What a waste of time and money. A situation like this can be avoided with good communication between the trades.

Common methods of communicating in the construction industry

A career in construction means that you will often have to use written documents such as drawings, specifications and schedules. These documents can be very large and seem very complicated but, if you understand what they are used for and how they work, using such documents will soon become second nature.

The reasons for clear communication

Clear communication is vital for efficient relations between everyone who may be involved in a business, from the employer and employees through to clients and suppliers. You will have seen throughout this unit that there are several different methods to ensure good communication, and that there are procedures in place to avoid major problems developing in the workplace due to unclear communication.

Most of the crucial moments when you will need to use good, clear and effective communication relate to decisions that will have a wider effect on the business and those working around you. Some examples of these include:

- **Alterations to drawings** – it is important to communicate any changes to these to everyone involved, as all the planning, estimating, material orders and work programmes will be based in part on these drawings. Not communicating changes could lead to mistakes in all these areas.
- **Variations to contracts** – the contract with the client is the crucial document that dictates all decisions that are made on a worksite. Changes to this document must be made known throughout a business.
- **Risk assessments** – the results of these assessments have a direct impact on the safety of workers on site, and should be made known to all.
- **Work restrictions** – these should be communicated to everyone as a restriction is put in place for a specific reason. The restrictions may be put in place for safety reasons. This would mean the area is unsafe so everyone who may be affected needs to be told.

Functional skills

Planning drawings for construction will give you the opportunity to practise the interpreting elements of functional skills, e.g. FM 1.3.1: Judge whether findings answer the original problem; FM 1.3.2: Communicate solutions to answer practical problems.

Working life

James is about to draw a kitchen plan for a client. Where would you begin if you were in his shoes?

Think about who to consult when planning a drawing. When talking to the client, what should James ask about? Appliances, the positioning of electrical points, and the way the client intends the kitchen to be used are as important as budget and design choices.

What other considerations are there? James will need to take into account openings for doors and windows, as well as supplies for essential services like water, gas, and electricity.

What other things would you include when drawing up plans?

FAQ

How many different forms are there?

A lot of forms are used in the building industry and some companies use more than others. You should ensure you get the relevant training on completing any form before using it.

How do I know what scale the drawing is at?

The scale should be written on the title panel (the box included on a plan or drawing giving basic information such as who drew it, how to contact them, the date and the scale).

How do I know if I need a schedule?

Schedules are only really used in large jobs where there is a lot of repeated design information. If your job has a lot of doors, windows etc., it is a good idea to use one.

Check it out

1. What information must be in your contract of employment? Write a list, explaining what each piece of information means.
2. Explain who draws up the plan, and their role in the construction process.
3. State three different types of drawings and give a suitable scale for each one. Draw up an example of each type of drawing you have selected.
4. State three of the main contract documents, and explain briefly what is important about each of them and the information they contain.
5. Explain the main purpose of a specification, and the information it contains.
6. What is the purpose of the bill of quantities?
7. What is a penalty clause? Describe a situation where a penalty clause might be used.
8. What is a confirmation notice?
9. Why when calculating quantities of materials do you allow for wastage? Give an example of wastage on site and calculate how you might need to take this into account.
10. Name a job in each of the four construction employment areas: professional; technician; building craft worker; building operative. Prepare a brief job description for the job you have selected.
11. Explain why the client is the most important member of the building team.
12. Show with the aid of a sketch, how the area and circumference of a circle is worked out.

Getting ready for assessment

The information contained in this unit, as well as continued practical assignments that you will carry out in your college or training centre, will help you with preparing for both your end of unit test and the diploma multiple-choice test. It will also aid you in preparing for the work that is required for the synoptic practical assignments.

Working with contract documents such as drawings, specifications and schedules is something that you will be required to do within your apprenticeship and even more so after you have qualified.

You will need to know about and be familiar with:

- interpreting building information
- determining quantities of material
- relaying information in the workplace.

To get all the information you need out of these documents you will need to build on the maths and arithmetic skills that you learnt at school. These skills will give you the understanding and knowledge you will need to complete many of the practical assignments, which will require you to carry out calculations and measurements.

You will also need to use your English and reading skills. These skills will be particularly important, as you will need to make sure that you are following all the details of any instructions you receive. This will be the same for the instructions you receive for the synoptic test, as it will for any specifications you might use in your professional life.

Communication skills have been a particular focus of this unit. This unit has shown who the key personnel involved in the communication cycle are and demonstrated how poor communication between these people can have a bad effect on business and teamwork. You will need to be sure that you follow these guidelines for clear communication. Teamwork is a very important part of all construction work and can help work to run smoothly and safeguard people's safety.

This unit has also explained the advantages and disadvantages of different types of communication. You will need to make sure that you always choose the most appropriate method of communication for the situation you are in. You also need to be confident in using all the different methods (letters, e-mail, telephone, signs etc.) of communication.

You have seen that clear communication is vital for teams to work effectively. You will need to be able to demonstrate how the key personnel should communicate effectively.

The communicational skills that are explained within the unit are also vital in all tasks that you will undertake throughout your training and in life.

Good luck!

Knowledge check

1 The abbreviation ct stands for:

a) cast iron

b) cement

c) column

d) concrete

2 Which of the following abbreviations is a timber?

a) pbd

b) swd

c) pvc

d) fnd

3 The purpose of a specification is:

a) to tell you how long a job will take

b) to tell you the quality of work and sizes not shown on the drawing

c) to tell you the quantity of materials you will need

d) to tell you how much the job will cost

4 How is the area of a circle calculated?

a) πd^2

b) $d\pi^2$

c) πr^2

d) $r\pi^2$

5 A written warning is a form of:

a) mediation

b) disciplinary

c) procedure

d) hierarchy

6 Day work rate means that you get paid:

a) at the end of every day

b) you get paid the same amount no matter what you do

c) you get paid only for the work you do

d) weekly

7 What site paperwork is used to record hours worked?

a) day work sheet

b) job sheet

c) timesheet

d) variation order

8 To what scale are site plans usually drawn?

a) 1:500 or 1:200

b) 1:2500 or 1:1250

c) 1:100 or 1:50

d) 1:10 or 1:5.

9 The abbreviation 'pbd' as used on a drawing represents:

a) plasterboard

b) plaster

c) polythene

d) polyvinyl acetate

10 What is the contract document that deals with repeated design information?

a) specification

b) schedule

c) plans and drawings

d) conditions of contract

UNIT 2003

Knowledge of building methods and construction technology 2

Whatever type of building is being constructed there are certain principles and elements that must be included.

These basic principles are applied across all the work carried out in construction and will apply to nearly all the projects you could work on. The primary areas this unit will look at are the principles behind walls, floors, roofs and internal work. This unit also supports NVQ Unit VR02 Conform to Efficient Work Practices and NVQ Unit VR45 Place and Finish Non-Specialist Concrete.

This unit contains material that supports TAP Unit 2: Set Out for Masonry Structures. It also contains material that supports the delivery of the five generic units.

This unit will cover the following learning outcomes:

- Principles behind walls, floors and roofs

- Principles behind internal work

- Material storage and delivery of building materials.

Remember

When drawings are completed the correct keys, symbols, abbreviations and hatchings are used so that the various components used in construction are easily recognised and can be constructed

Key term

Stress – a constant force or system of forces exerted upon a body resulting in strain or deformation

K1. Principles behind walls, floors and roofs

All construction work requires working plans and drawings to complete the work. Drawings were covered earlier in Unit 2002 (page 54).

It is important to realise that when buildings are designed at the planning stage the different types of materials, methods of construction and principles behind all components are discussed and the most suitable materials and methods are chosen.

Principles of construction

Before looking at the range of different structures it is important to understand some of the key principles of construction. These are insulation and structural stability.

Structural loading

The main parts of a building that are in place to carry a load are said to be in a constant state of **stress**.

There are three main types of stress:

- **Tension** – pulls or stretches a material and can have a lengthening effect.
- **Compression** – squeezes the material and can have a shortening effect.
- **Shear** – occurs when one part of a component slips or slides over another causing a slicing effect.

To cause one of these types of stress a component or member must be under the strain of a load. Within construction there are two main types of loading:

- **Dead load** – the weight of the building itself and the materials used to construct the building, including components such as floors and roofs.
- **Imposed loads** – any moveable loads such as furniture, as well as natural forces such as wind, rain and snow.

To cope with the loads that a building must withstand there are load-bearing structural members strategically placed throughout the building.

There are three main types of load-bearing members:

- **Horizontal members** – one of the most common types of horizontal member is a floor joist, which carries the load and transfers it back to its point of support. The horizontal member, when under loading, can bend and be in all three

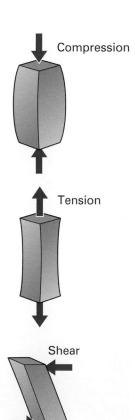

Figure 3.1 The three types of stress

types of stress, with the top in compression, the bottom in tension and the ends in shear. The bending can be contained by using correctly stress-graded materials or by adding a load-bearing wall to support the floor.

- **Vertical members** – any walls or columns that are in place to transfer the loads from above (including from horizontal members) down to the substructure and foundations have vertical members. Vertical members are usually in a compression state.

- **Bracing members** – bracing members are usually fitted diagonally to form a triangle which stiffens the structure. Bracing members can be found in roofs and even on scaffolding. Bracing is usually in compression or tension.

Damp proof course (DPC)

With sustainability and energy efficiency being talked about more and more the need to ensure that construction work is done with this in mind is vital. One of the main ways of ensuring that energy efficiency is maintained is by using correct insulation and a damp proof course (DPC).

A damp proof course (often shortened to DPC) or damp proof membrane (DPM) is a layer of non-absorbent material bedded on to a wall to prevent moisture penetrating into a building. There are three main ways moisture can penetrate into a building:

- rising up from the ground
- through the walls
- moisture running downwards from the top of walls around openings or chimneys.

There are three types of DPC:

- flexible
- semi-rigid
- rigid.

Flexible DPC

Flexible DPC comes in rolls of various widths to suit requirements. Nowadays most rolls are made of pitch-polymer or polythene but bitumen can still be found. Metal can be used as a DPC (in copper and lead) but because of the cost is mainly used in specialised areas. The most widely used and economic DPC material is polythene. Flexible DPC should always be laid upon a thin bed of mortar and lapped by a minimum of 100 mm on a corner or if joining a new roll.

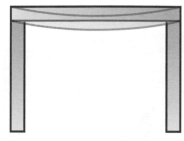

Figure 3.2 Horizontal structural members

Figure 3.3 Vertical structural members

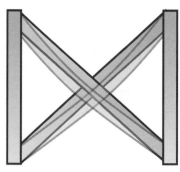

Figure 3.4 Bracing structural members

Knowledge of building methods and construction technology 2 **Unit 2003**

Semi-rigid DPC

This type of DPC is normally made from blocks of asphalt melted and spread in coats to form a continuous membrane for tanking for basements or underground work.

Rigid DPC

Rigid DPC uses solid material such as engineering bricks or slate, which were the traditional materials used. Slate is more expensive to use than other DPC materials and has no flexibility. If movement occurs the slate will crack, allowing damp to penetrate. Engineering bricks could be used for a garden wall if a DPC was required.

Modern insulation materials

Insulation, or more correctly thermal insulation, is a general term used to describe products that reduce heat loss or heat gain by providing a barrier between areas that are significantly different in temperature. There are a number of items in the home that benefit from insulation, such as central heating boilers and hot water pipes. However, buildings themselves need some extra help to make them more energy efficient. Home insulation therefore reduces the amount of heat that escapes from a building in the winter and protects it from getting too warm in the summer.

There are several different types of insulation available. These include:

- **Rigid foam** – this has a high compressive strength and is usually used where it needs to support weight (e.g. under a floor, or in lofts as a storage solution). As well as strength and durability, rigid foam insulation can also provide additional properties such as fire resistance and acoustic insulation to minimise the level of sound travelling through walls and floors.
- **Sheep's wool** – this is a fairly new insulation product. However, before it is used as an insulation material, it must undergo an intensive cleaning process in order to remove the dirt and oils from the wool. The chemicals and energy used during this process must be taken into account when measuring its environmental impact, putting sheep's wool behind mineral wool in terms of its overall eco-credentials.
- **Polystyrene boards** – a high density polystyrene sheet is usually cut to fit between ceiling joists. Safe and easy to install, these boards easily meet the required insulation values with minimal board thickness.

Functional skills

Becoming familiar with building and construction methods means you will need to become familiar with FE 1.2.1 – 1.2.3 which relate to reading and understanding information. FM 1.2.1b relates to interpreting information from sources such as diagrams, tables, charts and graphs.

Mineral wool insulation is the most common type of insulation.

Mineral wool insulation

There are two main types of mineral wool insulation. These are:

- **Glass mineral wool** – the world's most popular and widely used insulation material, glasswool is made from recycled glass bottles. This means it is ultra-eco-friendly. It is easy to handle and install, plus it is the most cost-effective insulation available.

- **Rock mineral wool** – rock mineral wool has a more solid structure, so it is ideal for situations where it may be under compression, e.g. on a flat roof.

Mineral wool insulation products are available in rolls of different widths and thicknesses for quick and simple DIY installation, for example, between the rafters in a roof or joists in a ceiling or floor.

It can be produced as lightweight 'slabs' for installing into the cavity walls when building new houses. 'Loose' mineral wool can also be used to fill cavity walls and is blown in through a hole drilled in the wall after it is built.

Installing mineral wool insulation is also an effective fire safety measure, as it does not burn easily, and can therefore prevent fire spreading. In fact, rock mineral wool can resist temperatures above 1000°C.

Other methods of insulation

As well as the insulation detailed above, certain other areas also require insulation. This can range from installing special double glazing units with thermal properties to ensuring that water pipes are correctly insulated (lagged).

Insulating water pipes is vital as it prevents them from freezing. Freezing can cause the pipes to crack and, in worst case scenarios, flood an entire building. Pipes are lagged either with a foam tube that slips over the pipe or with a mineral/rock wool blanket that is wrapped around them.

Cavity wall insulation is mentioned above in the cavity wall section but older buildings may not have insulation in the cavity. In these instances retro fitting of insulation is done by drilling holes into the exterior leaf of the cavity, filling it with a loose fill mineral wool and then resealing the holes.

Figure 3.5 Glass mineral wool

Figure 3.6 Rock mineral wool

Did you know?

There are in place at the moment various government grants in conjunction with energy providers that allow a house to be insulated for a minimal charge or even for free.

This is current, but for how long?

Substructure

All buildings start with the substructure – all the structure below ground level, up to and including the DPC. The substructure receives the loads from the main building and transfers them safely down to a suitable load bearing layer of ground.

Setting out

Setting out refers to the marking out and positioning of a building. It is a very important operation as the setting out of a building must be as accurate as possible. Mistakes made at the setting out stage can prove very costly later. To appreciate the need for careful and accurate setting out, we have to understand and visualise the finished building and its requirements. When setting out a building, you must make sure that it is in the right place, it is level and it is square.

Planning foundations

Before any foundation can be formed, there must be extensive exploration, testing and preparation of the ground on which the building is to be erected.

As an apprentice, it is unlikely that you will find yourself involved in the design process of foundations for a particular building or structure, as this will be left to the architect and the structural design team. However, an appreciation of factors influencing the design of any foundation will help you to understand why there are different foundation types.

As already stated, the design of any foundation depends on a number of important factors:

- ground conditions
- soil type
- location of drains in relation to the proposed structure
- location of trees in relation to the proposed structure
- combined loads to be put on the ground directly beneath the proposed structure.

The purpose of foundations

The foundations of a building ensure that all dead and imposed loads are safely absorbed and transmitted through to the natural foundation or sub-soils on which the building is constructed. Failure to adequately absorb and transmit these loads will result in the stability of the building being compromised and will undoubtedly cause structural damage.

Did you know?

The natural foundation is also referred to as the sub-foundation

Find out

Do some research into the types of load that may be imposed on a building structure

Foundations must also be able to allow for ground movement brought about by shrinkage or expansion of the soil as it dries out or becomes wet. The severity of shrinkage or expansion depends upon the type of soil being built on.

Frost may also affect ground movement, particularly in soils that hold water for long periods. Freezing of this retained water can cause expansion of the sub-soil.

Find out

What is the term given to the effect on sub-soil when retained water freezes?

Types of soil

As you can imagine there are many different types of soils. For foundation design purposes, these have been categorised as follows:

- rock
- gravel
- clay
- sand
- silt.

Each of these categories of sub-soil can be broken down even further, for example:

- clay which is sandy and very soft in its composition
- clay which is sandy but very stiff in its composition.

This information will be of most interest to the architect, but nonetheless is of the utmost importance when designing the foundation of a building.

A number of calculations are used to determine the size and make-up of the foundation. These calculations take into account the **bearing capacity of the soil**. Calculations for some of the more common types of foundations can be found in the current *Building Regulations*. However, these published calculations cannot possibly cover all situations. Ultimately it will be down to the expertise of the building design teams to accurately calculate the bearing capacity of the soil and the make-up of the foundation.

Key term

Bearing capacity of soil – the load that can be safely carried by the soil without any adverse settlement

In the early stages of the design process, before any construction work begins, a site investigation will be carried out to ascertain any conditions, situations or surrounding sites which may affect the proposed construction work. A great deal of data will need to be gathered during site investigations, including:

- position of boundary fences and hedges
- location and depth of services, including gas, electricity, water, telephone cables, drains and sewers

Find out

Look at the different methods and equipment used to locate and identify various hidden services

Find out

How are the different soil tests carried out?

Did you know?

Site investigations or surveys will also establish the contours of the site. This will identify where certain areas of the site will need to be reduced or increased in height. An area of the site may need to be built up in order to mask surrounding features outside the boundaries of the proposed building project

Find out

How can plant growth affect some structures?

- existing buildings which need to be demolished or protected
- position, height, girth and spread of trees
- types of soil and the depths of these various soils.

The local authorities will normally provide information relating to the location of services, existing buildings, planning restrictions, preservation orders and boundary demarcation. However, all of these will still need to be identified and confirmed through the site investigation. In particular, hidden services will need to be located with the use of modern electronic surveying equipment.

Soil investigations are critical. Samples of the soil are taken from various points around the site and tested for their composition and for any contamination. Some soils contain chemicals that can seriously damage the foundation concrete. These chemicals include sodium and magnesium sulphates. The effects of these chemicals on the concrete can be counteracted with the use of sulphate-resistant cements.

Many different tests can be carried out on soil. Some are carried out on site; others need to be carried out in laboratories. Tests on soil include:

- **penetration tests** – to establish density of soil
- **compression tests** – to establish shear strength of the soil or its bearing capacity
- **various laboratory tests** – to establish particle size, moisture content, humus content and chemical content.

Once all site investigations have been completed and all necessary information and data has been established in relation to the proposed building project, site clearance can take place.

Site clearance

The main purpose of site clearance is to remove existing buildings, waste, vegetation and, most importantly, the surface layer of soil referred to as topsoil. It is necessary to remove this layer of soil, as it is unsuitable to build on. This surface layer of soil is difficult to compact down due to the high content of vegetable matter, which makes the soil soft and loose. The topsoil also contains various chemicals that encourage plant growth, which may adversely affect some structures over time.

The process of removing the topsoil can be very costly, in terms of both labour and transportation. The site investigations will determine the volume of topsoil that needs to be removed.

In some instances, the excavated topsoil may not be transported off site. Where building projects include garden plots, the topsoil may just need to be stored on site, thus reducing excessive labour and transportation costs. However, where this is the case, the topsoil must be stored well away from areas where buildings are to be erected or materials are to be stored, to prevent contamination of soils or materials.

Once the site clearance is complete, excavations for the foundations can start and the concrete foundations can be constructed.

Construction of concrete foundations

Trench excavation

In most modern-day construction projects, trenches are excavated by mechanical means. Although this is an expensive method, it reduces labour time and the risks associated with manual excavation work. Even with the use of machines to carry out excavations, an element of manual labour will still be needed to clean up the excavation work: loose soil from both the base and sides of the trench will have to be removed, and the sides of the trench will have to be finished vertically.

Manual labour is still required for excavating trenches on some projects where machine access is limited and where only small strip foundations of minimum depths are required.

Trenches to be excavated are identified by lines attached to and stretched between profiles. This is the most accurate method of ensuring trenches are dug to the exact widths required.

Excavation work must be carefully planned as workers are killed or seriously injured every year while working in and around trenches. Thorough risk assessments need to be carried out and method statements produced prior to any excavation work commencing.

Potential hazards are numerous and include: possible collapse of the sides of the trench, hitting hidden services, plant machinery falling into the trench and people falling into the trench.

One main cause of trench collapse is the poor placement of materials near the sides of the trench. Not only can such materials cause trench collapse, but they may also fall into the trench onto workers. Materials should not be stored near to trenches unless absolutely necessary. Where there is a need to place materials close to the trench for use in the trench itself, always ensure that these are kept to a minimum, stacked correctly and used quickly; most importantly, ensure that the trench sides are supported.

Figure 3.7 Removing soil from a site

Figure 3.8 Trenches are often excavated by mechanical means

Trench support

The type and extent of support required in an excavated trench will depend predominantly on the depth of the trench and the stability of the soil.

Traditionally, trench support was provided by using varying lengths and sizes of timber, which can easily be cut to required lengths. However, timber can become unreliable under certain loadings, pressures and weather conditions and can fail in its purpose.

More modern types of materials have been introduced as less costly and time-consuming methods of providing the required support. These materials include steel sheeting, rails and props. Trench support can be provided with a mixture of timber and steel components.

Here you can see the methods of providing support in trenches with differing materials and a combination of these materials.

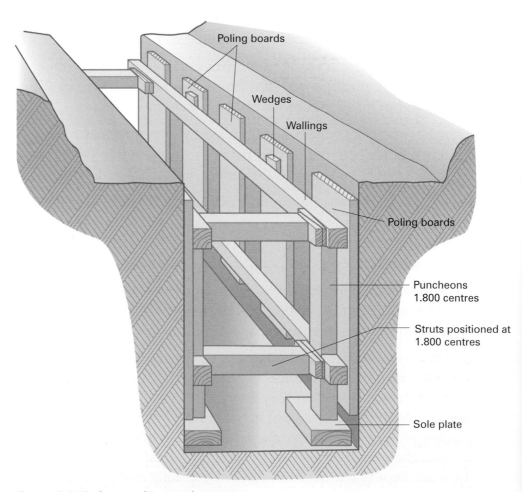

Figure 3.9 Timber used in trench support

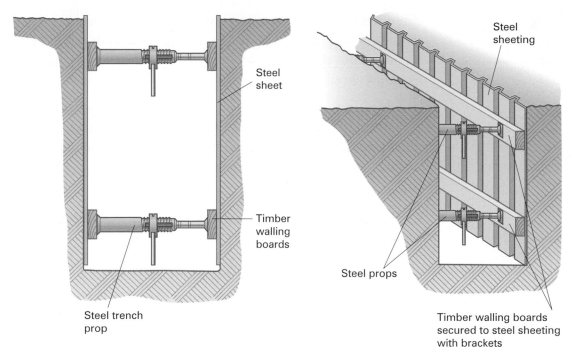

Figure 3.10 Combination of timber and steel used in trench support

The amount of timber or other materials required to provide adequate temporary support will be determined by the characteristics of the soil and the soil's ability to remain stable during the time over which the work is carried out. The atmospheric conditions will also affect the soil's ability to remain stable. The longer the soil is exposed to the natural elements, the more chance there is of the soil shrinking or expanding.

Without support, soil will have a natural angle of repose – the angle at which the soil will rest without collapsing or moving. Again, this will be affected by the natural elements to which the soil is exposed. It is virtually impossible to establish accurately the exact angle at which a type of soil will settle, so it is always advisable to provide more support than is actually required.

Site engineers will carry out various calculations in relation to the support requirements for trenches.

Temporary barriers or fences should also be provided around the perimeters of all trenches, to prevent people falling into the trenches and to prevent materials from being knocked into them. Good trench support methods will incorporate

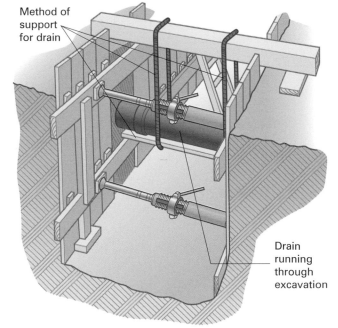

Figure 3.11 Support for drains running through an excavation

extended trench side supports, which provide a barrier – similar to a toe board on a scaffold – to prevent materials being kicked or knocked into the trench. Where barriers or fences are impractical, trenches should be covered with suitable sheet materials.

In addition to the supports already mentioned, any services which run through the excavated trenches (in particular drains and gas pipes) need to be supported, especially where the ground has to be excavated underneath them.

Where trenches have to be excavated close to existing buildings, it may be necessary to provide support to the elevation adjacent to the excavation. This is because, as ground is taken away from around the existing foundations, the loads will no longer be adequately and evenly distributed and absorbed into the natural or sub-foundation, which may cause the structure to collapse. This support is known as shoring.

One other factor that can affect the safety of workers in excavations and the stability of the soil is surface water. Surface water can be found at varying levels within the soil and, depending on their depth, trenches can easily cause flooding. Where this occurs, water pumps will need to be used to keep the trench clear. Failure to keep the trench free of water during construction will not only make operations difficult, but may also weaken and loosen the support systems due to soil displacement.

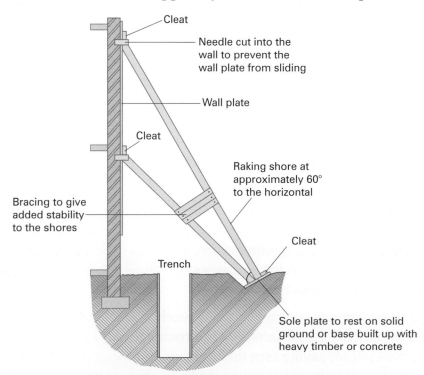

Figure 3.12 Raking shores used to support an existing building

Concrete

Concrete is a mixture of cement, aggregates and water. The aggregate is normally in two parts:

- **fine aggregate** – sand and limestone dust
- **coarse aggregate** – gravel or limestone chippings.

The coarse aggregate is the bulk of the concrete, while the fine aggregate fills in the voids between the larger particles.

The cement is the binder that holds all the aggregates together. Water is required to cause a chemical reaction (hydration) that changes the dry cement powder into an adhesive.

Cement

The most common type of cement used for concrete is Ordinary Portland Cement (OPC). Over the years, however, several types of Portland cement have been developed which are more suited to certain circumstances. These include:

- Rapid-Hardening Portland Cement (RHPC), which gives strength more quickly than OPC.
- Sulphate-Resisting Portland Cement (SRPC), which should be used in ground containing a high level of sulphates, as sulphates would damage OPC.
- Low Heat Portland Cement (LHPC), which produces less heat during hydration. This makes it more suitable than OPC where large masses are needed: large masses of OPC could produce high temperatures, which might lead to the concrete cracking.

Fine aggregates

Fine aggregates can be obtained from riverbeds or sand pits, or dredged from the seabed. Dredged aggregates must be washed to remove any mud and weed. Seashore sand must not be used due to the high salt content.

The shape and size of the grains can affect the strength of the concrete. The particles should be irregular in shape (not rounded) and well graded, with the size not larger than 5 mm. Also, if the grain size is too small it will increase the total surface area so that the designed quantity of cement becomes insufficient, causing a weakness in the finished mix.

Clay and silt particles prevent the cement from bonding to the aggregate, so each load delivered to the site should be tested for 'cleanliness'. The amount of silt must not be more than 10 per cent of the volume of aggregate. The silt test is used to check this.

> **Remember**
>
> All aggregates should be 'well graded' – they should range from small to large grains – so they fill in all the voids in the concrete

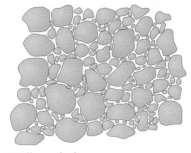

Well graded

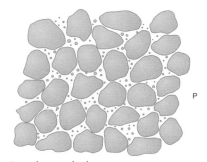

Poorly graded

Figure 3.13 Well graded and poorly graded concrete

Step 1 Ingredients being added to water

Example

If we measure the sand to be 45 mm and the silt thickness to be 5 mm:

$$\frac{5}{45 + 5} \times \frac{100}{1}$$

$$\frac{5}{50} \times \frac{100}{1}$$

$$0.1 \times 100$$

$$= 10\%$$

Conclusion – this sample would be suitable.

Silt test

The following materials and equipment are needed for this test:

- a sample of sand
- water
- salt
- a glass jar or measuring cylinder
- a tape measure.

Step 2 Jar after shaking

Step 3 Jar after three hours

- **Step 1** – place 25 mm of water in the jar, add 1 teaspoon of salt and gradually add the sand until the level of the top of the sand reaches 50 mm.

- **Step 2** – shake the jar for one minute.

- **Step 3** – leave to settle for three hours. Measure the height of the aggregate and the thickness of the silt layer.

To work out the percentage of silt in the aggregate the following sum must be calculated:

$$\frac{\text{Thickness of silt}}{\text{Total height of aggregate and silt}} \times \frac{100}{1}$$

Coarse aggregates

Coarse aggregates are the larger particles of a concrete mix. They can be made from gravel or crushed rock. If gravel is to be used, this should also be crushed as the irregular shape of the crushed particles gives a better bond with the cement than if they are left smooth. The size of the coarse aggregate can range between 5 and 40 mm, but if it is to be used for reinforced concrete the size should be kept smaller than 20 mm.

Water

Water is used in the production of concrete to enable the cement to set and also to make the concrete 'workable'. Water must not contain any impurities which might affect the strength of the concrete. The general rule for the quality of water is that it should be drinkable (potable).

Mixes

Concrete is designed depending on where it is to be used. Mass concrete for normal strip foundations, oversite concrete, footpaths etc. should be mixed to a ratio of 1:3:6 of cement, fine aggregate and coarse aggregate. Concrete walls, beams and suspended floors etc., should have a ratio of 1:2:4 cement, fine aggregate and coarse aggregate.

For more structural concrete, the mixes are specified as a 'grade'. This grade is a number (usually between 7 and 30) and is the amount of pressure, in newtons (N), that has to be applied to each square millimetre of a cube of concrete before it is crushed in a test carried out after 28 days.

Batching

In order to produce concrete to a consistent strength and workability it is essential that each mix is accurately measured out, or batched, before being placed into the mixer.

The most accurate method of batching concrete is by weighing. On sites where large amounts of concrete are required each day, it is usual to use a mixer which can weigh the amount of aggregate placed in a hopper, before it is fed into the mixer.

Figure 3.14 Ready mix concrete can be delivered to site by lorry

Functional skills

Working with concrete mixes is good practice for FM 1.2.1h: Solve simple problems involving ratios.

Knowledge of building methods and construction technology 2 Unit 2003

Key term

Gauge box – a bottomless box which should hold the correct volume of aggregate needed to mix a 25 kg bag of cement

The ready mix concrete plants, which produce the concrete we see on the roads, in lorries and often on construction sites, would use a similar method, but on a larger scale.

Where weight batching is impossible, the next most accurate method is by volume. When volume batching, the amount of cement in a 25 kg bag would be 0.0175 m³, so if we needed a 1:3:6 mix we would require three times this volume of fine aggregate and six times this volume of coarse aggregate.

To ensure accurate proportions of the aggregates, a **gauge box** should be made for each of the aggregates.

The volume of the gauge box would be made to the ratios shown in Table 3.1 below.

Mix	Cement	Fine aggregate	Coarse aggregate
1:3:6	1 bag (25 kg)	0.050 m³	0.100 m³
1:2:4	1 bag (25 kg)	0.035 m³	0.070 m³

Table 3.1 Ratios for volume of gauge box

When batching the concrete, the boxes are placed on a clean, firm base, filled with the aggregate and levelled off at the top. The area is cleaned of all spillages and the boxes are lifted off. The aggregates are then loaded into the mixer along with a full bag of cement.

Water–cement ratio

Water is used when mixing the concrete to cause the cement to set and make the concrete 'workable'. The more water in the mix, the more workable the concrete will be. However, the cement will only require a certain amount of water to make it set.

Any excess water is called free water. This free water occupies space and when the concrete dries out voids are left behind, causing the concrete to become weak.

The amount of water that should be added to a mix is given as a ratio between the cement and water and this is called the water–cement ratio. This water–cement ratio is specified as a decimal number, usually between 0.4 and 0.8.

In order to work out the amount of water needed in a concrete mix, the water–cement ratio is multiplied by the weight of cement being mixed. This gives the amount of water in litres.

Did you know?

Many concreting jobs require mixes to be maintained at a constant strength and colour, so 'shovel fulls' are not an accurate enough method of batching. This is because a shovel full to one person may be more or less than a shovel full to another person who may mix the next batch. This would result in mixes with different proportions

For example, if a concrete mix has a water–cement ratio of 0.5 and contains 25 kg of cement, the amount of water needed for this mix would be:

$$0.5 \times 25 = 12.5 \text{ litres}$$

This is the total quantity of water that would be specified by an engineer.

Types of concrete

Before starting a concreting project, it must be decided whether to use ready mix concrete (mixed at a concrete plant and transported to site) or to self mix concrete. Each has advantages over the other.

Advantages of self mix:

- cost is much lower
- no need to order in advance (if materials are on site)
- project can be postponed without advance notice (e.g. owing to bad weather).

Advantages of ready mix:

- no need for storage of materials
- able to provide large batches of materials
- no need to employ labourers to mix the concrete.

Workability

Mixed concrete must be sufficiently **workable** so that it can be fully compacted. Workability is affected by:

- the water–cement ratio
- the cement–aggregate ratio
- the size of the coarse aggregate
- the shape of the aggregate.

Workability may be measured by the slump test. This takes a sample of a batch of concrete and places it in a steel cone 100 mm diameter at the top, 200 mm diameter at the bottom and 300 mm high, placed on a levelled base plate.

> **Remember**
>
> Allowances must be made for the quantity of water present in the aggregates (e.g. damp sand)

> **Remember**
>
> For ready mix to be an advantage, the concrete lorry must have good access to the pour area

> **Key term**
>
> **Workable** – easy to use

Unit 2003 Knowledge of building methods and construction technology 2

Step 1 Filling the cone

Step 2 Rodding

Step 3 Smoothing off

Step 4 Lifting off the cone

Step 5 Measuring the slump

- **Step 1** – standing on the foot pieces, fill the cone in four equal layers.
- **Step 2** – rod each layer 25 times with a 16 mm diameter, rounded rod.
- **Step 3** – smooth off the concrete when the cone is full.
- **Step 4** – slowly lift the cone straight up and off.
- **Step 5** – lay the rod across the upturned slump cone and measure the distance between the concrete and the rod. This distance is the slump.

There are three kinds of slump:

- normal
- collapse
- shear.

A concrete mix would have been designed to have a certain degree of slump. This would be given as the amount of workability. Table 3.2 shows the degrees of slump for concrete mixes.

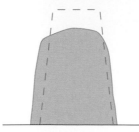
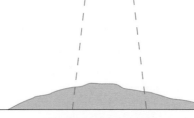
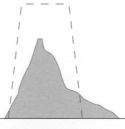

Normal   Collapse (too wet)   Shear (too dry)

Figure 3.15 Slump test results

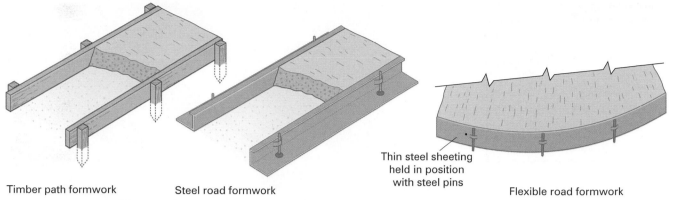

Timber path formwork   Steel road formwork

Thin steel sheeting held in position with steel pins

Flexible road formwork

Figure 3.16 Types of formwork

Workability	Slump	
Low	10–30 mm	If the slump does not meet the specified slump, it should not be used.
Medium	25–75 mm	
High	65–135 mm	

Table 3.2 Degrees of slump for concrete mixes

Formwork

The purpose of formwork is to hold the freshly placed and compacted concrete until it has set. To achieve this, the formwork should:

- be rigid enough to prevent bending
- be strong enough to carry the weight of the concrete
- be set in place to line and level
- have tight joints to prevent water or cement paste loss
- have suitable size panels to allow safe and easy handling
- be designed in such a way that air pockets are not trapped.

Formwork may be made from timber or steel. The choice of which to use usually depends on how many times the formwork is to be used. Steel formwork may be more expensive than timber initially, but it can be reused more times as timber can be easily damaged during the striking of the formwork.

Formwork for pathways

This formwork uses timber or steel road forms, with the height of the formwork being the same as the thickness of the concrete path. The formwork is positioned to align with the required amount of fall to allow for surface water drainage.

Pegs or steel pins are driven behind the formwork to prevent it from moving outwards when concrete is placed. Wedges may be used to adjust the alignment of the formwork.

Unit 2003 Knowledge of building methods and construction technology 2

Did you know?

Another reason for not using nails is that the amount of pressure on the formwork during compaction of the concrete could cause the joints to open, allowing the concrete to leak

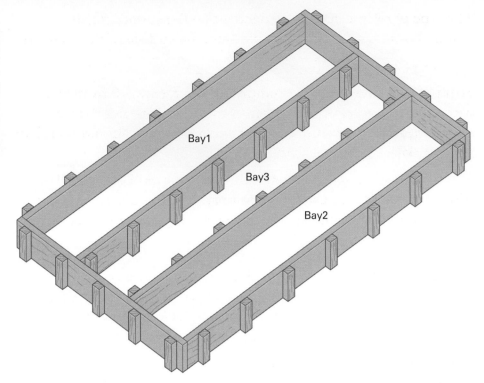

Figure 3.17 Alternative strip method used for large floor areas

Formwork for ground floors

Floors for buildings, such as factories and warehouses etc., have large areas and would be difficult to lay in one slab. Floors of this type are usually laid in strips up to 4.5 m wide, running the full length of the building (see Figure 3.17). The actual formwork would be similar to that used for paths.

Fixing formwork

The fixing of formwork may be made using nails, clamps or bolts. Clamps or bolts are preferred over nails as they are easier to strip off the formwork after completion, with less chance of anyone stepping on a nail which has been left sticking out of an old piece of formwork.

Release agent

To prevent damage to the concrete, and to allow for easier striking of the formwork, the surface of the formwork must be coated with a release agent before concrete is placed. Suitable release agents are:

- light oil
- chemical release agent
- mould cream emulsion
- water-based emulsion
- wax.

Remember

Steel tools should not be used to clean formwork as they can easily scratch the forms, which could show on the concrete surface

The type of release agent is dependent on the surface finish required; some of the agents could stain the surface of the concrete.

Striking of formwork

Striking of formwork is the removal of the formwork from the hardened concrete. Vertical sides of the formwork may be removed after 12 hours while soffits supporting lintels etc., should be left in place between 7 and 14 days.

All formwork should be cleaned as soon as it has been struck. A stiff brush should be used to remove any dust and cement grout. Stubborn bits of grout can be removed using a wooden scraper.

Reinforcement

Concrete is strong in **compression**, but weak in **tension** so, to prevent concrete from being 'pulled' apart when under pressure, steel reinforcement is provided. The type and position of the reinforcement will be specified by the structural engineer.

The reinforcement must always have a suitable thickness of concrete cover to prevent the steel from rusting if exposed to moisture or air. The amount of cover required depends upon the location of the site with respect to exposure conditions, and ranges from 20 mm in mild exposure to 60 mm for very severe exposure to water.

To prevent the reinforcement from touching the formwork, spacers should be used. Made from concrete, fibre, cement or plastic they are available in several shapes and various sizes to give the correct cover.

Expansion joints

Concrete expands and contracts as air temperatures rise and fall, so provision must be made for this variation in the length of the slab. These provisions are termed expansion joints and should be placed between 7 and 10 m apart. An expansion joint provides

Key terms

Compression – squeezing or squashing together

Tension – stretching

Figure 3.18 An example of concrete spacers

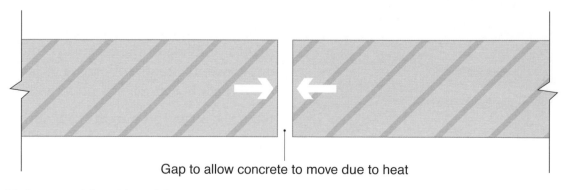

Gap to allow concrete to move due to heat

Figure 3.19 Concrete slabs without joint

a gap between adjoining slabs, allowing each slab to take up this space as it expands and so preventing the concrete from cracking.

The expansion joint is formed using a 12 mm thick fibreboard, 25 mm below the surface. The top of the expansion joint is filled with a flexible sealant. These materials are most suitable as they can be compressed.

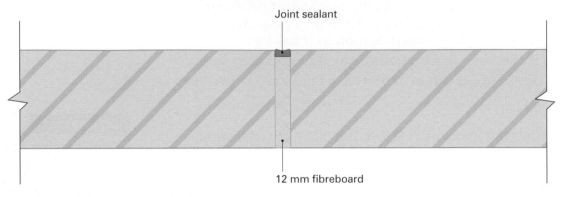

Joint sealant

12 mm fibreboard

Figure 3.20 Concrete slabs with expansion joint

Compacting

When concrete has been placed, it contains trapped air in the form of voids. To get rid of these voids we must compact the concrete. The more workable the concrete, the easier it will be to compact. However, if the concrete is too wet, the excess water will reduce the strength of the concrete.

Failure to compact concrete results in:

- reduction in the strength of the concrete
- water entering the concrete, which could damage the reinforcement
- visual defects, such as honeycombing on the surface.

Figure 3.21 Tamper board with handles

The method of compaction depends on the thickness and the purpose of the concrete. For oversite concrete, floors and pathways up to 100 mm thick, manual compaction with a tamper board may be sufficient. This requires slight overfilling of the formwork and tamping down with the tamper board. For larger spans the tamper board may be fitted with handles.

For slabs up to 150 mm thick, a vibrating beam tamper should be used. This is simply a tamper board with a petrol-driven vibrating unit bolted on. The beam is laid on the concrete with its motor running and is pulled along the slab.

For deeper structures, such as retaining walls, a poker vibrator would be required. The poker vibrator is a vibrating tube at the end of a flexible drive connected to a petrol motor. The pokers are available in various diameters from 25 mm to 75 mm.

The concrete should be laid in layers of 600 mm with the poker in vertically and penetrating the layer below by 100 mm. The concrete is vibrated until the air bubbles stop and the poker is then lifted slowly and placed 150 to 1000 mm from this incision, depending on the diameter of the vibrator.

Surface finishes

The following surface finishes may be used for slabs:

- **Tamped finish** – simply using a straight edge or tamper board when compacting the concrete will leave a rough finish to the floor. This is ideal for a path or drive surface, because it will provide grip for vehicles and pedestrians. This finish may also be used if a further layer is to be applied, to give a good bond.
- **Float and brush finish** – after **screeding** off the concrete with a straight edge, the surface is floated off using a steel or wooden float and then brushed lightly with a soft brush (see photo below). Again, this would be suitable for pathways and drives.
- **Steel float finish** – after screeding off using a straight edge, a steel float is applied to the surface. This finish attracts particles of cement to the surface, causing the concrete to become impermeable to water but also very slippery when wet. This is not very suitable for use outside but ideal for use indoors for floors, etc.

Figure 3.22 Vibrating beam tamper

Figure 3.23 Vibrating poker in use

> **Key term**
>
> **Screeding** – levelling off concrete by adding a final layer

Figure 3.24 Brushed concrete finish

Figure 3.25 Power float

Did you know?

The success of surface finishes depends largely on timing. You need to be aware of the setting times in order to apply the finish

Figure 3.26 Ribbed concrete finish

Remember

If the water is allowed to evaporate from the mix shortly after the concrete is placed, there is less time for the cement to 'go off'

- **Power trowelling/float** – three hours after laying, a power float is applied to the surface of the concrete. After a further delay to allow surface water to evaporate, a power trowel is used. A power float has a rotating circular disc or four large flat blades powered by a petrol engine. The edges of the blades are turned up to prevent them digging into the concrete slab. This finish would most likely be used in factories where a large floor area would be needed.

- **Power grinding** – this is a technique used to provide a durable wearing surface without further treatment. The concrete is laid, compacted and trowel finished. After 1 to 7 days the floor is ground, removing the top 1–2 mm, leaving a polished concrete surface.

Surface treatment for other surfaces may be:

- **Plain smooth surfaces** – after the formwork has been struck, the concrete may be polished with a carborundum stone, giving a polished water-resistant finish.

- **Textured and profiled finish** – a simple textured finish may be made by using rough sawn boards to make the formwork. When struck, the concrete takes on the texture of these boards. A profiled finish can be made by using a lining inside the formwork. Linings may be made from polystyrene or flexible rubber-like plastics, and give a pattern to the finished concrete.

- **Ribbed finishes** – these are made by fixing timber battens to the formwork.

- **Exposed aggregate finish** – the coarse aggregate is exposed by removing the sand and cement from the finished concrete with a sand blaster. Another method of producing this finish is by applying a chemical retarder to the formwork, which prevents the cement in contact with it from hardening. When the formwork is removed, the mortar is brushed away to uncover the aggregate in the hardened concrete.

Curing

When concrete is mixed, the quantity of water is accurately added to allow hydration to take place. The longer we can keep this chemical reaction going, the stronger the concrete will become.

To allow the concrete to achieve its maximum strength, the chemical reaction must be allowed to keep going for as long as possible. To do this we must 'cure' the concrete. This is done by keeping the concrete damp and preventing it from drying out too quickly.

Curing can be done by:

- Spraying the concrete with a chemical sealer. This dries to leave a film of resin which will seal the surface and reduce the loss of moisture.

- Spraying the concrete with water, which replaces any lost water and keeps the concrete damp. This can also be done by covering the concrete with a layer of sand or hessian cloth or other similar material, and dampening this layer.

- Covering the concrete with a plastic sheet or building paper, will prevent water from evaporating into the air due to wind and sun. Any evaporated moisture due to the heat will condense on the polythene and drip back onto the concrete surface.

Concreting in hot weather

When concreting in temperatures over 20°C, there is a reduction in workability due to water loss through evaporation. The cement also tends to react more quickly with water, causing the concrete to set rapidly.

To remedy the problem of the concrete setting quickly, a 'retarding mixture' may be used. This slows down the initial reaction between the cement and water, allowing the concrete to remain workable for longer.

Extra water may be added at the time of mixing so that the workability will be correct at the time of placing.

Water must *not* be added during the placing of the concrete, to make it more workable, after the initial set has taken place in the concrete.

Concreting in cold weather

Water expands when freezing. This can cause permanent damage if the concrete is allowed to freeze when freshly laid or in hardened concrete that has not reached enough strength (5 N/mm^2, which takes 48 hours).

Concreting should not take place when the temperature is 2°C or less. If the temperature is only slightly above 2°C, mixing water should be heated.

After being laid, the concrete should be kept warm by covering with insulating quilts. This allows the cement to continue its reaction with the water and prevents it from freezing.

Remember

In hot weather, concrete must be placed quickly and not left standing for too long

Safety tip

In hot weather, take precautions against the effect of the sun on your skin, for example, wear sun block and a T-shirt

Find out

The Cement & Concrete Association (C&CA) offers a service of technical information and advice, based on the work at its Research Station, combined with wide practical experience and the collection of information on a worldwide basis. The Association's training centre provides an extensive range of courses on concrete practice. Information is passed through publications and films

Types of foundation

Concreting will be used to create a range of different foundation types. As previously stated, the design of a foundation will be down to the architect and structural design team. The final decision on the suitability and depth of the foundation, and on the thickness of the concrete, will rest with the local authority's building control department.

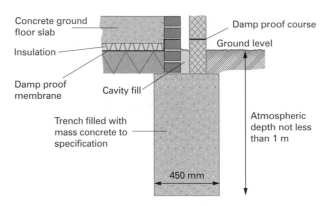

Concrete ground floor slab

Damp proof course

Insulation

Ground level

Damp proof membrane

Cavity fill

Trench filled with mass concrete to specification

Atmospheric depth not less than 1 m

450 mm

Figure 3.27 Narrow strip foundation

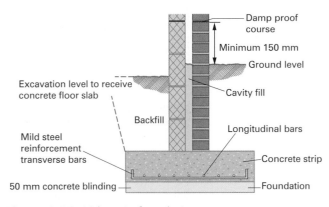

Damp proof course

Minimum 150 mm

Ground level

Excavation level to receive concrete floor slab

Cavity fill

Backfill

Mild steel reinforcement transverse bars

Longitudinal bars

Concrete strip

50 mm concrete blinding

Foundation

Figure 3.28 Wide strip foundation

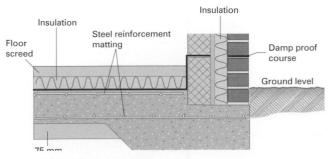

Insulation

Insulation

Steel reinforcement matting

Floor screed

Damp proof course

Ground level

75 mm

Figure 3.29 Raft foundation

Strip foundations

The most commonly used strip foundation is the 'narrow strip' foundation, which is used for small domestic dwellings and low-rise structures. Once the trench has been excavated, it is filled with concrete to within 4–5 courses of the ground level DPC. The level of the concrete fill can be reduced in height, but this makes it difficult for the bricklayer due to the confined area in which to lay bricks or blocks.

The depth of this type of foundation must be such that the soil acting as the natural foundation cannot be affected by the weather. This depth would not normally be less than 1 m.

The narrow strip foundation is not suitable for building with heavy structural loading or where the soil is weak in terms of supporting the combined loads imposed on it. Where this is the case, a wide strip foundation is needed.

Wide strip foundations

Wide strip foundations consist of steel reinforcement placed within the concrete base of the foundation. This removes the need to increase the depth considerably in order to spread heavier loads adequately.

Raft foundations

These types of foundation are used where the soil has poor bearing capacity, making the soil prone to settlement. A raft foundation consists of a slab of concrete covering the entire base of the structure. The depth of the concrete is greater around the edges of the raft in order to protect the load-bearing soil directly beneath the raft from further effects of moisture taken in from the surrounding area.

Pad foundations

Pad foundations are used where the main loads of a structure are imposed only at certain points – for example, where brick or steel columns support the weight of floors, or roof members, and walls between the columns are of non-load bearing cladding panels. The simplest form of pad foundation uses individual concrete pads placed at various points around the base of the structure, with concrete ground beams spanning across and between them. The individual concrete pads will absorb the main imposed loads, while the beams will help to support the walls.

The depth of a pad foundation will depend on the load being imposed on it. In some instances, there may be a need to use steel reinforcement to prevent excessive depths of concrete. This type of pad foundation can reduce the amount of excavation work required, as trenches do not need to be dug out around the entire base of the proposed structure.

Piled foundations

There are a large number of different types of piled foundation, each with an individual purpose in relation to the type of structure and ground conditions.

Short bored piled foundations are the most common piled foundations. They are predominantly used for domestic buildings where the soil is prone to movement, particularly at depths below 1 m.

A series of holes are bored, by mechanical means, around the perimeter of the base of the proposed building. The diameter of the bored holes will normally be between 250 and 350 mm and can extend to depths of up to 4 m. Once the holes have been bored, shuttering is constructed to form lightweight reinforced

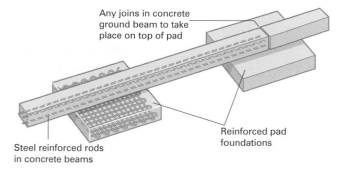

Figure 3.30 Square pad foundation with spanning ground beams

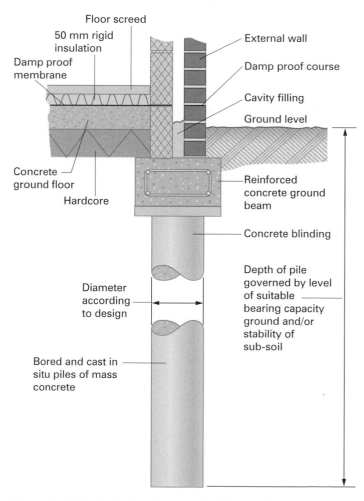

Figure 3.31 Typical short bored piled foundation

concrete beams, which span across the bored piles. The bored holes are then filled with concrete, with reinforcement projecting from the top of the pile concrete, so it can be incorporated into the concrete beams that span the piles.

As with pad foundation, short bored piled foundations can significantly reduce the amount of excavated soil, because there is no need to excavate deep trenches around the perimeter of the proposed structure.

Stepped foundations

A stepped foundation is used on sloping ground. The height of each step should not be greater than the thickness of the concrete, and should not be greater than 450 mm. Where possible, the height of the step should coincide with brick course height in order to avoid oversized mortar bed joints and eliminate the need for split brick courses. The overlap of the concrete between any given step, and the step below it, should not be less than 300 mm or less than the thickness of the concrete.

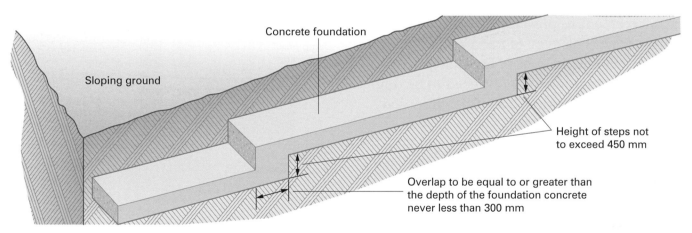

Concrete foundation

Sloping ground

Height of steps not to exceed 450 mm

Overlap to be equal to or greater than the depth of the foundation concrete never less than 300 mm

Figure 3.32 Typical stepped foundation

Superstructure

The superstructure covers everything above the substructure, from floors to walls to roofing. The purpose of the superstructure is to enclose and divide space, as well as spread loads safely into the substructure.

Within the superstructure, you will find the primary, secondary and finishing elements, as well as the services.

Floors

There are two main types of floor: ground and upper.

Ground floors

There are a few main types of ground floor. These are the ones you will most often come across.

- **Suspended timber floor** – a floor where timber joists are used to span the floor. The size of floor span determines the depth and thickness of the timbers used. The joists may be built into the inner skin of brickwork, sat upon small walls (dwarf/sleeper wall), or suspended from some form of joist hanger. The joists should span the shortest distance and sometimes dwarf/sleeper walls are built in the middle of the span to give extra support or to go underneath load-bearing walls. The top of the floor is decked with a suitable material (usually chipboard or solid pine tongue and groove boards). As the floor is suspended, usually with crawl spaces underneath, it is vital to have air bricks fitted. These allow air to flow under the floor, preventing high moisture content and timber rot.

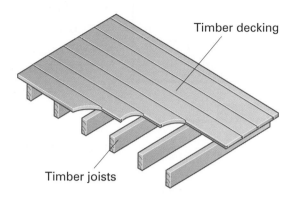

Figure 3.33 Suspended timber floor

- **Solid concrete floor** – concrete floors are more durable and are constructed on a sub-base incorporating hardcore, damp proof membranes and insulation. The depth of the hardcore and concrete will depend on the building and will be set by the *Building Regulations* and the local authority. Underfloor heating can be incorporated into a solid concrete floor. Great care must be taken when finishing the floor to ensure it is even and level.

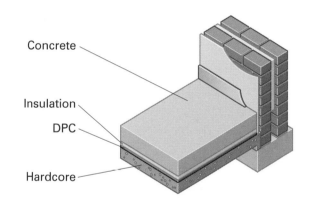

Figure 3.34 Solid concrete floor

- **Floating floor** – basic timber floor construction that is laid on a solid concrete floor. The timbers are laid in a similar way to joists, though they are usually 50 mm thick maximum as there is no need for support. The timbers are laid on the floor at predetermined centres and are not fixed to the concrete base (hence floating floor). The decking is then fixed onto the timbers. Insulation, or underfloor heating, can be placed between the timbers to enhance the thermal and acoustic properties.

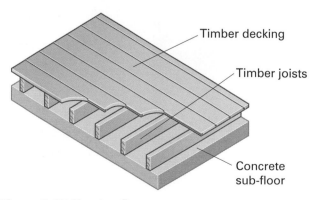

Figure 3.35 Floating floor

Knowledge of building methods and construction technology 2 **Unit 2003**

Key term

Regularised joists – joists that are all the same depth

Upper floors

Again, solid concrete slabs such as pre-cast beams can be used in larger buildings, but the most common type of upper floor is the suspended timber floor. As before, the joists are either built into the inner skin of brickwork or supported on some form of joist hanger. Spanning the shortest distance, with load-bearing walls acting as supports, it is vital that **regularised joists** are used, as a level floor and ceiling are required. The tops of the joists are again decked out, with the underside being clad in plasterboard and insulation placed between the joists to help with thermal and acoustic properties.

Walls

There are two main types of wall within a building: external and internal.

External walls

External walls come in a variety of styles, but the most common is cavity walling. Cavity walling is simply two brick walls built parallel to each other, with a gap – the cavity – between them. The cavity wall acts as a barrier to weather, with the outer leaf (or skin) preventing rain and wind from penetrating the inner leaf. The cavity is usually filled with insulation to prevent heat loss.

Timber kit houses are becoming more and more common as they can be erected to a wind and watertight stage within a few days. The principle is similar to a cavity wall: the inner skin is a timber frame clad in timber sheet material and covered in a breathable membrane to prevent water and moisture penetrating the timber. The outer skin is usually face brickwork.

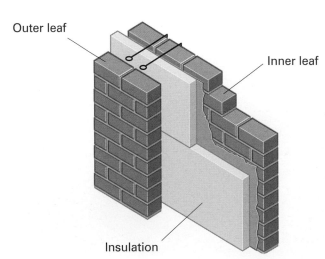

Figure 3.36 A cavity wall

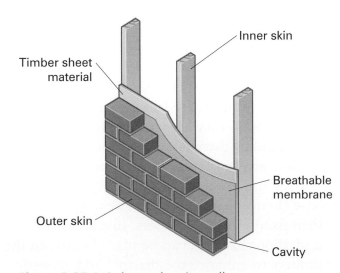

Figure 3.37 A timber and cavity wall

There are also other types of exterior walling, such as solid stone or log cabin style. Industrial buildings may have steel walls clad in sheet metal.

Internal walls

Internal walls are either load-bearing or non-load-bearing.

The difference between the two is that load-bearing walls will support the weight of any upper floors or roofs; in a house there will usually be at least one load-bearing wall. Non-load-bearing walls are simply used to divide the area into separate rooms.

Internal walls come in a variety of styles. Here is a list of the most common types.

- **Solid block walls** – simple blockwork walls, sometimes using fairface blockwork. These may be covered with plasterboard or plastered over to give a smooth finish, to which wallpaper or paint is applied. Solid block walls offer low thermal and sound insulation qualities. However, advances in technology mean that materials such as thermalite blocks can give better sound and heat insulation.

- **Solid brick walling** – usually made with face brickwork as a decorative finish. It is unusual for all walls within a house to be made from brickwork.

- **Timber stud walling** – more common in timber kit houses and newer buildings. Timber stud walling is also preferred when dividing an existing room, as it is quicker to erect. Clad in plasterboard and plastered to a smooth finish, timber stud partitions can be made more fire resistant and sound/thermal qualities can be improved with the addition of insulation or different types of plasterboard. Another benefit of timber stud walling is that timber noggins can be placed within the stud to give additional fixings for components such as radiators or wall units. Timber stud walling can also be load bearing, in which case thicker timbers are used.

- **Metal stud walling** – similar to timber stud, except that metal studs are used and the plasterboard is screwed to the studding.

- **Ground lats** – timber battens that are fixed to a concrete or stone wall to provide a flat surface, to which plasterboard is attached and a plaster finish applied.

Safety tip
Load bearing walls must not be altered without first providing temporary supports to carry the load until the work has been completed

Figure 3.38 Solid block wall

Figure 3.39 Solid brick wall

Figure 3.40 Timber stud wall

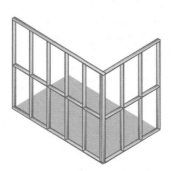

Figure 3.41 Metal stud wall

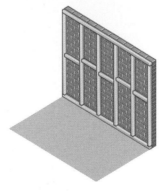

Figure 3.42 Ground lats

Knowledge of building methods and construction technology 2 **Unit 2003**

Cavity walling

Cavity walls are mainly used for house building and extension work to existing homes and flats. They consist of two separate walls built with a cavity between, joined together by metal ties. In most cases the outer wall is made of brick and the inner skin is made of block.

The main reason for this type of construction is to protect the inside from water penetration. The cavity forms a barrier. If the outer wall becomes wet (through rain, snow etc.), water is not passed through because the two walls do not touch. Air circulating around the cavity dries the dampness caused, as well as keeping the inner wall dry. Where the walls do meet, for example at door and window openings, a DPC is used to stop water penetration. The cavity can be insulated either partially or fully to make the building warmer and more energy-efficient.

Roofs

Although there are several different types of roofing, all roofs will technically be either a flat roof or a pitched roof.

Flat roofs

A flat roof is a roof with a pitch of 10 or less. The pitch is usually achieved through laying the joists at a pitch, or by using **firring pieces.**

The main construction method for a flat roof is similar to that for a suspended timber floor, with the edges of the joists being supported via a hanger or built into the brickwork, or even a combination of both. Once the joists are laid and firring pieces are fitted (if required), insulation and a vapour barrier are put in place. The roof is then decked on top and usually plasterboarded on the underside. The decking on a flat roof must be waterproof, and can be made from a wide variety of materials, including fibreglass or bitumen-covered boarding with felt layered on it.

Drainage of flat roofs is vital. The edge to which the fall leads to must have suitable guttering to allow rainwater to run away, rather than down the face of the wall.

> **Key term**
>
> **Firring pieces** – tapered strips of timber

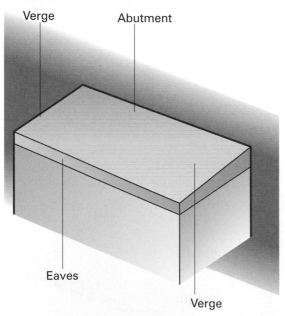

Figure 3.43 Flat roof terminology

Pitched roofs

There are several types of pitched roof, from the basic gable roof to more complex roofs such as mansard roofs. Whichever type of roof is being fitted to a building, it will most likely be constructed in one of the following ways.

- **Prefabricated truss roof** – as the name implies, this is a roof that has prefabricated members called trusses. Trusses are used to spread the load of the roof and to give it the required shape. Trusses are factory-made, delivered to site and lifted into place, usually by a crane. They are easy and quick to fit – either they are nailed to a wall plate or held in place by truss clips. Once fitted, bracing is attached to keep the trusses level and secure from wind. Felt is then fixed to the trusses and tiles or slate are used to keep the roof and dwelling waterproof.

- **Traditional/cut roof** – as an alternative to trusses, the cut roof uses loose timbers that are cut in-situ to give the roof its shape and to spread the relevant load. More time-consuming, and difficult to fit than trusses, the cut roof uses rafters that are individually cut and fixed in place, with two rafters forming a sort of truss. Once the rafters are all fixed, the roof is finished with felt and tiles or slate.

Metal trusses can also be used for industrial or more complex buildings.

To finish a roof where it meets the exterior wall (eaves), you must fix a vertical timber board (fascia) and a horizontal board (soffit) to the foot of the rafters/trusses. The fascia and soffit are used to close off the roof space from insects and birds.

Ventilators are attached to the soffits to allow air into the roof space, preventing rot, and guttering is attached to the fascia board to channel rainwater into a drain.

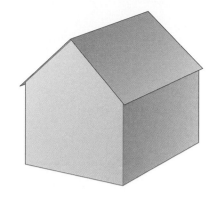

Figure 3.44 Duo pitch roof with gable ends

Did you know?

Due to the fact that heat rises, the majority of heat loss from a building is through its roof. Insulation such as mineral wool or polystyrene must be fitted to roof spaces and ideally to any intermediate floors as well

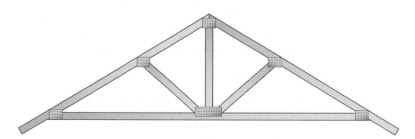

Figure 3.45 Prefabricated wooden roof truss

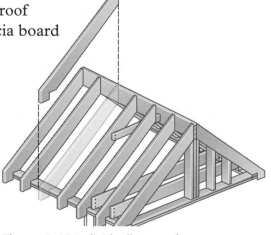

Figure 3.46 Individually cut rafters

Insulation materials in roofs

Due to the fact that heat rises, the insulation materials contained within a roof space, whether it be a flat or pitched roof, have a vital impact on the energy efficiency of the building.

Using the wrong type or size of insulation can vastly reduce the efficiency of the building. The type and size of insulation that should be used will be decided at the early planning stage and the architect should state what is to be used.

On smaller jobs where there is no architect, or on jobs where installing insulation is the only job, it is important that you read the manufacturer's information. This should be contained on the packaging, but if in doubt telephone the manufacturer to check.

Finishing elements

Finishing elements are the final surfaces of an element, which can be functional or decorative.

The main finishing elements are:

- plaster
- render
- paint
- wallpaper
- felt and battens for roofs
- flooring.

Finishing for walls

Plaster

Plaster can be used on a variety of wall surfaces to give a smooth and even finish. The plaster comes in powder form, usually bagged, and is mixed with water until it reaches a consistency that allows it to be applied to the surface and trowelled smooth. Ready-mix plaster is also available, but is more expensive, especially when a lot of surfaces have to be plastered.

These are the main surfaces to which plaster is applied.

- **Brick/blockwork** – prior to application, a bonding agent must be applied to the wall (usually a coat of watered down PVA), to help the plaster adhere to the surface. Usually a first coat of bonding plaster is applied to the wall to give it a level and flat surface. When this is dry, a second, finish coat is applied. As the finish coat is drying, the plasterer will work on the wall, smoothing it out until it is as smooth as glass.

Safety tip

To prevent dermatitis, ensure that you wear gloves when working with plaster, render or cement

- **Plasterboard** – as plasterboard is a flat surface to begin with, a bonding coat is rarely used. Generally, the plasterboard is fixed with the back face (the face with the writing) exposed to give better adhesion. Whether it is a wall or a ceiling, the plasterer will again work the finish coat to a very smooth surface.
- **Lath and plaster** – this is usually found in old properties. The laths are thin strips of wood, which are fixed to the wall with small gaps between to give the plaster a **key.** Once the laths are fixed the plasterer will apply bonding and finish coats as before.

Plasterboard with a tapered edge can also be fixed to the walls. In this case, instead of plastering the entire wall, the plasterer will simply fill the nail/screw holes, fit tape where the plasterboard joins are, and fill only the joints. Pre-mixed plaster is usually used for this; when it is dry, a light sanding is required to give a smooth finish. This method is preferred in newer buildings, especially timber kit houses.

Not all walls are plastered smooth, as some clients may require a rough or patterned finish. Although not technically a plaster, Artex™ is often used to give decorative finishes, especially on ceilings.

Render

Render is similar to plaster in that it is trowelled on to brick or blockwork to give a finish. Applied to external walls, the render must be waterproof to prevent damage to the walls. Different finishes are available, from stippling to patterning.

Paint

Paint is applied to various surfaces and is available in many different types to suit specific jobs. Paint is applied for a variety of reasons, the most common being to:

- **protect** – steel can be prevented from corroding due to rust, and wood can be prevented from rotting due to moisture and insect attack
- **decorate** – the appearance of a surface can be improved or given a special effect (for example marbling, wood graining)
- **sanitise** – a surface can be made more hygienic with the application of a surface coating, preventing penetration and accumulation of germs and dirt, and allowing easier cleaning.

Key term

Key – the end result of a process that prepares a surface, usually by making it rough or grooved, so that paint or some other finish will stick to it

Figure 3.47 Lath and plaster

Figure 3.48 Plaster being applied and trowelled

Paint is either water-based or solvent-based. When a paint is water-based, it means that the main liquid part of the paint is water; with a solvent-based paint, a chemical has been used instead of water to dissolve the other components of the paint.

Water-based paint is generally used on walls and ceilings, while solvent-based paint is used on timber mouldings, doors, metals, etc.

There are other surface finishes besides paint such as varnish (used on wood), masonry paint (used on exterior walls) and preservatives, which are used to protect wood from weather and insect attack.

Wallpaper

Wallpapers are used to decorate walls – thicker wallpapers can also hide minor defects. Basic wallpapers are made from either wood pulp or vinyl.

Wood-pulp papers can be used as preparatory papers or finish papers. Preparatory papers are usually painted with emulsion to provide a finish, or they can be used as a base underneath finish papers. Types of wood-pulp paper include plain, coloured and reinforced lining paper, as well as wood chip.

Vinyl wallpaper is a hard-wearing wallpaper made from a PVC layer attached to a pulp backing paper. Types of vinyl paper include patterned, sculptured or blown vinyl.

Wallpaper is hung on a wall using a paste. Not all pastes have the same strength, so make sure you choose the correct paste for the type of paper you are using.

Finishing for roofs

Finishing for a roof requires the laying of felt over the trusses or rafters to provide a weatherproof barrier. On top of the felt, battens are placed horizontally along the roof. This not only helps to keep the felt in place but, more importantly, allows a fixing and gives an angle for either a tile or slate finish.

Figure 3.49 Builder laying felt on a roof

Flooring

Flooring is traditionally finished with carpets in the majority of rooms, with a vinyl or linoleum material used in the kitchen and bathroom. Today, however, there is a larger choice in how floors are finished, with the main types of floor finish being:

- **Carpet** – still preferred in a large number of homes, as it feels warmer and more comfortable than other finishes. Some carpets are more moisture resistant and can be fitted in any room.
- **Linoleum** – a plastic-based floor covering that is glued down and comes in a variety of patterns or colours. Not so popular nowadays, as many people prefer laminated flooring.
- **Laminated flooring** – a solid MDF style base with a thin layer, or veneer, placed on top which can be wood grained or tiled. This is popular as it is hard wearing, comes in short lengths which click together and is easily fitted. If fitting laminated flooring in an area of high moisture, such as a kitchen or bathroom, ensure that the flooring you buy is suitable.
- **Tile** – it has recently become popular, especially in kitchens, to use traditional large floor tiles. These are very hard wearing and care needs to be taken when installing them to ensure that they are laid level.

Solid wood flooring

There are two methods in which a finish can be achieved for this type of flooring.

If you have old wooden tongue and groove floorboards, you can remove the existing floor covering, sand down the floorboards and then cover them with a suitable varnish. This is not a very energy efficient method as heat will escape from the gaps between the floorboards.

Alternatively, where chipboard flooring has been used, fitting solid tongue and groove boarding on top of the chipboard or instead of it will give you a more traditional look.

Figure 3.50 Chipboard flooring

K2. Principles behind internal work

Types of materials

Materials were covered earlier in this unit. You can refer back to previous pages for more detailed information on properties and storage of materials.

There are several types of material that you will use for internal work. These include the materials shown in the table below.

Material	Use
Polyurethane	A polymer that is used in a wide variety of building materials ranging from varnish to adhesive.
Glass fibre quilt	Used mainly to insulate areas within the buildings such as roof spaces and the areas between floors and walls.
Common brick	A basic brick that can be used in any type of walling.
Common block	A block made from concrete that can be used in any type of walling.
Aggregates	Covers a wide range of materials such as sand, chippings etc. Used in the creation of cements, concretes and renders.
Plasterboard	Man-made board that is used to clad walls and ceilings.
Concrete	Mixed from aggregates. Can be used to create formwork for floors, pillars, etc.
Metals	Used widely on large sites as a means of support. On some commercial/industrial buildings the entire skeleton of the frame can be made from metal.
Mineral wool	Similar uses to glass fibre quilt, acting as insulation.
Softwood	Used for a variety of joinery purposes from doors to stairs to roofs.
Hardwood	Used where a higher class of finish is needed (such as doors). Very rarely used in roofs unless the beams are exposed.
Facing brick	Used on the outer skin of a cavity wall – more decorative than common brick.
Thermal block	Used on the inner skin of a cavity wall to provide better thermal insulation.
Glass	Used in windows and doors to allow natural light to enter the premises.
Plaster	Used to cover over plasterboard or brick/block walls to give a smooth finish ready for decoration.
Engineering brick	Used in the same ways as common or facing bricks, but where more strength is required.

Internal components

Secondary elements are not essential to the building's strength or structure, but provide a particular function, such as completing openings in walls, etc.

The main secondary elements are:

- stairs
- frames and linings
- doors
- windows
- architrave and skirting.

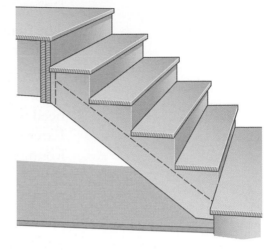

Stairs

Stairs are used to provide access between different floors of a dwelling or to gain access to a higher/lower area. Stairs are made up of a number of steps and each continuous set of steps running in the same direction is known as a flight. Steps are made of vertical boards called risers and horizontal boards called treads.

Figure 3.51 A simple staircase

There are various types of stair, ranging from spiral staircases (often fitted where there is a lack of space) to multi-flight staircases, such as dog-leg or half-turn stairs.

Stairs are strictly governed by the *Building Regulations* and there are numerous requirements that must be adhered to when constructing and installing them.

Stairs are generally made from four types of material:

- **timber** – the most common material, used widely in almost all buildings
- **in-situ-cast concrete** – a wooden frame is constructed around the stairwell and concrete is poured into the frame, forming the staircase
- **pre-cast concrete** – concrete is cast in large moulds to form the staircase; usually found in the stairwells of blocks of flats and in other areas of heavy use
- **steel** – usually found on the exterior of buildings in the form of fire escapes, etc.

Frames and linings

Frames and linings are fitted around openings and are used to allow components such as windows and doors to be fitted. The frame or lining is fitted to the wall and usually finished flush with the walls. The joint between the frame or lining and the wall is covered by the architrave.

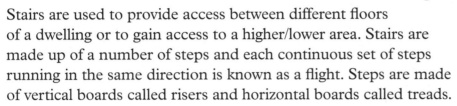

Doors

The main purpose of a door is to provide access from one room to another and to allow a space to be closed off for security/thermal/ sound reasons.

Doors come in many varieties, shapes and sizes. The type you need will be determined by the location and purpose of the door. Exterior doors are generally thicker and are fitted with more ironmongery such as letter plates and locks. Some interior doors will have locks fitted as well, such as bathroom doors or doors that need to be secure.

Doors can be solid timber or have glass in them and may be graded for fire resistance.

Windows

Windows are fitted to allow natural light to enter the building with minimal loss of heat. Again, windows come in a variety of shapes and styles. Glass that is fitted in a window can be decorative and heat-loss resistant.

Architraves and skirting

Architraves are decorative mouldings used to hide the gap between frames and the wall finish. Skirting is moulding that covers the gap between the floor and the base of a wall. These mouldings come in a variety of **profiles** such as torus and ogee.

Other mouldings can also be used, such as picture and dado rails.

> **Key term**
>
> **Profile** – the shape of a moulding when you cut through it

Substance damage to building materials

There are a number of substances which can have a negative effect on building materials when they come into contact with them.

Water

Water can cause a range of problems for materials and can have a number of detrimental effects on them. Water can cause components to expand, which can add additional stress to joints etc. and cause cracks or gaps to appear. Water can also cause some components to rust, reduce the effectiveness of insulation properties and damage interior finishes such as paint. Water in materials will increase the chances that they will be attacked by mould, fungi or insects.

Frost

Frost will have a similar effect to water once it has thawed, but during the freezing process materials will shrink with the cold. When the temperature rises and the ice begins to thaw and melt, this change can cause cracks. With some materials this can cause severe problems, particularly with copper plumbing pipes.

Chemicals

Chemicals can have a very detrimental effect on building materials. Most will cause some damage, and certain chemicals can corrode, or even completely break down and destroy some materials.

Heat and fire

Heat will cause materials to expand, which can cause minor problems, such as doors not shutting correctly. It can also affect things such as paint finishes, the thermal properties of materials and the effectiveness of certain glues. Fire will destroy the majority of building materials, including steel, if hot enough and left to burn.

Reducing the risk of damage

Materials can be treated to prevent or reduce the effects of these elements. The type of treatment used is usually chemical and care needs to be taken to ensure that the treatment will not cause other damage to the material. Don't make matters worse when you are trying to improve them!

Products that provide protection to materials will come with manufacturers' instructions – be sure to follow these instructions.

Rectifying material deterioration

If any materials have deteriorated and need to be repaired or replaced then it is vital that the cause of deterioration is found and steps are taken to prevent reoccurrence.

This may mean treating the replacement materials or, in the case of water damage, repairing any leaks. The main methods used to protect and repair the main groups of materials are as follows:

- Timber can be protected by cutting out damaged parts. A protective coating, based on water, tar or solvents, can be placed on wood. These products are known as preservatives.
- Metal materials can be given protective coatings. Steel and iron can be coated in zinc, which will prevent rusting. This is known as galvanic protection.
- Concrete and masonry are protected by expansion joints, which were covered on pages 105–106.

Find out

Use the Internet to research some common chemicals and the effects that they can have on a range of materials

Safety tip

Chemicals can be dangerous – don't put yourself at risk and always follow instructions

Safety tip

All wood preservatives are toxic and should be handled with care

K3. Storage and delivery of building materials

Stock rotation and delivery times

When dealing with certain materials it is important to know about stock rotation, which ensures that the materials do not go past their use-by date. Materials such as plaster or cement have a use-by date on them. Generally, such materials will set or go off about this date. To prevent this, it is vital that the materials are used before this happens.

When taking delivery of materials, place the newest materials at the back. This will mean that the older materials are used first and will reduce the risk of materials reaching their use-by date.

Delivery dates are also important. You want to ensure that materials are there when they need to be used, but you don't want them delivered weeks before they are needed as they will take up valuable storage space and can get damaged or expire.

The main types of materials affected by this are:

- cement
- plaster
- glue
- paints
- preservative coatings

Checking deliveries to sites

When a delivery is made to a site, security will check that the delivery is due and that the materials are indeed for that site. The foreman or site agent will then look at the delivery note and check it against the order to ensure that what is being delivered is what was ordered.

The unloading of the materials can then take place, usually with a designated person checking the quality of the materials, as well as checking the quantity against the delivery note. The materials should then be stored appropriately.

Tools used to transport materials

When handling materials it is important to know the best way to carry things safely. Manual handling should be avoided if at all possible and mechanised equipment such as forklifts should be used instead.

If this is not possible or available, hand tools should be used. These include:

- wheelbarrows
- pallet trucks
- bag trolleys
- skips.

In some cases there is only one way that a material can be carried, e.g. mixed cement should only be moved in a wheelbarrow.

FAQ

How do I know if the materials I am using are strong enough to carry the load?

The specification will give you the details of the sizes and types of material that are to be used. You will need to use this document when you need to know which materials to use for the job.

Do I have to fix battens to a wall before I plasterboard it?

No. The method called dot and dab can be used where plaster is dabbed onto the back of the plasterboard and then pushed onto the wall.

Check it out

1. Describe the process that should happen before any construction work commences on a building project.
2. State three key factors that influence the design of a foundation and explain why.
3. Explain what is meant by the terms 'dead load' and 'imposed load'.
4. During a site investigation, certain data needs to be collected. Give a list of the key information that must be recorded during this investigation.
5. Why must excavation work be carefully planned before it is carried out?
6. Name three categories of soil.
7. Name three types of foundation. Complete sketches to show the key features of these types of foundation.
8. Explain how surface water can affect excavation work.
9. In a stepped foundation, what is the recommended maximum height of each concrete step?
10. State four of the main principles of building and briefly explain what each of them is.
11. List the three main types of stress.
12. Give a brief description of external walling.
13. What are the four main secondary elements? Why are they secondary?
14. Give a brief description of the process involved with lath and plaster.
15. What are the three main services?

Getting ready for assessment

The information contained in this unit, as well as continued practical assignments that you will carry out in your college or training centre, will help you with preparing for both your end of unit test and the diploma multiple-choice test. It will also aid you in preparing for the work that is required for the synoptic practical assignments.

The information in this unit will build on the information that you may have acquired during Level 1 Unit 3 and will help you understand the basics of your own trade as well as the basic information on several other trade areas.

You will need to be familiar with:

- the principles behind foundations, walls, floor and roofs
- the principles behind internal work
- storage and delivery of building materials.

It is important to understand what other trades do in relation to you and how their work affects you and your work. It is also good to know how the different components of a building are constructed and how these tie in with the tasks that you carry out. You must always remember that there are a number of tasks being carried out on a building site at all times, and many of these will not be connected to the work you are doing. It is useful to remember the communication skills you learnt in Unit 2002, as these will be important for working with other trades on site. You will also need to be familiar with specifications and contract documents, to know the type of construction work other crafts will be doing around you on site.

For learning outcome one, you saw the range of different structures and how they maintain structural stability and quality of insulation. It is important that the working drawings are precise in order to complete the structure accurately. You will need to be able to sketch a section through building elements and components.

This unit has explained the different construction methods for foundations, walls, floors and roofs. Although you will not be working on all these elements, you need to be familiar with the work undertaken on them in order to plan when to carry out your own work. You will need to be able to complete a programme of work for a simple two-storey construction. To do this you will need to understand the jobs that other trades have to carry out on these parts of the building.

Remember, a sound knowledge of construction methods and materials will be very useful during your training as well as in later life in your professional career.

Good luck!

Knowledge check

1 What is the most popular and widely used insulation?

a) polystyrene sheets
b) rigid foam
c) glass mineral wool
d) rock wool

2 One of the main causes of trench collapse is:

a) incorrect methods used in the excavation work
b) poor placement of materials near to the sides of the trench
c) the type of soil
d) presence of tree roots or other vegetation

3 The final decision for the suitability and in particular the depth of the foundation and thickness of concrete will rest with whom?

a) structural design team
b) architect
c) local authority
d) client

4 The type of foundation used for a small domestic dwelling or low rise structure is:

a) wide strip foundation
b) short bored piled foundation
c) pad foundation
d) narrow strip foundation

5 In a stepped foundation, the overlap of the concrete to that below should not be less than:

a) 250 mm
b) 300 mm
c) 450 mm
d) 600 mm

6 Which of the following are primary elements?

a) roofs
b) windows
c) foundations
d) all of the above

7 Flat roofs are constructed in a similar way to:

a) suspended timber floors
b) floating floors
c) truss roofing
d) cut roofing

8 Which of the following secondary elements are decorative mouldings?

a) frames
b) linings
c) windows
d) architraves

9 Which of the following are finishing elements?

a) plaster
b) glazing
c) dado rail
d) all of the above

10 Which of the following can be water or solvent based?

a) paint
b) plaster
c) wallpaper
d) render

UNIT 2045

How to interpret working drawings to set out masonry structures

Setting out refers to the marking out and positioning of a building. It is a very important operation as the setting out of a building must be as accurate as possible. Mistakes made at this stage can prove very costly later. To appreciate the need for careful and accurate setting out, we have to understand and visualise the finished building and its requirements.

This unit also supports NVQ Unit VR41 Set Out Masonry Structures and VR43 Lay Domestic Drainage.

This unit contains material that supports TAP Unit 2: Set Out for Masonry Structures. It also contains material that supports the delivery of the five generic units.

This unit will cover the following learning outcomes:

- How to interpret information to establish setting out requirements

- How to prepare construction sites for setting-out activities

- How to select resources for setting out work

- How to set out regular shaped masonry structures on level ground.

Remember

There may be restrictions on the building you are planning. The local authority will be able to inform you about any planning restrictions that might apply to a proposed build

Key terms

Building lines – imaginary lines set by the local authority to control the positioning of buildings

Boundary lines – lines that indicate ownership, for example, lines between properties

Functional skills

When reading and understanding the text in this unit, you are practising several functional skills:
FE 1.2.1 – Identifying how main points and ideas are organised in different texts.
FE 1.2.2 – Understanding different texts in detail.
FE 1.2.3 – Read different texts and take appropriate action, e.g. respond to advice/instructions.
If there are any words or phrases you do not understand, use a dictionary, look them up using the Internet or discuss with your tutor.

Remember

Working drawings are drawn to a scale, not real-life size. You will need to work with this scale, in order to work out how many blocks you need

K1. Interpret information to establish setting out requirements

The types of drawing used and the main information they supply was covered earlier in this book. Please turn to the following pages for more information on:

- types of drawing and use of symbols and abbreviations (pages 54–57)
- purpose of different types of drawing (pages 54–57)
- purpose of using datums (page 57).

All this information will be used to set out the correct dimensions and location of a building.

Finding the right place to set out sounds like an obvious thing to state, but it is so important that this is done absolutely correctly. Buildings have sometimes had to be completely demolished because they were put up in the wrong place! This is because **building lines** and **boundary lines** are often involved and there are very strict regulations governing these.

The building line shows exactly where you have permission to set out and construct the building. If you set out the building outside of this line, you will be placing it in an area where you do not have permission, or the right, to construct the building.

You must make sure that you are within boundary lines and that you are setting out as the architect and client intended within these lines. Failure to do so could lead to an expensive and time-consuming correction of the mistake.

Reading and taking measurements from drawings

With any wall that you build, you will need a drawing in the workshop. The drawing should have a plan and an elevation so you can see what you will be building as well as any measurements or block lengths marked. From this, you can work out what materials you will need. For example, if the wall is six blocks long and four blocks high, you will need 24 blocks.

On more complicated tasks you may have an opening, such as a window or door. You will need to know the size of the opening. If the drawing is based just on measurements, you will need to measure a block and remember its size in order to calculate the number required.

There are some methods of taking measurements that are specific to the type of drawing you may have as a reference.

Checking measurements

Regular checks of measurements should be carried out while setting out. This is to ensure that all walls, trenches and other constructions are in the correct positions and that they are square before any excavations are carried out. Once excavations are dug out, it is very difficult to change them other than to carry out extra digging work. This will cost more money for tasks, such as extra soil removal, or materials, such as more concrete.

If the error is spotted at this point, it will remove the risk of the substantial cost of making corrections after concreting. There are a number of problems that can be caused by incorrectly placed setting out, for example, walls not sitting on the foundations.

Reporting inaccuracies in information

Sometimes information given to you may be wrong or have mistakes in it. For example, this can be an oversight on measurements or lead to material requirements not being suitable for the job. These inaccuracies should be reported immediately to your line manager and you will need to explain what the problem is.

Your manager may be able to give you the correct information straight away, but in most circumstances they will probably need to speak to their line manager, who could be the site foreman, or in turn may need to speak to the clerk of works or the architect, if the problem is related to drawings. These people may, in turn, need to speak to the client to resolve the problem. However, no work should be carried out until this is resolved.

K2. Prepare construction sites for setting out activities

In the early stages of the design process, before any construction work begins, a site investigation will be carried out to ascertain any conditions, situations or surrounding sites that may affect the proposed construction work. A great deal of data will need to be established during the site investigation, including:

- position of boundary fences and hedges
- position, height, girth and spread of trees
- uneven or sloping ground
- existing buildings that need to be demolished or protected

Functional skills

When taking measurements you will need to use a range of information sources. This will allow you to practise FM 1.2.1b which relates to interpreting information from sources such as diagrams, tables, charts and graphs.

Remember

From the point of view of your training in the workshop and the drawings you will be using there, your supervisor will probably be best placed to resolve your problem

- types of soil and the depths of any different soils
- location and depth of services, including gas, electricity, water, telephone cables, drains and sewers.

Although the local authorities will normally provide information relating to the location of services, existing buildings, planning restrictions, preservation orders and boundary lines, all of these still need to be identified and confirmed through the site investigation.

Once all site investigations have been completed and all the necessary information and data in relation to the proposed building project has been established, site clearance can take place.

Reasons for site clearance

The main purpose of site clearance is to remove from the area covered by the site plan existing buildings, waste, vegetation and, most importantly, the surface layer of soil, referred to as top soil, because it is unsuitable to build on.

Once a site has been cleared of all these obstacles and content, it will be suitable to build on and excavations for the foundations can be started.

Resources for site clearance

Site planning and positioning resources

Site planning is a very important process. Offices, canteens, toilets and storage areas, for example, all have to be taken into account when putting the plan for a site together. The positioning of all these facilities needs to be clearly established. They must also be clearly placed in such a way that they do not stop or get in the way of the day-to-day work of the site.

Storage areas need to be positioned on site where delivery and recovery of material from them will involve the least amount of transportation. This is not only delivery from external suppliers, but also transportation across the site and between material compounds. Storage areas also need to be monitored to maintain health and safety, as well as to reduce the risk of theft of materials.

Offices need to be positioned directly near the main site entrance with clear directions to them. This means that any visitors – either for deliveries or other visitors to the site – are obliged to report directly to authorised staff before they enter the site. When they report to reception, visitors should state their reasons for being on

Figure 4.1 An example of an onsite office for a building site

Figure 4.2 An example of storage facilities for building materials

site. The staff in the office will also be able to ensure that visitors are covered for insurance purposes. Welfare facilities, canteens, toilets, drying rooms and so on should also be in this area. This means that the staff will also comply with the health and safety on site, especially as regards the wearing of PPE.

Once you have a drawing to work to, you will need to look at preparing your working area and the positioning of materials. After working out the quantity or volume of the different materials required, you will have to stack them in your area. Each site has different rules for arranging materials. On smaller sites, materials are often positioned close by, ready for use. On bigger sites, all materials may be held in a compound until needed and then transported by fork lift to positions as required.

Your supervisor will explain the correct method of setting out the job. You will need to use the drawings and measurements given to you by your supervisor.

Walk-over survey

A walk-over of the site should be carried out before you begin any work. This is essential as it will give you a chance to spot any problems or hazards within the area before you begin work. Possible hazards on the site could include broken glass, spikes, obstacles or holes. If not identified and dealt with, these problems and hazards could endanger workers or cause damage to machinery later on.

Unidentified problems or hazards can lead to delays in the project. They also reflect badly on the company's safety record. In serious cases, they could lead to legal action.

Remember

Every material on site has specific requirements for use and storage. You will have to make sure that the site plan you are using allows for these materials to be stored correctly and safely

Figure 4.3 Trees and the surrounding area are protected on site

The results of the walk-over survey need to be recorded and submitted to your manager so that the results can be shared with the entire team working on the site as well as with the site management.

Clearing and planting hedges and trees

It will also be necessary to remove hedges and trees from the site area. These will need to be uprooted and moved to a new location or disposed of.

Large trees may need to be cut down to allow for the construction. In most instances, the existence of trees will have been taken into account at the planning stages of a project. This is particularly the case if there are preservation orders on certain trees. In that case, the trees and the immediately surrounding area will need to be protected while the work is being carried out in other areas on site.

Did you know?

Preservation orders are used to preserve and protect trees from damage. They are placed by the local authority. Removing or damaging protected trees can lead to prosecution. Not all trees are protected and individual decisions are made on each tree depending on its age, position, species and size

Working life

Lewis is involved in carrying out a site survey on a plot of land and setting out the new building on the site. The ground is fairly flat with little vegetation except two large sycamore trees directly in the area to be excavated for the foundations of the building.

- What should he do?
- Who should he contact?
- What organisations would need to be contacted about the trees?
- What impact could this have on the type of foundation to be used?
- What impact could this have on cost and timescales?

In other instances, new trees and hedges may be introduced before the job is finished. This may be to allow them to take root and create a pleasant environment ready for the buildings being used.

Level stripping

If the ground is uneven or sloping, level stripping will be required. In some cases, it would be too costly to level the whole area, so banked or stepped areas are left. These would normally be determined on the survey before stripping begins and incorporated into the finished design of the site.

The ground is normally cleared and levelled using a digger. Sometimes dug material may be stock piled on site, but in other instances it is removed so as not to block areas planned for storage or building.

Demolition

Some sites require the removal of an existing building. This process is called demolition. The materials and debris are often carefully removed as it is sometimes possible to use these again. In some instances, a building may be removed and re-erected elsewhere on site or even in a new location.

Demolition is dangerous and should be carried out by specialist contractors.

Most buildings are only two or three storeys high. For these, demolition is relatively simple. The building can be pulled down both manually and mechanically. For larger buildings, a wrecker ball may be needed. This is effective for demolishing masonry, but can be less efficient for other materials.

Safety should always be a key concern during demolition work. A site safety officer should work with the demolition crew to ensure that all the rules and regulations are being followed.

Existing services

The services are specialist components within a building ranging from running water to electricity. The main services in a standard house are:

- **Electrical** – covers all electrical components within the building from lights and sockets to security and communication systems. Electrical installation and maintenance work must be undertaken by a fully trained specialist as electricity can kill.
- **Mechanical** – covers items such as lifts. As with electrical services, work on mechanical services should only be undertaken by a specialist.

Did you know?

Site investigations or surveys will establish the contours of the site. This will identify where certain areas of the site will need to be reduced or increased in height. For example, an area of the site may need to be built up in order to mask surrounding features outside the boundaries of the proposed building project

Safety tip

Any live gas, electricity or water supplies to a building that will be demolished need to be cut off in advance

Figure 4.4 Demolition taking place on site

Remember

All service work must be carried out by fully trained and competent people

- **Plumbing** – can cover gas as well as running water, but only if the plumber is qualified and CORGI registered as a gas installation expert.

It is essential to ensure that all these services have been located and the supply to them has been cut off before any work on site starts and particularly when excavating trenches and doing ground work. As much information as possible should be gathered to avoid damage, danger to workers and the public, and expensive repairs.

If a mechanical digger is carrying out the excavation, then damage to an existing service can happen extremely quickly. The digger bucket can go through the ground and the service without much effort. This can cause delays to the work due to the time it will take to carry out repairs, which will add extra costs to the project.

Damage to existing services will probably also cause a great deal of inconvenience to the people in the surrounding area, who may be left with no electricity, gas or water for a long period of time until the service has been repaired.

Locating existing services

The local authorities will normally provide information relating to the location of services. However, all of these still need to be identified and confirmed through the site investigation. In particular, hidden services will need to be located with the use of modern electronic surveying equipment.

There are several scanning devices available that can be used to locate any existing services and these should be used to survey the land before any excavation work begins. A survey of the area will need to be conducted to locate:

- gas pipes
- water pipes
- electricity cables
- telephone cables
- drainage pipes
- television cables
- tree roots and other buried objects.

Other hazards

Some sites contain gases (methane) and there must be an awareness of this before starting work so that necessary precautions can be taken. These problems often occur on land previously used as landfill sites, which have been left to settle for a number of years and are now ready for building purposes.

Another important consideration in excavations is the lack of oxygen. This can occur in confined spaces or deep excavations and sometimes tests have to be carried out to monitor the oxygen levels.

Methods for isolating services

If any disconnection or connection of services is required, it must always be carried out by the relevant supplier of the service. The person working on the service must be trained and competent.

Connecting services

The other main reason for locating services is to make connections from the existing service pipes and cables to the new construction. For example, all domestic dwellings need water, gas and electricity!

Each service provider will normally attend to any new connections. The exception is drainage, which is normally carried out by the ground workers associated with the site itself. They may also be asked to expose services ready for connections to be made. However, any exposed pipes or cables must be protected from damage and any trenches left open must be secured by barriers and clearly indicated by signs.

Any service should only be exposed for the minimum amount of time to allow connections to be made.

Once the connection has been made, the trench should be back filled and compacted as best as possible to avoid shrinkage and settlement at a later date. The trench may require more reinstatement work later, especially if tarmac is to be used as a top finish.

Safety around the trench

There are some very simple things you can do to make sure that the trench is as safe as possible:

- Keep excavated material cleared away from edges of trenches to stop the excess weight causing the ground to collapse.
- Store pipes at right angles to the trench so they do not roll in.
- Put up warning signs and guardrails as required to protect workers.
- Inspect the trench carefully if there has been a change in the soil conditions, for example after a heavy rainfall.

Trench timbering

Trench timbering is the operation of supporting the sides of a trench. In drainage, operatives will spend a considerable amount of time in the trench during the laying of the pipes, so their safety

Safety tip

The longer a pipe or cable is exposed, the more the chance of damage to it and the greater the hazard risk to workers

Did you know?

Most operations now use steel sheets with timber bracing as this is much stronger than timber alone

Figure 4.5 Trench timbering

must be ensured by the prevention of trench collapse. Drain trenches can be quite deep and all excavations 1.2 m deep and over should have some kind of support. Even shallow trenches may need support in certain soils, and remember that operatives may have to kneel or lie down to carry out some operations.

Reclamation of materials

Reclaimed materials have been taken from demolished constructions or moved soil and re-used in a new building. This process involves minimal changes or alterations to their original use, with the materials being re-used for a similar but new purpose. Reclaimed materials can be cut to size, adapted, cleaned or refurbished, but are fundamentally unaltered.

This is part of introducing **sustainability** to building design and construction. It is important to consider what materials can be recycled in new constructions. Examples of this include:

- slates or tiles being re-used for roofing
- masonry being crushed and re-used for general site fill
- timber sections being re-used for panel products
- cleaned bricks being crushed and re-used as hardcore.

Drainage systems

Drainage systems are pipe work, usually underground, which carry away waste matter and water from a building. They are a very important part of the construction process, as all waste materials have to be carried from a building safely to prevent the spread of disease.

It is required that a drain should be:

- designed to suit its intended purpose
- laid out as simply as possible
- sloped enough to take away waste
- airtight and/or watertight
- able to prevent gases entering the building
- ventilated to get rid of the gases
- accessible for inspection and cleansing.

Setting out the gradient of a drainage system

To perform this operation a certain amount of information is required before you start. It is acceptable to start at the lowest point and work to the highest so the starting point must be known.

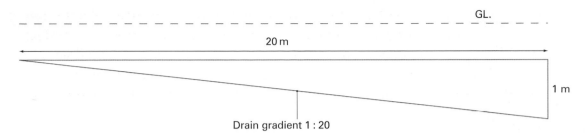

GL.

20 m

1 m

Drain gradient 1 : 20

Figure 4.6 Drain gradient

The starting point must be:

- an existing local authority sewer
- a branch drain left on the sewer
- an existing inspection chamber
- a septic tank.

When the starting and finishing points have been found the 'path' of the drain can be established.

Gradients of drainage

For a drain to work efficiently, the right slope is essential. The gradient is a ratio and is obtained by dividing the length of the drain by the amount of fall. For example, if a drain run is 20 m long and falls 1 m then the gradient is $20 \div 1 = 1{:}20$.

Figure 4.7 A traveller is used to check drain gradient

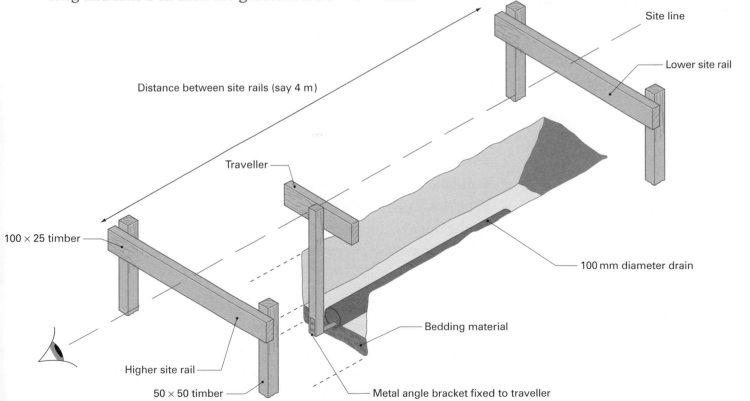

Site line

Lower site rail

Distance between site rails (say 4 m)

Traveller

100 × 25 timber

100 mm diameter drain

Bedding material

Higher site rail

50 × 50 timber

Metal angle bracket fixed to traveller

Figure 4.8 Gradient of drain showing traveller

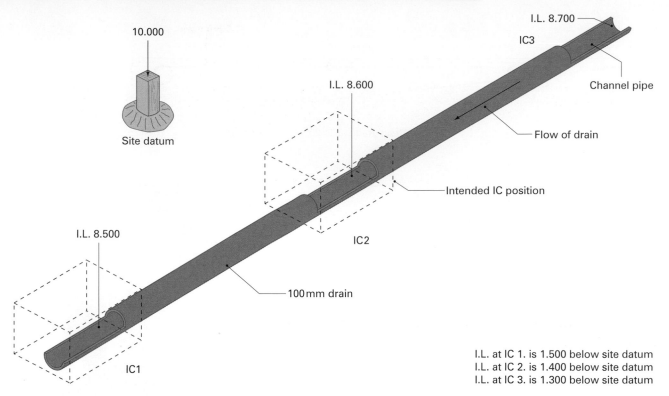

10.000

Site datum

I.L. 8.700

IC3

Channel pipe

I.L. 8.600

Flow of drain

Intended IC position

IC2

I.L. 8.500

100 mm drain

IC1

I.L. at IC 1. is 1.500 below site datum
I.L. at IC 2. is 1.400 below site datum
I.L. at IC 3. is 1.300 below site datum

Figure 4.9 Invert levels at inspection chambers

To maintain the correct gradient of a run of pipes, site rails are set up at the end or at intervals along the drain and the invert levels of the drain. Pipes can be checked by the means of a traveller (a T-shaped rod).

Maintaining gradients

In order to maintain gradient:

- fix lower site rail (any height)
- divide distance between site rails by gradient (1:40)
  = 4000 ÷ 40 = 100 mm
- set higher site rail 100 mm higher than lower site rail
- determine length of traveller at lower end of drain (invert level to site line)
- lay each pipe and sight traveller as shown to maintain gradient.

Invert levels

When calculating gradients the invert of the pipe is used as the reference point and this can be related to the site datum. When a drainage layout is designed, the architect or draughtsman will usually give the invert level at each inspection chamber, which will of course contain channel pipes. The invert level will be in metres to three decimal places, for example 7.675 m. The inspection chambers on a drain are placed at changes of

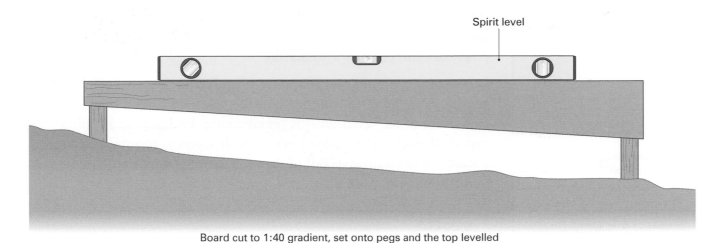

Spirit level

Board cut to 1:40 gradient, set onto pegs and the top levelled

Figure 4.10 Gradient board on pegs

direction or gradients, so it is practical to place site rails near inspection chambers.

Gradient boards

Another way of setting out a gradient is with the use of a gradient board. It is a tapered piece of timber, which is placed onto pegs within the trench or laid on the pipes after laying to check the gradient. A spirit level is used on top of the gradient board to check the position.

Pipes entering buildings

Where a pipe passes through a wall to enter a building, certain precautions are necessary to prevent damage to the drain:

- the wall above the pipe must be adequately supported to prevent any weight of the structure settling on the pipe
- a 50 mm gap should be maintained all around the pipe
- a rigid sheet material should be placed both sides of the hole to prevent vermin entering the building and backfill entering the 50 mm clearance.

Types of drainage system

There are two types of drainage system:

The combined system

In this type of drainage system the foul and surface water is carried in the same pipe.

The separate system

In a separate system the foul and surface water are kept separate by the use of two drainage systems. The foul water is discharged

> **Remember**
> Gradient boards are only really suitable for short drain runs and would not be accurate on long runs

> **Did you know?**
> Concrete lintels are normally used as support when bridging an opening

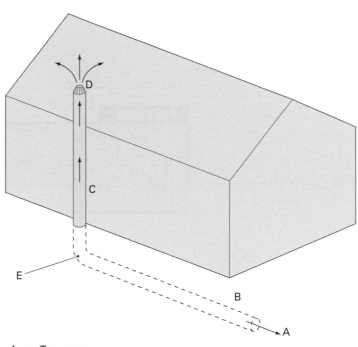

A = To sewer
B = 100 mm diameter drain
C = Soil and vent pipe
D = Pipe guard
E = Rest bend

Figure 4.11 Drainage ventilation

into a company sewer (local water authority) or type of container, and the surface water is carried away to a water course (canal, river, stream, etc.) or a soakaway.

In the modern era great planning is undertaken to collect and **treat** as much waste water as possible to meet the demands of every one of us. Whether it is for drinking, bathing, or keeping our clothes clean, a vast supply of fresh water is required in every country just to survive. All of this is generated through climatic conditions (e.g. rainfall, etc.).

Drainage ventilation

Drainage ventilation is very important for two main reasons:

- to allow gases to escape from the drain
- to equalise pressure so that the air pressure in the drain is the same as outside the drain.

In a building with an upstairs toilet, the outlet connection joins on to the soil and vent pipe, which then carries on above the roof level, to vent the gases. A pipe guard is put in to the top to prevent birds nesting at the top and causing a blockage.

Drainage pipes and fittings

Pipes

The materials used for pipes are:

- clay
- uPVC
- concrete
- iron.

The minimum diameter of a pipe carrying soil water is 100 mm.

Most straight pipes are circular in section and contain a slight chamfer on each end to enable easy entry into the joining coupling.

Fittings

These are components used in drainage, other than straight pipes. There are numerous fittings available – some of the common ones are shown in Figure 4.12.

Fittings are usually the same material as the pipes being used, but can differ with various adapters.

The main locations for fittings are:

- at a junction
- at a bend
- at the end of a drain
- in an inspection chamber.

Rigid pipe joints

Rigid joints refer to joints made with sand and cement (in the ratio of 1:2). The spigot is inserted into the socket and 'centred' by tarred yarn or rope. This joint has the disadvantage that the slightest movement of the pipe could fracture the joint and cause a leak.

- Used when a branch drain meets a main drain
- Not recommended on soil drainage

- Used when a drain changes direction
- Should be avoided where possible on soil drainage

- Used to terminate the end of a drain and receive sink wastes and remainder pipes
- Water seal remains in bottom of gully to prevent gases excaping

- Used in an inspection chamber where a branch drain meets a main drain
- Aids cleansing and inspection

Figure 4.12 Types of drainage fitting

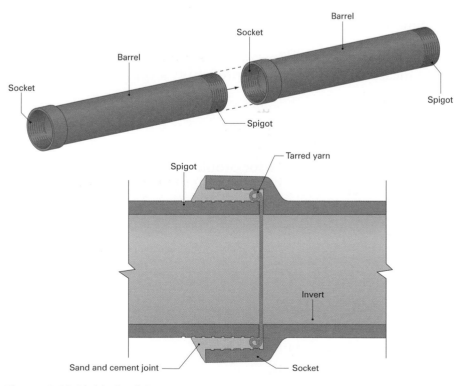

Figure 4.13 Rigid pipe joints

Figure 4.14 Flexible drainage pipe joint

Flexible pipe joints

Flexible joints have many advantages over rigid joints as they:

- can move slightly without leaking
- can be laid faster and more efficiently
- are not damaged by freezing temperatures
- can be tested immediately after laying
- are easily aligned.

Pipe bedding and surrounds

Pipe bedding and surrounds are very important as they have a two-fold purpose. They must:

- protect the pipe from receiving any loads that may break or damage the drain
- allow movement of the pipe within the ground.

K3. Select resources for setting out work

Materials you will need to set out a building

The exact materials you will need to set out a building will vary depending on the size of the job. The following list would be adequate for, say, a small detached house:

- plans and specifications
- two measuring tapes (30 m), preferably steel
- optical level
- site square (optional)
- 50 mm × 50 mm timber pegs
- 25 mm × 100 mm timber for profiles
- lump hammer
- claw hammer
- hand saw
- a line
- concrete (ballast and cement) to secure pegs (although sometimes unnecessary)
- sand (for marking out trenches)
- 50 mm round-head nails
- 75 mm round-head nails.

Did you know?

Flexible pipes are normally bedded and surrounded with pea gravel but in some cases solid concrete is used

Functional skills

To set out correctly you will need to use a wide range of measurements and resources. This will allow you to practise FM 1.2.1b which relates to interpreting information from sources such as diagrams, tables, charts and graphs. You will also be able to practise solving problems requiring calculations with common measures including length, weight and capacity.

Ranging lines

Ranging lines are the lines used on profiles to check that the correct positions and measurements are in place before any excavation work is carried out. They are also used to check and maintain the squareness of the building. Once set up to the nails or saw cuts on the profiles, they show the outline of the foundation trenches or walls.

These lines can be transferred to the ground for excavation work or the building of walls.

Optical level

An optical level is a levelling device that comprises a camera, a tripod and a staff or grade rod. The camera swivels on a pin projecting from the top of the tripod. There are many different models currently on the market and their accuracy differs over varying distances. The average optical level is accurate to within 6 mm over a distance of approximately 30–40 m.

Once placed in position on the tripod and adjusted for level, the optical level projects a level line across the distance between the datum peg and the point to where this datum level is to be transferred.

Transit level

Transit levels are also used for the purpose of transferring levels. However, they can also be used for providing vertical plumb lines and checking verticals for plumb.

> **Remember**
>
> When using optical levels and other electronic levelling devices, the tripod should not be disturbed during levelling. To avoid internal damage to the level, never carry the level while on the tripod

Figure 4.15 An optical level   **Figure 4.16** A transit level

Laser level

Laser levels are the more modern technology in construction, taking over from the Cowley and dumpy levels. They are very accurate and easy to set up. The level is fixed to a tripod. Press the button and it automatically finds level, shooting a red dot that can be picked up on the staff giving the reading. Laser levels can be used for all types of levelling throughout the course of the work, from setting foundations and floor heights, to setting suspended ceiling levels or even putting in straight plumbing pipework. Some are accurate up to 100 m and, if the level is knocked, it gives notification of movement.

Figure 4.17 Laser level

Spirit levels

Made from aluminium, spirit levels come in various sizes from 225 mm to 1200 mm, with 1200 mm being the main size that a bricklayer uses. They are used for levelling things horizontally and for plumbing vertically, having bubbles that give a reading between set lines and to determine accuracy of the work. Some levels have an adjustable bubble at the bottom for levelling angled work.

Great care must be taken when using levels as they can easily go out of **true**, which can result in work seeming to be level or plumb by the reading, but actually being wrong. This could result in work having to be taken down and re-done.

Straight edge

A straight edge is a tool with a very accurate straight edge. It is used for drawing or cutting straight lines. A ruler is a good everyday example of a straight edge. Straight edges can be made from wood or metal, but must be rigid and fixed so as to provide straight lines.

Builder's square

This is the most commonly used way of setting out a corner if no optical square is available on site. It is made of timber, is usually

Figure 4.18 Spirit level

Figure 4.19 Straight edge tool

Figure 4.20 Builder's square

made on site, and has to be practical enough to be carried and held in place for checking corners easily.

The above list is not exhaustive, but gives you a good idea of what is required. After checking on the size of the job, you should adjust the list as appropriate.

Checking resources for levelling

All resources used for levelling should be checked on a regular basis. The checks on this equipment should be as follows.

- Straight edges should be checked by laying the edge on a flat surface and seeing if any areas of it don't touch. This type of check is most commonly done by eye. By looking down the length of a straight edge you can see if there are any bows or if warping has taken place. You will also be able to identify any surface damage.

- Spirit levels should be checked by setting the level on a flat surface. Then check the bubble position. Rotate the level through 180° and set it down in the same place. The bubble should be in exactly the same position. If not, the level is out of true.

- Optical levels can be checked by taking a reading from a given point to mark a new point. Then move the level and reset it to take a reading at the new point. Then transfer the level back to the first position – this should have the same reading.

Using calculations to set out buildings

We will look at the steps involved in setting out over the next few pages. Listed below are a few golden rules you should always observe during the setting out process.

- Make sure you know where the building line and boundaries are.
- Check your equipment before commencing.
- Establish a datum where it will not be disturbed.
- Always use the measurements given and avoid scaling.
- Set out a base line (e.g. front of house). Make sure you do not infringe on or over the building line.
- Be aware of any underground pipes, etc.
- Check the drawings for errors.
- Take all measurements with care and accuracy.
- Check and double-check setting out after completion.

Functional skills

Setting out a building will allow you to practise several functional mathematic skills. These include FM 1.2.1b relating to interpreting information from sources such as diagrams, tables, charts and graphs; FM 1.2.1c: Drawing shapes; FM 1.2.2: Checking accuracy of results; FM 1.3.1: Judging whether findings answer the original problem and FM 1.3.2: Communicating solutions to answer practical problems.

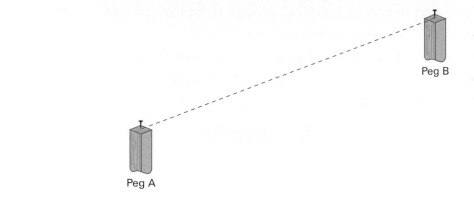

Peg B

Peg A

Datum peg

Figure 4.21 Step 1 Establish front base line (frontage)

Step 1 Establish front base line

- Peg A to peg B.
- The nails indicate the corners of the building.
- The pegs should be reasonably level with each other.
- The pegs must be secure and not move.

Step 2 Establish peg C

Assume sizes are 4 m × 2 m:

$$X^2 = 4^2 + 2^2$$
$$X^2 = 16 + 4$$
$$X^2 = 20$$
$$X = \sqrt{20}$$
$$X = 4.472 \text{ m}$$

Two tapes can be used now from A and B to find C.

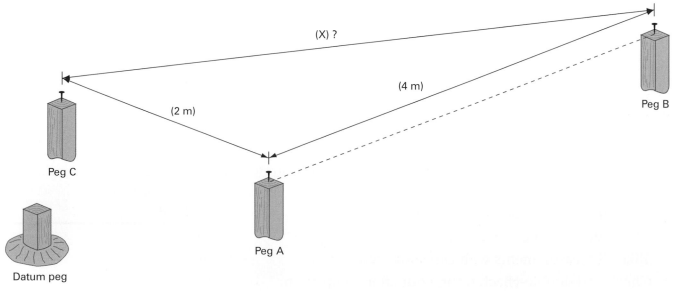

(X) ?

(4 m)

(2 m)

Peg C

Peg B

Datum peg

Peg A

Figure 4.22 Step 2 Establish peg C (using a site square, builder's square or the 3:4:5 method)

Step 3 Establish peg D

1. Use two tapes and measure from pegs C and B.
2. Check the diagonals A–D and C–B.
3. The building is square if the diagonals are the same.

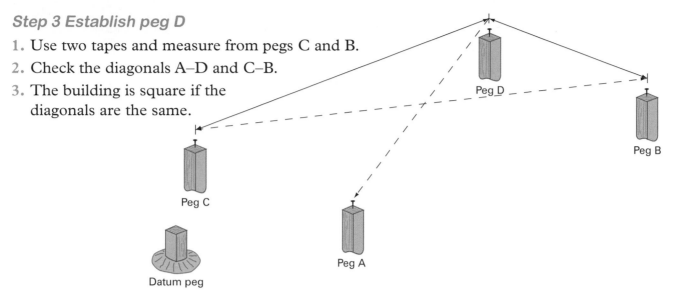

Figure 4.23 Step 3 Establish peg D

Step 4 Erect profiles at E and F

1. Project line from nails in pegs A and B.
2. Mark profiles with nails or saw cuts.
3. The profiles should be 1 m minimum away from the face – further if machine digging.

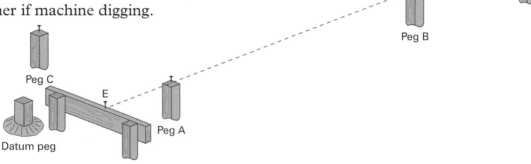

Figure 4.24 Step 4 Erect profiles at E and F

Step 5

The profile at peg D showing alternative.

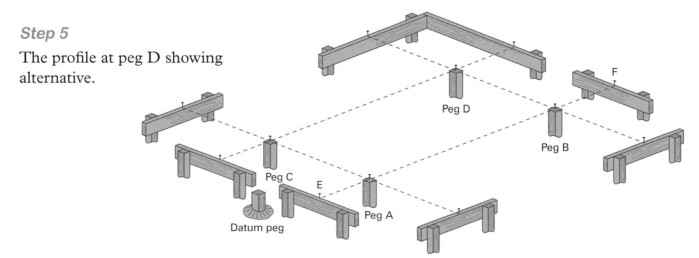

Figure 4.25 Step 5 Repeat step 3 for remaining profiles

Step 6 Remove corner pegs

1. Attach the continual line as shown.
2. The line represents the face line(s).
3. The line should not 'bind' on crossing.

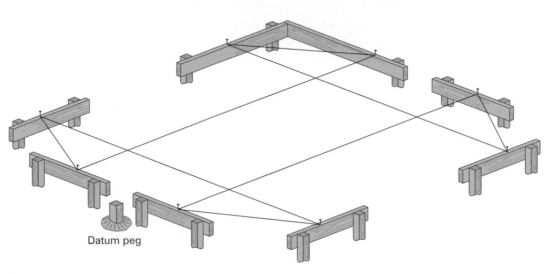

Datum peg

Figure 4.26 Step 6 Remove corner pegs

Step 7 Edges of foundations marked on profiles

1. Attach a line.
2. Plumb down and mark on the ground with sand (shown dotted).
3. Excavate trenches.

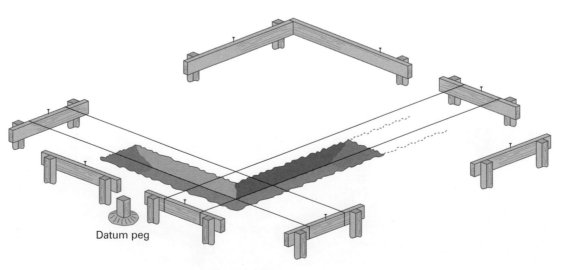

Datum peg

Figure 4.27 Step 7 Edges of foundations marked on profiles

K4. Set out regular shaped masonry structures on level ground

The setting out of masonry structures will be familiar to you from Level 1. This section will give you a brief recap of the skills and methods you will need to use in order to set out a building and make sure you are building in the right place.

Dimensional accuracy

Dimensions must follow the drawings and measurements will be checked periodically on site to make sure work is correct. If it does not match the drawings, work will have to be taken down and re-built. It is very important that a building has square (90°) corners. The setting out of a building must be square to avoid problems in the future – such as the roof not fitting!

There are no set industrial standards for dimensions – the only time standards are used is for training purposes. Here standards are given to plus or minus millimetres.

Buildings must also be kept level through using datum points. These use the Ordnance Survey benchmark system as a reference to create a site datum, which gives a fixed level from which all the construction is measured, to ensure that all the walls and floors are at the same level.

Remember

There are sometimes exceptions to the square rule, such as circular buildings or a building on an awkwardly shaped site

Setting out right angled corners

These can be marked out with a builder's square by placing two pegs in the ground with a line between them. By setting the builder's

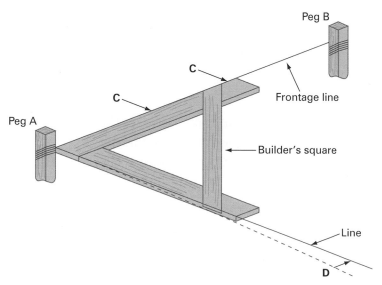

Figure 4.28 Right angle set out with a builder's square

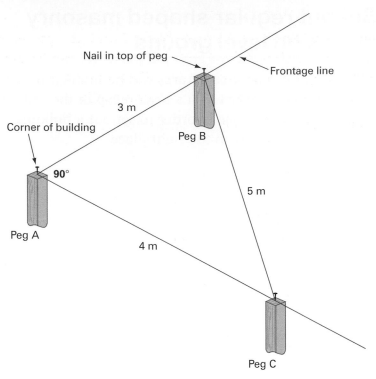

Figure 4.29 Right angle set out using 3:4:5 method

square parallel with this line, you will be able to place another peg with a line attached at a 90° angle from the original line.

You can also use what is known as the 3:4:5 method. If you use three lines, one 3 cm, one 4 cm and another 5 cm long, and then joint them in a triangle, you will automatically create a perfect right angle opposite the longest line.

Single and corner profiles

Corner profiles are used for setting out the main corners. Corners can be joined together to make a strong profile. This means there is less chance of pulling when lines are attached.

Pulling occurs when the lines are attached to a single wooden profile and the line is then stretched so tightly that it can start to pull the pegs that the profile rail is attached to. This can give a distorted or false line. A good way of avoiding this is to have two profiles joined together. This gives more strength to the line and the profiles.

However, in some cases, machinery may be used to dig out the correct positions of trenches and other similar tasks. To give the machine enough space to move, single profiles may have to be used. Single profiles would also have to be used for marking out any internal wall foundations.

Locating walling and trench positions on profiles

Once the centre lines have been established onto the profile you have used, the trench positions and wall positions can be marked onto them, using the drawing and specification to determine the cavity size, wall thicknesses and foundation width.

These measurements can then be added to the profile by the use of nails or saw cuts.

Working in excavations

The working space required between profiles depends on the method of excavation. When machines are used in excavations, there needs to be space to allow them to move. Spoil needs to be placed in piles within reach of a machine bucket arm. If the profiles are too close together, they will be damaged by these machines. For hand digging, less room will be needed.

Transferring information onto foundation concrete

Once the foundation concrete has been laid, the wall positions can be marked onto the concrete. This can be done by using spray paint, chalk or mortar to mark the position lines. The lines used for marking out the trenches should now be positioned on the nails/saw cuts marked on the profiles for the walls. These should be set on the external positions so that the lines cross to show the external corner positions.

Depending on what you are building, this should now give you the outline of the building with the four corner points clearly visible. Use a level plumb down onto the concrete foundation, with the top of the level just about touching the line. Be careful not to push the line, as this will give an incorrect position when marked. If the level will not reach to the line, a straight edge can be used to gain the height required. The level is then placed against the straight edge to plumb.

Once the position is achieved, mark the bottom of the level or straight edge on the side that is against the line. Repeat against the other corner line. From these markings, you can now mark the internal wall positions.

Overcoming setting out problems

Most of the problems associated with setting out are related to measurements on the drawings of boundaries. At this stage of setting out, if any problems are found, they should be reported to the site supervisor or manager.

Remember

If profiles are moved in any way, the measurements on them will be altered. Once concreted, walls may not fit onto the foundation. This will be very expensive to correct

Did you know?

It is good practice to mark a position approximately 900 mm along each line from the corner to give a line to build the corners to. Draw or mark the two lines, which should meet at the corner. Repeat this for all external corners

Remember

Care should be taken while using levels so as not to knock or damage them in any way. Damage to levels could lead to incorrect measurements being taken and building depths being incorrect

FAQ

Why not just write the full words on a drawing?

This would take up too much space and clutter the drawing, making it difficult to read.

Why are drain systems tested twice?

The first test checks for leaks before backfilling (filling the excavation) and the second test makes sure no pipe work has been damaged during backfilling. Clearly you don't want to find any leaks after backfilling so filling the excavation must be done with care.

With so many different types of level available, which is the best type to use when setting out?

A laser level is probably the best type of level available as they are very accurate and easy to set up. They can also be used for all types of levelling throughout the course of the work, from setting foundations to ceiling levels. However, you may be limited by the technology on site. A transit level is probably the next best type of levelling equipment available. Whatever you use, make sure you check it first and use it correctly.

Check it out

1. Explain why a walk-over site survey is carried out when setting out. Write a method statement, stating the best way of carrying out this survey.
2. Draw a sketch of a corner profile. Describe what the corner profile is used for and suggest some key points to remember when using it.
3. Name eight pieces of equipment or tools required for setting out. Describe what this equipment is used for and suggest the points when they would be used.
4. Explain why sulphate resistant cement may be used underground. What makes this type of cement different from the other types of cement?
5. Name five types of sub-soils and describe what needs to be done differently to work with each one.
6. Explain how to check a level for accuracy. Prepare a method statement describing how you would make these checks.
7. Name four services that are normally found underground. Prepare a risk assessment for working with these services.
8. Describe why it is important to check measurements regularly whilst setting out. Describe who to report any problems to and suggest a possible process for making these reports.

Getting ready for assessment

The information contained in this unit, as well as continued practical assignments that you will carry out in your college or training centre, will help you with preparing for both your end of unit test and the diploma multiple-choice test. It will also aid you in preparing for the work that is required for the synoptic practical assignments in setting out.

You will need to be familiar with:

- how to understand and work to drawings
- how to set out corners using different methods
- why it is important to carry out checks in measurements
- understanding the materials and equipments required to set out
- how to find and transfer different levels associated with setting out.

All these points will be needed for the synoptic test when carrying out the building of the different walls required. For learning outcome two, this unit has identified the resources required for carrying out site clearance, as well as identifying the reasons why this is important. You will need to use this knowledge to create your own checklist of resources required to prepare sites for clearance activities, as well as carrying out calculations required for site clearance activities.

As part of preparing for site clearance, you will need to carry out a walk-over survey to establish site conditions, as well as recording the results of this survey. You have seen the importance of locating and isolating existing services. The results of your walk-over survey, alongside this knowledge, will need to be used to establish the requirements on site to do this safely. This unit has covered the methods used to locate and isolate existing services and you will need to use this knowledge to draw up your plan for site clearance.

Before you start work on the synoptic practical test it is important that you have had sufficient practise and that you feel that you are capable of passing. It is best to have a plan of action and a work method that will help you. You will also need a copy of the required standards, any associated drawings and sufficient tools and materials. It is also wise to check your work at regular intervals. This will help you to be sure that you are working correctly and help you to avoid problems developing as you work.

Your speed at carrying out these tasks will also help you to prepare for the time limit that the synoptic practical task has. But remember, don't try to rush the job as speed will come with practise and it is important that you get the quality of workmanship right. Check your marking list to ensure your tolerances are correct on the areas of setting out and levelling as you progress.

Always make sure that you are working safely throughout the test. Make sure you are working to all the safety requirements given throughout the test and wear all appropriate personal protective equipment. When using tools, make sure you are using them correctly and safely.

Good luck!

Knowledge check

1 When setting out, how can you check if the building is square?

a) Check the widths

b) Check the perimeter

c) Check the lengths

d) Check the diagonals

2 What organisation could give you information about planning restrictions?

a) HSE

b) Local authority

c) Local historians

d) BIS

3 Why should materials not be stacked next to a trench after heavy rain?

a) This is the wrong place

b) It is too close to work with machines

c) The stack could cause a collapse into the trench

d) The stack will stop you from getting into the trench

4 Who has produced detailed documents relating to safety in excavations?

a) Local authority

b) HSE

c) Local council

d) CITB

5 What is the supporting of trenches called?

a) Profiling

b) Ranging

c) Shoring

d) Trenching

6 What would be used to transfer levels over long distances?

a) Straight edge and level

b) Optical levels

c) Site square

d) Level

7 Why is it important to check measurements regularly when setting out?

a) So you know what you are doing

b) So no errors are allowed to occur

c) To be sure that you are getting the levels right

d) To make sure the foundations are deep enough

8 What do the letters 'TBM' stand for?

a) Temporary benchmark

b) Temporary building manager

c) To be moved

c) Temporary Barrier Membrane

9 Why do you need to locate underground services before excavations?

a) To protect them against the elements

b) To reconnect the services

c) To avoid damage and costly repairs

d) To replace them

10 What are most problems with setting out related to?

a) Levels

b) Heights

c) Measurements

d) Depths

UNIT 2046

How to carry out thin joint masonry and masonry cladding

Thin joint masonry is a clean, fast and accurate system of construction. The demand for higher build quality, greater productivity, improved thermal performance, air tightness and waste reduction is helping to make thin joint masonry more popular in the UK construction industry.

This unit also supports NVQ Unit VR42 Erect Masonry Cladding and VR44 Erect Thin Joint Masonry Structures.

This unit contains material that supports TAP Unit 4: Provide Details to Masonry Structures, Unit 5: Carry Out Masonry Cladding to Timber Frames and Unit 6: Co-ordinate Self and Others to Erect Complex Masonry Cladding.

This unit will cover the following learning outcomes:

- How to construct buildings using thin joint blockwork to required specification

- How to construct masonry for use with timber-framed buildings to required specification

- How to construct masonry for use with concrete- and steel-framed buildings to required specification.

Key term

Aircrete – a product name for blocks manufactured from autoclaved aerated concrete

Key term

Swimming effect – this is where the blocks that have been laid float on the wet mortar bed as the weight upon them increases. This dramatically affects the setting time of the blockwork structure and restricts the height to which blocks can be laid in any one day

K1. Construct buildings using thin joint blockwork to required specification

Features of the thin joint system

Tests carried out by leading manufacturers and suppliers of thin joint systems and by representatives of the industry have concluded that the benefits of the system are invaluable to an industry where clients, developers and external agencies continue to demand improved quality of the end product, at the same time as increased production.

Benefits of the thin joint system

The thin joint method uses a combination of lightweight **Aircrete** blocks and a fine sand- and cement-based, quick drying mortar.

The main benefits of using the thin joint system include:

* speed
* improved quality of the finished product.

Speed

Blockwork structures can be constructed much more quickly than traditional methods. This is due to a number of factors.

* The quick bonding time of the mortar reduces the **swimming effect** caused by the weight of the blockwork on the courses below.
* The accuracy and uniformity of the Aircrete blocks, combined with the accuracy of the thin joint, reduces the time spent on levelling individual blocks.
* With less mortar being used, the bond strength of the blockwork is enhanced. This again allows for more stability during the construction process and also allows other aspects of the construction work to continue within a short space of time, after the blockwork structure has been completed.
* The thin joint system enables the inner leaf of a cavity wall structure to be built, in its entirety, prior to the outer leaf being built. This makes it possible to provide a waterproof work environment for other trades to carry on with the work programme.
* The availability of larger format blocks also increases the speed at which walls can be built.

Improved quality of the finished product

The quality of the finished product is improved due to a number of factors.

- Aircrete blocks are produced to very accurate sizes, resulting in the finished product having a cleaner and more uniform appearance.

- As the inner leaf of cavity structures can be built first, it is easier to maintain a clean cavity and avoid the bridging of wall ties with mortar.

- The thermal insulation properties of the structure are improved because the mortar joints are thinner and the area of blockwork is greater. Where larger format blocks are used, even better thermal insulation is achieved.

- Aircrete blocks have high sound insulation properties due to the material used and the structure of the block.

- There is less wastage of materials due to the ease and accuracy with which the blocks can be cut. Also thin joint mortar is supplied pre-mixed in 25 kg bags, allowing for just the right amount to be mixed for the job in hand, as and when required.

Resources required to carry out the thin joint construction process

Aircrete blocks

These are made from autoclaved aerated concrete. This is a lightweight material which makes the blocks easy to handle and to cut, but at the same time has a high compressive strength. The main ingredients combined to form this material are lime, sand of quartz, water and cement. As the name suggests, Aircrete also contains between 60 and 80 per cent of air by volume, with thousands of tiny air bubbles being produced during the 'baking' process. Once this process is complete and the material has been allowed to set, it is cut into blocks of the required size using mechanical wires. In order to obtain the maximum strength of the blocks, they are cured in autoclaves. This is where the blocks are subjected to saturation with high pressured steam at temperatures up to 200°C.

Aircrete blocks are available in a variety of sizes ranging from the standard sized block of 440 mm × 215 mm up to an extra large block with a face size of approximately 610 mm × 270 mm. These blocks are also available in varying thicknesses and grades to suit the work being carried out.

Figure 5.1 Aircrete blocks

Safety tip

It is recommended that you use suitable hand protection when using thin joint mortar. As this type of mortar is cement-based, there is a risk of developing dermatitis and/or burns and irritation to the skin through prolonged exposure to it

Did you know?

Always clean the mixer thoroughly after use, using either water or ballast and gravel to prevent future material from sticking to the drum sides so easily

Did you know?

Although occasional stirring or remixing of the thin joint mortar can be carried out following the initial mix, no additional water should be added as this will significantly weaken the bonding properties of the mix

Thin joint mortar

Mortar is covered in greater detail on pages 198–200. It is formed from a number of resources:

- sand
- cement
- water
- plasticisers (for brickwork)
- colouring agents (where coloured mortar is desired).

It usually requires mixing, either by hand or machine, although certain mortar products can be purchased pre-mixed and ready for use.

Thin joint mortar is a combination of fine ground sand (silica) and Portland cements. It is available under a number of different trade names and is produced by various manufacturers as part of their thin joint systems. It is normally supplied in 25 kg bags and then added to water and mixed until the correct consistency is obtained. Guidance for mixing is given on the packaging.

Thin joint mortar remains workable for a number of hours – up to four hours in most instances – while still in the bucket. However, once spread on the block, the mortar will begin to set within 10 to 20 minutes. Full setting of the mortar is reached after approximately 1 to 2 hours, depending on the product. Thin joint mortar is spread at a thickness of 2–3 mm. The tools used for the mixing and application of the mortar are explained later in this unit (see pages 164–165).

Machine mixing

Mixing by machine can be carried out by using an electric, petrol or diesel mixer. Always set the mixer on level ground.

Fill the mixer with approximately half of the water recommended, adding the plasticiser if it is being used. Add half of the cement and half of the sand required to the water. Allow them to mix and then add the remaining cement, then the sand. Add more water if required, allowing at least two minutes for the mix to become workable and to ensure that all the materials are thoroughly mixed together.

Once the mix has been taken out of the mixer, part fill the mixer with water and allow the water to run for a couple of minutes to remove any mortar stuck to the sides.

Wall ties for thin joint systems

Wall ties used in traditional brick and block structures are not suitable for use in thin joint systems as they are too thick to fit into the thin mortar joints. However, there are a variety of ties compatible with thin joints currently on the market. The majority of them are made from stainless steel. Some of the most common include:

- twist ties
- flat steel ties
- abutment wall ties
- movement joint ties.

Twist ties

These are used for cavity walls where the inner leaf has been built and the outer leaf is still under construction. They are driven into the Aircrete block work at a height to suit the outer leaf courses as they are laid. These ties will also take insulation clips, which secure partial fill cavity insulation batts. Twist ties are available in various sizes to suit up to 150 mm cavities.

Figure 5.2 Twist tie

Flat steel ties

These are available for use when joining the inner and outer leaves of a cavity wall where the two leaves which are constructed at the same time and are of the same course height. The ties are bedded into the blockwork in the same way as traditional methods.

Flat steel ties are also available for connecting blockwork at junctions, where perimeter walls join partition or dividing walls.

Abutment wall ties

These are also used for connecting blockwork at junctions where courses are not at the same level. The tie is fixed to the perimeter wall using a suitable fixing and the other end of the tie sits into the bed joint of the adjoining wall.

Figure 5.3 Insulation clips/discs

Figure 5.4 Flat steel ties

Figure 5.5 Abutment wall tie

Unit 2046

How to carry out thin joint masonry and masonry cladding

Find out

Find out if there are any variations to the ties mentioned that are also suited to the thin joint system

Remember

On large sites, or in instances where a large number of cuts are required for the job, a mechanical hand saw or circular saw may be used to cut blocks

Movement joint ties

As the name suggests, these are used to tie walls together where the continuous length has been broken up to allow for movement joints. They allow for contraction and expansion between the two walls to avoid any damage to the blockwork caused by movement.

Figure 5.6 Movement tie

Tools and equipment used for the thin joint system

Scoop

This is used to spread thin joint mortar, producing a consistent joint thickness of 2–3 mm. The scoop is available in varying sizes of between 75 and 200 mm.

Figure 5.7 Scoop

Sledge

As with the scoop, this tool is also used to spread thin joint mortar. However, the sledge is for use where the width of the block exceeds 200 mm. This tool is available in sizes between 200 and 300 mm.

Figure 5.8 Sledge

Masonry hand saw

This is used to cut Aircrete blocks to the required size.

Block cutting square

This is used as a marking guide when cutting blocks.

Figure 5.9 Masonry hand saw

Figure 5.10 Block cutting square

Sanding board

The sanding board is used to remove any imperfections in the bed course. As the thin joint system requires a very accurate bed thickness to be maintained, it is important that any raised areas in the bed course are removed prior to applying the thin mortar joint.

Block rasp

The block rasp is used to trim any areas of the block that are raised and too big to be removed with a sanding board. These raised areas may occur when there has been inaccurate cutting and will affect the accuracy of the thin joint thickness.

Figure 5.11 Sanding board

Figure 5.12 Block rasp

Whisk attachment

The whisk is attached to a powered drill and is used to mix the thin joint mortar in a large tub or bucket.

Bonding for blockwork

Blockwork should be set out to use as many full blocks as possible. At an internal corner, a 100 mm section of block should be used to gain half bond. Never use brick on an internal corner, as the thermal value of a brick is not to the same as a block and will cause a 'cold spot' to the finished area, possibly showing through the plaster on completion.

Damp proof barriers

The techniques used for this are the same as for cavity walls. This will be covered in Unit 2048.

Working with materials

Positioning materials

Before beginning construction work, you will need to position and stack the components you need to work with on the construction site.

Each site will have different rules for arranging materials, either placing them nearby or keeping them in a holding compound until needed. There may be written instructions for storing and placing materials, or you may be given verbal instructions by a site manager. In both cases, it is important to check any information you find confusing and to confirm that you have understood how materials are to be placed.

Decisions on material placement affect everyone on site, as everyone needs to know how to access them. Placing materials in the wrong place could also lead to health and safety issues.

Figure 5.13 Whisk attachment

> **Remember**
>
> Because of the cost of bricks, most walls above 215 mm thick usually incorporate blocks as they are more cost-effective and have the strength required

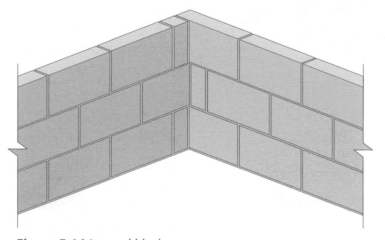

Figure 5.14 Internal block corner

Health and safety and risk assessments

One of the main health and safety issues is the risk of mortar coming into contact with the skin or splashing into the eyes when it is being used. There is also a risk of inhaling dust or fumes from mortar. Appropriate PPE (personal protective equipment) such as gloves, safety goggles and a respiratory mask should be worn.

Blocks should be unloaded and transported around the site by forklift. If being used on scaffolding, they should also be lifted by forklift, not carried up ladders by hand or on a shoulder.

Blockwork should not be built too high without proper security being in place as this may cause structural collapse. This is particularly important if working in windy conditions as walls can be blown down, causing damage to property or people. Another reason to avoid laying too high is that you will not be able to see the line correctly. If the block touches the line, it will move and cause the wall to bow. You could also cause yourself damage by reaching too high, pulling muscles in your back or stomach.

Wall ties must not be left exposed, as there is the danger that workers and site users may snag themselves on the ties.

You must conduct a risk assessment of the area you are working in to identify any site-specific risks that may exist. You will then be able to put work practices into effect to protect you from the risks.

Safety tip

Guidance on the dangers of working at height can be found on pages 27–33

Cutting components

When preparing to build walls, you may need to cut and prepare blocks. There are three different methods that can be used:

- by hand using a hammer and bolster chisel
- by hand using a saw
- by machine using a portable disc cutter or fixed table saw.

The method used sometimes depends on the type of block being used. For example:

- A hand saw would be no good to cut concrete blocks, but perfect for lightweight blocks.
- A hammer and bolster are adequate for concrete blocks, but can chip the edges of the cut. If the cut blocks are to be covered by another material, this would be acceptable, but if the blocks have a face finish, then machine cutting would be the better option, especially if a large number of cuts are required.

Safety tip

As well as your normal PPE, always wear goggles, gloves and a face mask when cutting blocks

Protecting materials and completed work

After completing a day's work, the bricklayer must take precautions to prevent damage to the wall from the weather.

Rain will cause mortar joints to run over the face of the wall, causing unsightly stains. To prevent rain damage, walls should be covered with a polythene sheet or tarpaulin. A scaffold board or bricks can be used to secure the cover in place. The sheeting should be kept clear of the wall to allow for ventilation.

Cold weather could cause the water in the mortar to freeze, damaging the bonds between blocks and bricks, making the wall weak and possibly causing the wall to be taken down. To prevent the mortar from freezing, newly built walls should be covered if there is a sudden drop in temperature to below 3°C. The covering should consist of a layer of hessian or insulation slabs, with a waterproof tarpaulin or plastic sheeting on top.

Maintaining industrial standards

Industrial standards are the standards and tolerances allowed on site, or in the workshop, covering the plumbness, level and finish of a wall, if it is to **gauge**, if the joints on courses run true and plumb, as well as the cleanliness of the wall once built.

> **Key term**
>
> **Gauge** – the blockwork course heights; for a block size of 215 mm, this would be the size plus the 10 mm joint – 225 mm; gauge can be maintained by using a gauge rod

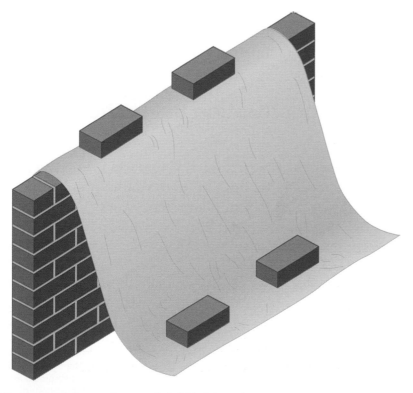

Figure 5.15 Protecting newly laid brickwork

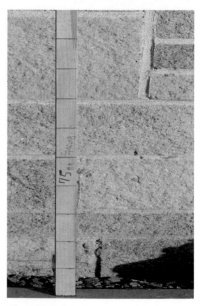

Figure 5.16 Gauge rod in use

> **Remember**
>
> The standard block size is 440 mm x 215 mm

> **Safety tip**
>
> Always remember the basics of kinetic lifting techniques when handling blocks, particularly the larger size blocks available with the thin joint system

> **Remember**
>
> It is essential that the bed course is level and free from imperfections prior to laying the first bed of the thin joint mortar

> **Remember**
>
> You must always ensure that the course that is to receive a bed of thin joint mortar is free from dust as this can adversely affect the adhesion of the mortar

> **Key term**
>
> **Superstructure** – work above the DPC

Forms of construction where the thin joint system can be used

The structure and composition of Aircrete blocks make them a very versatile material. When they are used in conjunction with the thin joint mortars that are now available, the thin joint system becomes suitable for most aspects of construction normally associated with the more traditional types of materials. The thin joint system can be used for any of the following:

- foundations
- partition walling
- external solid walling
- cavity walling
- separating or party walls.

As the thin joint system has high resistance to both water penetration and frost, few problems are encountered when it is used for external solid walling. However, it is recommended that the external face of the blockwork is finished with either cladding or a traditional rendered finish, particularly where the wall is constantly exposed to inclement weather, such as rain and frost.

The thin joint system also has a high resistance to fire and good sound insulation qualities, making it highly suitable for the construction of partition walling and separating walls.

The strength and sulphate resistant properties of the system, also make it suitable for foundation walls in most types of soil and ground conditions.

Methods of construction using the thin joint system

If constructing a cavity wall structure, it is important to ensure that the substructure walls are built up to the damp proof course (DPC) prior to laying the inner thin joint blockwork. This enables any required openings to be set out accurately before work starts on the **superstructure**.

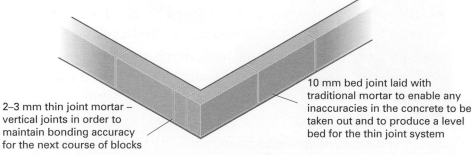

Figure 5.17 A bed course of blocks laid with traditional mortar bed and with thin joint mortar vertical joints

2–3 mm thin joint mortar – vertical joints in order to maintain bonding accuracy for the next course of blocks

10 mm bed joint laid with traditional mortar to enable any inaccuracies in the concrete to be taken out and to produce a level bed for the thin joint system

In most cases the first course or 'bed course' in the thin joint system should be laid using the normal sand/cement mortar. This will take out any inaccuracies that are present within the floor slab or foundation masonry.

In order to maintain accuracy in the courses above the bed course, thin joint mortar may be used for the **perps** (vertical joints) of the bed course. Once the bed course is sufficiently stable, work with the thin joint system can commence.

Bonding arrangements and the installation methods are much the same as the traditional block laying methods.

When erecting the corners of block walls built using the thin joint system, it is vitally important to ensure accuracy in the levelling, plumbing and gauging of the blocks. With the thin joint system there is no option of opening up joints to compensate for inaccuracies you might have caused during the build.

Once the corners have been erected, the blocks can be run into a line as normal. The thin joint mortar is applied to the blocks using a scoop or a sledge depending on the width of the block (see the descriptions of these tools on page 164). Both tools provide a consistent 2–3 mm layer of mortar across the bed and vertical joints.

As the individual blocks are laid, they should be firmly pushed against the vertical, mortared face of the previously laid block and at the same time lowered onto the mortared bed below. It is important to ensure that full joints are maintained at all times to retain the effectiveness and stability of the thin joint system. Where there is a need to tap blocks into place to ensure full uniform joints that are accurately laid to the line, a rubber mallet should be used in order to prevent damage to the blocks.

As previously stated, when constructing cavity walls, the inner leaf can be built in its entirety prior to work commencing on the outer leaf. This has a number of advantages:

- a watertight structure is provided at a much earlier stage of the project
- partial or full fill insulation can be fitted much more easily and will not be affected by excess mortar protruding from joints
- wall ties can be fixed once the insulation is in place – the insulation is then secured by the wall tie being driven into the pre-erected blockwork and secured with suitable insulation clips
- it is easier to keep a clean cavity as the outer leaf is constructed.

Key term

Perps – the vertical joints between two bricks or blocks

Did you know?

Bond arrangements for the thin joint system are the same as those used in the traditional brick and block methods

Did you know?

Where a single skin of walling is built in its entirety and is not supported by other walls, it should be supported or propped up until the mortar has fully set and is sufficiently stable. If this is not done, particularly during adverse weather conditions, the wall may collapse

Did you know?

Where wall ties are to be driven into the newly constructed inner leaf, it is recommended that the blockwork has been stabilised by the installation of the floor joists at the head of the wall

Remember

The spacing of wall ties is the same as when constructing cavity walling with traditional methods

Unit 2046

How to carry out thin joint masonry and masonry cladding

Forming openings in walling

There are many types of opening in cavity walling. Openings for doors and windows are covered in Unit 2048 on page 244.

Reveals

Reveals are formed in much the same way as with traditional construction methods. The Aircrete blocks can be cut to the required dimensions of the reveal, however the first reveal block may require support to enable the remaining blocks to be laid on top.

Arches

Arches have been used for many centuries in very different types of construction including bridges, viaducts, aqueducts, castles, as well as the simplest and most modern forms of housing structures.

The curved shape of an arch allows the weight of the masonry above it (the load) to be distributed evenly down through the walls at each side. The arch is not exposed to tensile stresses (forces that pull apart), because it is wedged between the walls on each side, and therefore will not collapse when a load is placed above it.

There are certain terms used when referring to parts of an arch, particularly during its construction, all of which you will come across in this unit. Figure 5.18 shows many of the different parts of an arch and Table 5.1 describes what these are.

Find out

Are there any other materials from which reinforcement for thin joint systems can be made?

Functional skills

Working with arches in buildings will allow you to use a range of functional skills, including FM 1.2.1b: Interpreting information from sources such as diagrams, tables, charts and graphs and FM 1.2.1d: Calculate perimeters and areas of simple 2D and 3D objects.

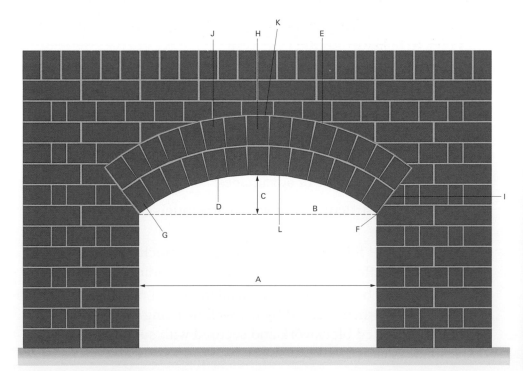

Figure 5.18 The parts of an arch

Letter	Part	Letter	Part
A	**Span** – the distance between the **abutments** that support the arch	G	**Springer** – the first brick of the arch seated on the springing line
B	**Springing line** – the line at which the arch sits on the abutments	H	**Key** (or key brick) – the central brick or stone at the top of an arch
C	**Rise** – the height of the arch from the springing line to the soffit	I	**Skewback** – the angle at the springing point, on the abutments, at which the arch ring bricks will be laid
D	**Intrados** – the interior lower line or curve of the arch ring	J	**Collar joint** – the horizontal or bed joint separating the arch rings
E	**Extrados** – the outside line of the arch ring	K	**Crown** – the very top point of the extrados
F	**Springing point** – the point at which the arch meets the abutments	L	**Soffit** – the underside face of the arch

Table 5.1 Arch construction terminology

> **Key term**
>
> **Abutments** – the walls or structures through which the weight above the arch is distributed, as well as the walls or structures supporting the ends of the arch

Some other important arch construction terminology includes:

- **Haunch** – the bottom part of the arch ring from the springing point to half-way up the ring.
- **Radius** – the distance from the central point on the springing line (known as the striking point) to the intrados.
- **Striking point** – the central point of the springing line from which the arch radius is struck.
- **Voussoirs** – the wedge-shaped bricks/stones of which the arch is made.

Methods of constructing simple arches

Two of the most common shapes of arch are the segmental (Figure 5.19) and semi-circular (Figure 5.20). Both shapes can be constructed by using either the rough ringed arch or axed arch methods.

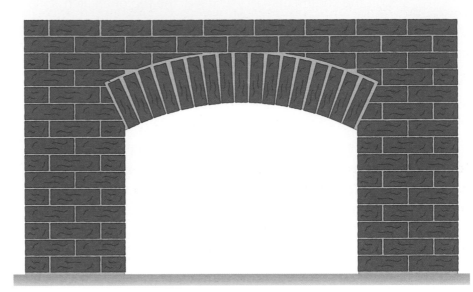

Figure 5.19 An example of a segmental arch

Figure 5.20 An example of a semi-circular arch

Rough ringed arch method

This method involves using wedge-shaped joints with standard sized bricks to form the arch ring. The size of the joints is determined by the **arch centre** or **turning piece.** The bricks used in the arch ring are normally laid as headers as opposed to stretchers (see Figure 5.21). If stretchers were used, the joints would need to be much wider to ensure that the desired shape was obtained and this could result in an unsightly appearance. The overall height of the arch is reached by using a number of arch rings.

Assuming that the turning piece, or arch centre, has been correctly positioned and adequately supported with props, and that the **folding wedges** are in place, the method of construction is as follows.

Identify the striking point on the timber turning piece or arch centre and plumb a vertical line up from this point to the top of the support. This will give you the centre point of the key brick's position. Mark the width of the key brick on the arch centre or turning piece. Then on either side of the key brick proceed to mark out, down the length of the intrados, equal brick spacings.

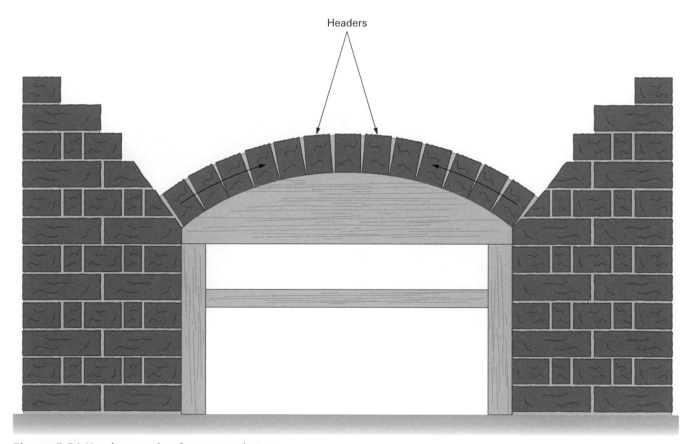

Figure 5.21 Headers used to form an arch ring

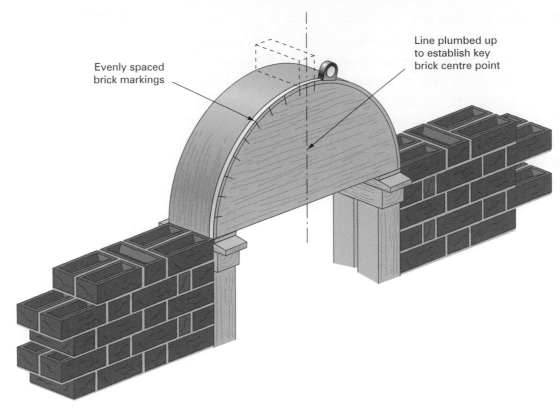

Evenly spaced brick markings

Line plumbed up to establish key brick centre point

Figure 5.22 The striking point

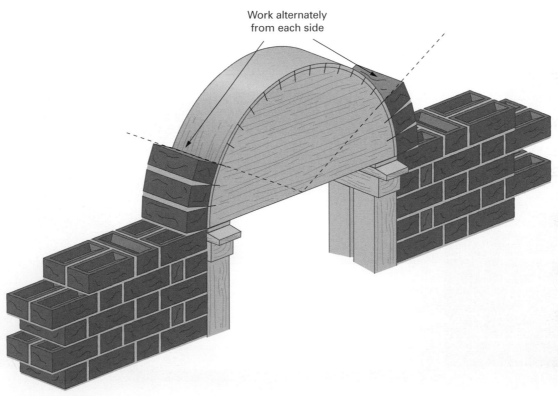

Work alternately from each side

Figure 5.23 Placing bricks

Note that these spacings must include allowance for mortar joints. The size of the joints may need to be altered slightly during bedding to allow for any deviation of brick size or to enable equal brick spacing around the timber support. Normally the joint size is slightly reduced from that of the standard 10 mm mortar joint in order to compensate for the widening of the joint at the extrados.

Commence with the placement of the bricks forming the arch ring, with the first brick being laid against the skewback angles on either side of the key brick.

It is important to ensure that there is no bedding between the brick and the timber centre, as this will result in difficulty in maintaining the correct curve of the arch bricks during construction and also stain the face of the bricks exposed once the support is removed. Packing may be introduced at the base of the

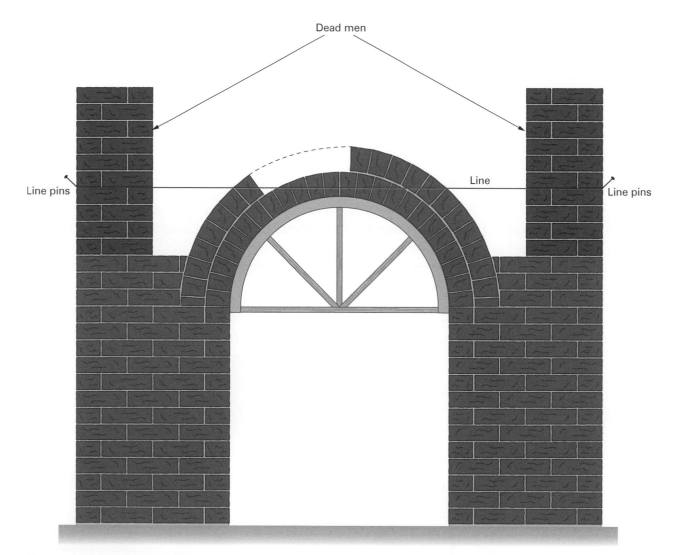

Figure 5.24 Dead men in use

Remember

Arch supports must not be removed until the bedding mortar has fully hardened

joint being formed to allow for ease of pointing once the support is removed.

Bricks should be laid alternately on either side of the key brick to ensure that there is no overloading on any particular side of the support. Once the key brick position has been reached you must ensure that this brick is placed accurately in the marked position on the centre and that there are fully compacted joints either side of it.

Throughout the construction of the arch rings you must also maintain the face plane of the brickwork. This can be done by using a suitable, accurate straight edge or by erecting temporary line supports on each of the abutments. These can be built in brick and are known as dead men (see Figure 5.24) or can consist of timber or metal profiles, accurately gauged and plumbed.

Axed arch method

This method is the total reverse to that of the rough ringed arch. In this method it is the bricks themselves that are cut to a wedge shape and the joints are uniform in shape and do not taper. The wedge-shaped bricks are referred to as voussoirs.

Functional skills

When faced with a problem on site, such as this problem with arch construction, you will have the opportunity to practise the interpreting elements of functional skills. This includes FM 1.3.1: Judge whether findings answer the original problem; FM 1.3.2: Communicate solutions to answer practical problems.

Working life

Max is setting out a semi-circular arch to form an archway to a garden wall. He has set the arch centre in place and is marking out the brick positions on the arch centre using a gauge of 75 mm. However, that creates a 15 mm gap to place a brick into.

How can Max get over this to make the arch correct? He will need to consider all the parts of the construction process. What might he need to do if the gap was larger?

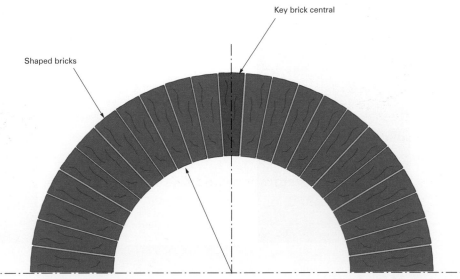

Key brick central

Shaped bricks

Figure 5.25 Section of an axed arch with shaped bricks

Insulation requirements for walling

Cavity walls are insulated mainly to prevent heat loss and therefore save energy. The *Building Regulations* tell us how much insulation is required in various situations and in most cases this would be set out in the specification in order for the relevant project to obtain planning permission from the local council.

There are three main ways to insulate the cavity:

* total or full fill
* partial fill
* injection (after construction).

Total or full fill

Figure 5.26 shows a section of a total fill cavity wall. The cavity is completely filled with insulation batts as the work proceeds. The batts are 450 mm × 1200 mm, made of mineral fibres and placed between the horizontal wall ties.

Partial fill

Figure 5.27 shows a partial fill cavity wall, where the cavity insulation batts are positioned against the inner leaf and held in place by plastic clips. More wall ties than usual are used to secure the insulation in place.

Injection

This is where the insulation is injected into the cavity after the main structure of the building is complete. The two main materials used are Rockwool fibreglass or polystyrene granules. On a new build, holes are drilled into the inner walls at about 1 m centres and the insulation is pumped into the cavity. If an older property were injected, then the holes would be drilled into the external mortar joints. The holes are then filled with mortar.

There are three key points regarding insulating cavity walls:

* handle and store insulation material carefully to avoid damage or puncturing
* the cavities should be clean
* read the drawing specifications and follow the manufacturers' instructions carefully.

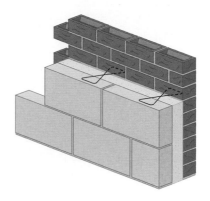

Figure 5.26 Wall with total or full fill

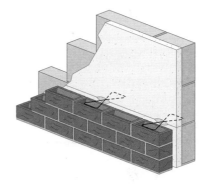

Figure 5.27 Wall with partial fill

Remember

When injecting insulation, great care must be taken not to drill the bricks as they will be difficult and costly to replace

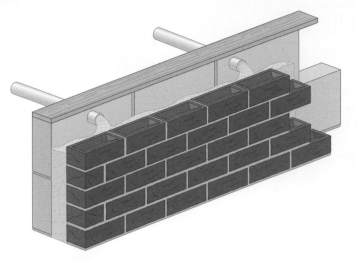

Figure 5.28 Wall being injected

Remember

Always check the specifications to determine the type and size of reinforcement required

Key term

Subsidence – the sinking in of buildings, etc.

Did you know?

Separating walls are also known as party walls

Figure 5.29 Reinforcement materials available for use in thin joint systems

Using reinforcement in walling

Brickwork is extremely strong in compression (being squashed), but weak in tension (being stretched). If there is any chance of brickwork being subjected to tensile forces (being stretched) some kind of reinforcement should be built into the wall.

Reinforcing can be done in several ways, but the most common way is to build in a steel mesh called expanding metal. The mesh is built into the bed joints. Various widths can be obtained for different thicknesses of wall. Brickwork can also be reinforced vertically with steel rods and concrete.

Some places where reinforced brickwork could be used are:

- over large span door or window openings
- where high security is required (such as a bank vault)
- in gate pillars
- in foundations where there is a possibility of **subsidence**
- in concrete columns.

Reinforcement for thin joint blockwork

Where thin joint blockwork is likely to be subjected to tensile forces, reinforcement can be built into the horizontal bed of the thin joint walling. However, only reinforcement material specially designed for use with the thin joint system should be used. Thin joint reinforcement is widely available and made from either stainless steel wire or galvanised steel with a zinc coating. It is supplied in rolls of up to 50 m in length and is approximately 1.2 mm thick.

Thin joint reinforcement must be bedded within the thin joint mortar. Where there is a need to overlap the reinforcement, the overlap should be a minimum of 225 mm. Where the reinforcement is used around openings, it should extend by at least 600 mm into the blockwork on both sides of the opening.

Reinforcement can also be used in lengths of thin joint blockwork over 6 m as an alternative to using movement joints. This is particularly effective for separating walls where movement joints cannot be used.

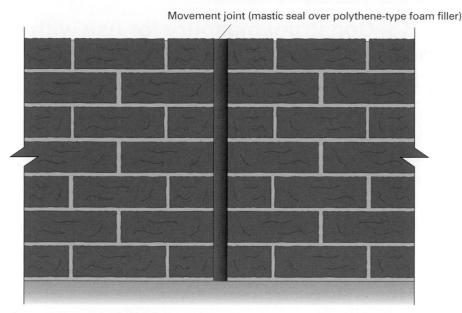

Movement joint (mastic seal over polythene-type foam filler)

Figure 5.30 Vertical movement joint

Using vertical movement joints

Architects and designers have found through experience that walls that are very long (10 m plus) can crack due to movement caused by:

- temperature change
- wetting and drying of the wall.

To solve the problem of movement, a wall can be divided into shorter lengths by introducing movement joints, which are actually an intended 'straight' joint filled with compressible (squashable) filler. This is then covered with mastic to seal the joint, preventing water penetration, but allowing movement.

Where the design of the structure requires the use of movement joints, manufacturers of Aircrete blocks recommend the following:

- the first movement joint should be no more than 3 m from the corner of a fixed end
- long lengths of walling should be made up of separate panels no longer than 6 m.

Movement joints can be formed either by introducing 10 mm gaps between the panels and filling with fibre boards, or by using specially designed ties to connect the two panels together, but allow movement of any panel that is subjected to tensile stress.

These specially designed ties are also available for use when tying walls together at junctions, for example where partition walls meet with perimeter walls and particularly those junctions that are susceptible to movement.

> **Find out**
>
> What is the maximum vertical distance between ties when used in a movement joint?

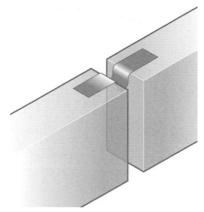

Figure 5.31 The use of movement ties

K2., K3. Construct masonry for use with timber-, concrete- and steel-framed buildings to required specification

With the introduction of timber-, concrete- and steel-framed structures into modern construction projects, cladding has become the ideal way of transforming these potentially drab and dreary buildings into structures that fully complement the aesthetic requirements of the environment in which they are built.

The skills for the use of masonry with these different building frames are the same, so we will look at these topics together:

- how to construct masonry for use with timber-framed buildings
- how to construct masonry for use with concrete- and steel-framed structures.

Types of cladding other than masonry cladding

There are a number of materials other than brick and block that can be used to clad a structure. The most common types of cladding used in modern construction are described below.

Traditional brick and block cladding

This type of cladding consists of an outer leaf of brick or block being constructed using the normal materials and methods associated with building cavity walling. It is tied back to the main structure using specially designed ties.

However, this type of cladding is restricted to low-rise buildings of no more than two or three storeys. This is because walls constructed in this way are incapable of adequately supporting their own weight above a certain height. The use of this type of cladding for taller buildings would also increase the risk of movement due to shrinkage of the main structural components, stress to the structure caused through wind pressures, settlement within the main structure, etc.

Pre-cast brick panels

These units are pre-cast and manufactured in production plants away from the construction site where they are to be used. They are usually much thinner in section than traditional brick outer leaves and are not designed to carry any structural loads.

Numerous pre-cast cladding systems of this type are available and each is fixed in its own special way, usually to the main structure

Figure 5.32 An example of pre-cast cladding panels

or one panel to another. In many instances, they are fixed in such a way that there is no need for traditional mortar courses and jointing methods.

In addition to the pre-cast units above, pre-fabricated brickwork is increasingly being used in modern construction projects. This type of brickwork consists of panels of traditional brickwork being built in a production plant and transported to site where it is lifted into position. This requires the brickwork to be pre-tensioned, with the use of steel reinforcement, so that the whole panel can be transported from the factory to the site without damaging or weakening it.

Brick slip and brick tile systems

This type of cladding consists of **brick slips**, or tiles of approximately 25–35 mm in thickness, fixed to a pre-fabricated panel, which is in turn fixed to the main structure.

The slips, or tiles, are fixed either by using a special adhesive or by mechanical fixing methods. All joint finishing is normally carried out once the installation is complete. Joint finishing is achieved by pumping a special cement-based mortar into the vertical and horizontal joints and then forming a joint finish in the normal way.

Alternative cladding materials

In addition to brick and block claddings, pre-cast panels can also be produced from materials such as concrete, stone, granite and slate. Of these, concrete cladding is the most common. It is normally in the form of pre-cast concrete panels reinforced with steel mesh and/or rods and available in a wide range of colours and finishes. The finish of these units can resemble a stone effect, standard rendered finishes and even a brick facing.

Masonry cladding

Traditional construction methods require the bricklayer to build outer and inner leaves of brick and blockwork with a gap of 50–75 mm separating them. The two separate leaves are tied together using galvanised steel ties. This is referred to as cavity wall construction. In most cases, cavity walls built in the traditional way are **load-bearing**. However, the traditional cavity walling construction is usually restricted to buildings of no more than two or three storeys in height.

Where buildings are built in excess of three or four storeys, an outer skin of facing brickwork may be used to cover the main framed structure. Traditionally, these multi-storey buildings have

Key term

Brick slips – these usually have the same length and height dimensions as standard clay bricks used in traditional construction methods. However, the thickness of the slip is normally no more than 25 mm. Generally brick slips are made from exactly the same material as standard clay bricks

Did you know?

Some manufacturers of brick slips and tiles are now producing this type of cladding in sizes larger than the standard brick sizes

Key term

Load-bearing – walls referred to as load-bearing support the load from roofs and floors

Remember

The main purpose or function of any masonry cladding is to provide the decorative finish to a structure

Remember

Whatever system you use, remember the manufacturer's installation instructions must be followed. Not only will these guide you on how to carry out the work, they will ensure that the cladding does its job and will not fail over time

Remember

In Scotland, a cavity barrier is also known as a firestop

been constructed from pre-cast concrete sections slotted together. The outer skin of brickwork is tied into the main structure using purpose-made fixings or metal support systems. A cavity still needs to be formed to ensure that the correct insulation properties required for the building are achieved. In most instances the outer skin is not required to carry any load imposed by floors or roofs, as this is supported by the main framed structure.

Where the brick outer skin is not required to support any load, it is known as masonry cladding.

Masonry cladding is also used to cover buildings of timber- and steel-framed construction. Timber-frame construction is becoming increasingly popular in modern house building. The inner leaf of timber-frame buildings consists of pre-formed panels made from structural timbers capable of supporting the loads imposed by the floors and roof. Steel-framed structures are more commonly used for buildings such as factory and warehouse units. As with the more traditional multi-storey concrete structures, the cladding will be tied back to the main structure using metal support systems.

In whatever situation masonry cladding is used, there are a number of different methods of installing and fixing the cladding to the main structure. A wide variety of fixing systems are available.

Health and safety issues

Whichever support system is used when installing cladding, it is of the utmost importance that the installation procedures are accurately followed. Failure to follow guidelines may result in failure of the support system and eventual weakening of the cladding sections and even collapse.

Preventing fire hazards

Regulations require that for any timber-frame dwelling, of two storeys or more, cavities must be closed at specified intervals with the use of cavity barriers. The spacing and positioning of these barriers will be identified within the specifications and drawings.

The following illustrations show examples of the positioning of cavity barriers in timber-frame construction.

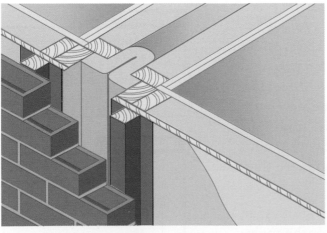

Figure 5.33 Cavity barriers at separating wall positions

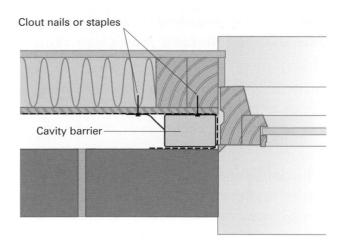

Figure 5.34 Cavity barriers at reveals

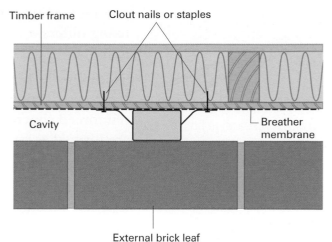

Figure 5.35 Cavity barriers at intervals within main cavity

Methods of supporting/fixing cladding

As previously mentioned, there are many new cladding systems being introduced into construction and each has their own particular installation procedures and fixing components. It is impossible to cover them all here, but the following section

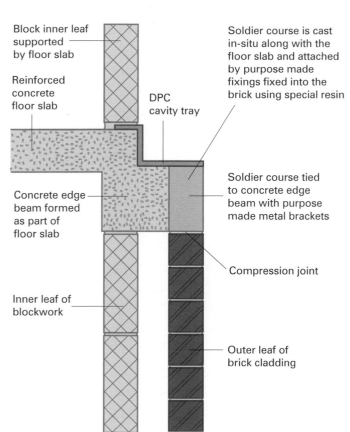

Figure 5.36 Typical concrete floor slab incorporating a reinforced edge beam

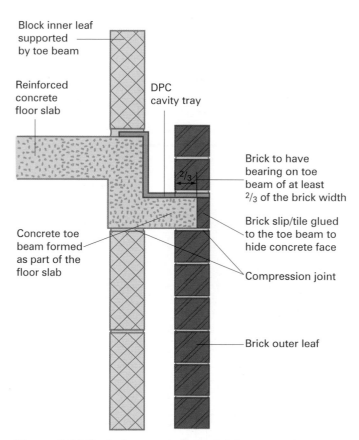

Figure 5.37 Typical concrete floor slab incorporating a reinforced toe beam

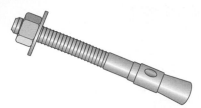

Figure 5.38 Expansion bolt for fixing a support beam to a concrete structure

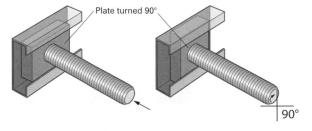

Plate turned 90°

90°

Figure 5.39 Purpose-made bolts slotting into a channel fixed to the main concrete structure

Did you know?

Horizontal movement joints are referred to as compression joints

provides an insight into the traditional methods of installing and fixing different types of cladding and the basic principles behind more modern methods.

Traditionally, brickwork cladding used on multi-storey concrete structures is supported at each floor level by specially formed and reinforced concrete toe or edge beams. These toe or edge beams are formed as part of the concrete floor slab.

However, with the introduction of metal support systems, the use of concrete support beams is becoming less common. Continuous lengths of metal supporting beams can be fixed to the structural concrete either by purpose-made expansion bolts or by specially designed bolts that fit into a channel slotted into or fixed to the surface of the concrete.

When fixing these types of metal supports to steel-framed structures, the support beam can be fixed directly to the steel frame without the need to use additional channelled fixing supports.

In most instances, brickwork cladding will be supported at each floor level when using the metal support systems. In addition to the metal supports, horizontal movement joints need to be incorporated. This is also the case when brick cladding is supported by concrete toe or edge beams. These movement joints are of vital importance to allow for the shrinkage or expansion over time of various materials such as concrete or brickwork.

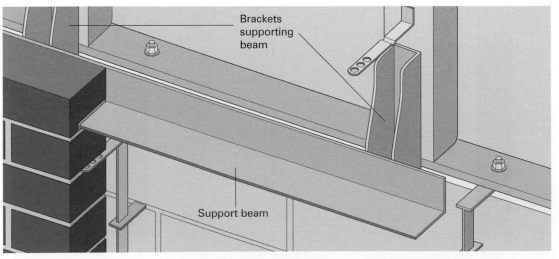

Brackets supporting beam

Support beam

Figure 5.40 Support beam attached directly to a steel frame

The horizontal movement joint should be provided between the underside of the metal angle and the course of brick beneath the angle (see Figures 5.36 and 5.37). The movement joint should be totally free from mortar, which is replaced by a special compressible strip or filler. In order to ensure water or moisture does not penetrate through this joint into the inner leaf, the filler or compression strip is set back from the face of the cladding by approximately 10–15 mm. The space is then filled with a waterproof, compressive sealant.

The thickness of the metal support beam will be determined by the amount or weight of brickwork cladding to be supported. Obviously the thicker the supporting beam is, the thicker the joint will be between the brickwork cladding above and below the beam. Where this joint is excessive, in other words above the normal 10 mm standard joint, a specially cut brick can be used to reduce the joint thickness. This brick is commonly referred to as a pistol brick. These are normally specially made for individual building projects.

A pistol brick is a standard size brick rebated on the underside to allow it to fit over the edge of the support beam, thus reducing the appearance of the excessive joint.

In instances where cavity widths exceed the normal 75 mm, which is becoming increasingly common particularly on cladded structures, the metal angle support is supported by individual metal brackets spaced at shorter distances apart and fixed to the structure. These individual brackets can be specially made to suit the cavity width. In addition, the thickness of the angle support beam can be reduced slightly due to the frequency in the spacing of the individual brackets, thus giving greater support. This type of bracket is normally supported by fixing into a channel that is pre-cast into the concrete structure or fixed directly to a steel structure.

> **Remember**
>
> If you do not ensure the supports are levelled at the time of fixing your brickwork, cladding will not be level and will look unsightly

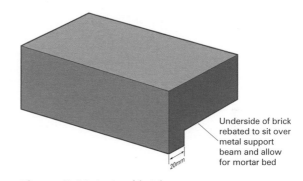

Underside of brick rebated to sit over metal support beam and allow for mortar bed

20mm

Figure 5.41 A pistol brick

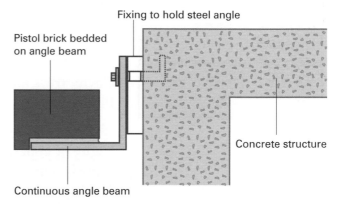

Pistol brick bedded on angle beam

Fixing to hold steel angle

Concrete structure

Continuous angle beam

Figure 5.42 A pistol brick positioned on the supporting metal beam

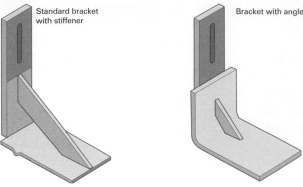

Standard bracket
with stiffener

Bracket with angle

Figure 5.43 Single support brackets

Where it is necessary to clad curved elevations or where there needs to be an arch or soldier course incorporated above an opening, single bracket supports are required. Continuous metal angles are not manufactured to suit this type of work.

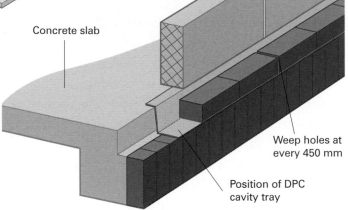

Concrete slab

Weep holes at every 450 mm

Position of DPC cavity tray

Figure 5.44 The positioning of cavity tray and weep holes

Damp proof barriers and cavity trays

Whether building traditional cavity walling or installing masonry cladding that incorporates a cavity-type construction, the principles of preventing water or moisture penetrating into the inner leaf of the building are the same.

Cavity trays and weep holes need to be positioned as shown in Figure 5.44.

When laying a course of bricks directly onto the metal support angle, or concrete support beam, the bricklayer must ensure there is a minimum of two-thirds of the brick's width actually bearing on the angle or beam. Pistol bricks may be used on this course to reduce the width of the oversized joint formed by the angle and the damp proof course (DPC).

Earlier in this unit we looked at the provision of horizontal movement joints to compensate for compressive forces imposed on the brick cladding sections. In addition to these movement joints, it is also important to take into consideration sideways movement caused by expansion or contraction of the brickwork. This can be compensated for by introducing vertical movement joints. These are introduced where the lengths of the brick cladding sections exceed 9 m.

Cladding above openings

Cladding above openings can be of either purpose-made sections or suspended brickwork, that is brick soldier courses.

Cladding panels can be produced by securing brick slips or tiles to a steel lintel section or a purpose-made load-bearing unit. The disadvantage of using this type of cladding is that the support angle can be seen where the opening is bridged.

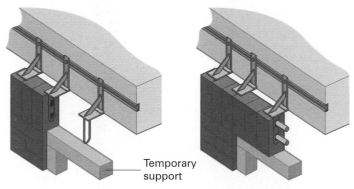

Temporary support

Figure 5.45 The use of stirrup brackets to suspend brickwork above an opening

In order to alleviate this problem, a brick soldier course can be suspended from the main structure above the opening using specially designed metal support brackets. These brackets are used one per brick and incorporate stirrups, which support steel rods threaded through the perforations in the suspended bricks.

Supporting suspended brickwork

During construction, the suspended brickwork must be supported temporarily to prevent it sinking or sagging. A timber frame, built to the size of the opening, is normally used as a support and is removed once the mortar has fully **cured**.

Whatever system is being used to support cladding, it is essential to ensure that it is fixed securely to the main structure. Manufacturers' guidelines will identify how tightly fixings are to be secured and how the various components of a particular fixing should be put together.

Additional support for cladding

In addition to supporting and securing cladding at storey height, it is also essential to provide **lateral** support. This will help to prevent the masonry cladding buckling under various stresses caused by **compressive forces**.

Key term

Cured – the mortar has set and reached its full strength

Key terms

Lateral – belonging to, relating to, located at or affecting the side

Compressive forces – these relate to the weight

Unit 2046

How to carry out thin joint masonry and masonry cladding

Lateral support is provided in two ways when installing masonry cladding. The first method is to tie the inner leaf to the outer leaf using traditional methods of positioning ties. Obviously the type of tie will be determined by the type of structure.

The second method used to provide lateral support is by tying the cladding to the structure using a lateral restraint tie system. For example, one such system comprises of a series of sliding ties fixed to a vertical support rod. The rod is then fixed to the main structural frame. The sliding ties can be positioned at appropriate points on the vertical rod and coincide with bed joints of the brick cladding as it is constructed.

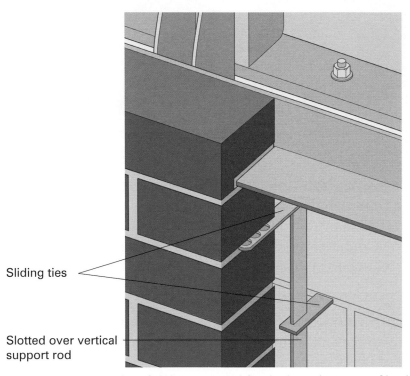

Sliding ties

Slotted over vertical support rod

Figure 5.46 Examples of sliding ties used for the lateral support of brick cladding

Working life

Ahmed, a young bricklaying apprentice, has been given the task of building the final section of brick cladding on a concrete structure while the experienced bricklayers carry out the setting out of an adjoining structure. Ahmed has almost completed the section when he realises that he has forgotten to put in place the lateral sliding support ties fixing the cladding to the main structure. However, he has put in place the lateral support ties connecting the inner and outer leaves of the cavity walling.

Ahmed talks to Carl, another apprentice. Carl tells him not to worry as long as he has incorporated the normal cavity ties.

What should Ahmed do? Is Carl right? Should Ahmed inform the experienced bricklayers and completely re-build the section? Or should he complete the work without sliding ties? Ahmed should be certain that what he is doing is right and at least check Carl's opinion with some of the more experienced bricklayers before making a decision.

What could be the impact of not using sliding ties? Are there are any health and safety impacts? What could be the impact on the project if the wall needs to be rebuilt?

Should Ahmed ask for advice? Is it his decision to make?

Functional skills

When working on-site you will be in a lot of situations where you will have different options for solving a problem.
These decisions give you the opportunity to practise the interpreting elements of functional skills, e.g. FM 1.3.1: Judge whether findings answer the original problem; FM 1.3.2: Communicate solutions to answer practical problems.

FAQ

Can thin joint mortar be used in conjunction with ordinary brickwork construction?

No, as this is specifically designed for use with Aircrete material.

Why is the first course laid out using sand and cement mortar and all the rest laid using a different mixture?

The first course is laid using sand and cement mortar so that any height or level discrepancies, especially if a block and beam floor system has been used, can be adjusted with the mortar joint. If a thin joint was used on the first course, then the maximum joint size would only be 3 mm, hence the course might not be level so as to continue above it.

Why are folding wedges used when positioning the arch support?

Folding wedges are used so that fine adjustments can be made to the height when positioning the arch support. They also make it easier to remove the arch centre when the mortar has set.

Why do you need to use a pistol brick to reduce the size of the joint between the angle and the course laid on top of it?

A joint which is excessive in size (above the normal 10 mm) will look unsightly and out of place, particularly where the brickwork is a prominent feature.

Check it out

1. Explain what a block rasp is used for.
2. Draw a sketch of a movement tie. What is this tie used for?
3. Draw a section of a box type lintel in place. Prepare a method statement showing how you put this in place. What other tasks would need to be carried out before you could install this lintel?
4. Draw a sketch of a Pistol brick and explain where it would be used in construction. Describe the advantages it has over other types of brick.
5. Explain how Aircrete blocks are made. Prepare a table showing the difference between aircrete blocks and other types of block.
6. Explain what swimming means. Prepare a method statement explaining how you could avoid swimming from happening.
7. Sketch a diagram of a floor slab, incorporating an edge beam. Describe how this is assembled and the benefits it brings to a building.
8. Name three types of ties used in thin joint masonry. Why are these ties used at different points? Explain why you would choose a particular tie.

Getting ready for assessment

The information contained in this unit, as well as continued practical assignments that you will carry out in your college or training centre, will help you with preparing for both your end of unit test and the diploma multiple-choice test. It will also aid you in preparing for the work that is required for the synoptic practical assignments in blockwork.

You will need to be familiar with:

- how to identify and calculate the materials and equipment required
- setting up your area
- learning how to set out, level, gauge and plumb blocks
- cutting blocks to given sizes, relating to cavity work
- understanding different types of cladding used in the industry.

All these points will be needed for the synoptic test when carrying out the building of the different walls required. This unit has shown the reasons for using, and methods of using, thin joint masonry. For example, for learning outcome three you have seen how to construct masonry for use with concrete- and steel-framed buildings to required specifications. This unit has shown the importance of putting together a checklist of resources and explained the methods of construction and cutting components. You will need to use this information to put together your own checklists, as well as selecting the method of construction and cutting of components that is most appropriate for your situation and the specifications. Producing a work method will be an important part of selecting the most appropriate method.

You will need to construct walling to form straight lengths, return and junctions. This will need to be carried out safely and you will need to use your knowledge in your practical work to identify the safest way of working. Carrying out a risk assessment will be an important part of this.

Before you start work on the synoptic practical test it is important that you have had sufficient practise and that you feel that you are capable of passing. It is best to have a plan of action and a work method that will help you. You will also need a copy of the required standards, any associated drawings and sufficient tools and materials. It is also wise to check your work at regular intervals. This will help you to be sure that you are working correctly, and help you to avoid problems developing as you work.

Your speed at carrying out these tasks will also help you to prepare for the time limit that the synoptic practical task has. But remember, don't try to rush the job as speed will come with practise and it is important that you get the quality of workmanship right. Check the marking list to ensure your tolerances are correct on the areas of plumbing gauge and levels as you progress.

Always make sure that you are working safely throughout the test. Make sure you are working to all the safety requirements given throughout the test and wear all appropriate personal protective equipment. When using tools, make sure you are using them correctly and safely.

Good luck!

Knowledge check

1 What tool is used to fine trim blocks ready for use or to prepare for block laying?

   a) Disc cutter

   b) Hand saw

   c) Sandpaper

   d) Block rasp

2 What materials make up the mortar for thin joint work?

   a) Sand and line

   b) Cement and aggregate

   c) Fine sand and cement

   d) Grit and cement

3 What is the average thickness size of joints used within the thin joint system?

   a) 1–2 mm

   b) 2–3 mm

   c) 3–4 mm

   d) 10 mm

4 What types of block are used in thin joint masonry?

   a) Concrete dense blocks

   b) Limestone blocks

   c) Clay blocks

   d) Aircrete blocks

5 What tool is used in place of a trowel to lay blocks under 200 mm wide?

   a) Rasp

   b) Scoop

   c) Whisk

   d) Sledge

6 If movement joints are required in the wall, what is the maximum distance allowed between joints?

   a) 4 m

   b) 3 m

   c) 6 m

   d) 7 m

7 What should be used to tap blocks into position?

   a) Club hammer

   b) Claw hammer

   c) Sledge hammer

   d) Rubber mallet

8 Other than brick and block, what material is most used as a cladding to a building?

   a) Concrete

   b) Aluminium

   c) Lead

   d) Cast iron

9 What is the normal thickness of a brick slip?

   a) 20–25 mm

   b) 25–35 mm

   c) 35–45 mm

   d) 50–55 mm

10 If cladding is used on a building, where could you get information on the correct methods of fixing of the product?

   a) Health and Safety Executive

   b) Local authority

   c) Manufacturers

   d) Codes of practice

UNIT 2047

How to build solid walling, isolated and attached piers

Solid walls are walls built entirely from bricks or blocks and mortar with no voids and with little or no other materials used. They range from 102 mm (or half a brick) thick up to 450 mm (or two bricks) thick. In exceptional situations walls may be thicker, but this is very rare today – thicker walls are more likely to be made from solid concrete.

This unit also supports NVQ Unit VR40 Erect Masonry Structures.

This unit contains material that supports TAP Unit 3: Erect Masonry Structures, Unit 4: Provide Details to Masonry Structures and Unit 6: Co-ordinate Self and Others to Erect Complex Masonry Cladding.

This unit will cover the following learning outcomes:

- How to plan and select resources for practical tasks
- How to erect solid walling to required specification
- How to erect isolated and attached piers to required specification.

K1. Plan and select resources for practical tasks

To determine the exact nature of the construction of solid walling and then carry out its construction, you will need to refer to the project drawings and plans. We covered this material earlier in Units 2002 and 2045, and the concepts will be the same for solid walling. Please refer back to this earlier section for more information on:

- type of drawings and conventions commonly used (pages 54–57)
- purpose of different types of drawing (pages 54–57)
- methods of interpreting measurements from drawings (pages 132–133)
- methods of reporting inaccuracies in information sources (page 133)
- reasons for checking datum points (page 57).

Resources used to carry out solid walling

Bricks and blocks

The key resources needed for solid walling are, of course, bricks or blocks.

Bricks

Most bricks are delivered pre-packed using either metal or plastic bands to stop the bricks from separating until ready for use. The edges are also protected by plastic strips to guard them during moving. Moving is usually carried out by forklift or crane. Bricks are also often shrink wrapped in plastic to protect them from the elements.

On site, bricks should be stored on level ground and not stacked more than two packs high. This is to prevent over-reaching or collapse, which could be a hazard to workers. On large sites, they may be stored further away and moved by telescopic-lifting vehicles to the position required for use.

The position of bricks in the kiln process can cause slight colour differences: the nearer the centre of the kiln the stronger the heat and the darker the colour of the brick. Therefore, bricks should be taken from at least three packs and mixed so that any differences in colour are less noticeable. If the bricks are not mixed, you could get whole sections of brickwork in slightly different shades.

This is called banding and in most cases is visible to the most inexperienced eye.

Blocks

Blocks are made from concrete and may be dense or lightweight. Lightweight blocks could be made from a fine aggregate that contains lots of air bubbles. The storage of blocks is the same as bricks.

Creating mortar

Mortar is used in bricklaying for bedding and jointing the bricks when building a wall. Mortar is made of sand, cement, water and plasticiser. The mortar must be 'workable' to allow the mortar to roll and spread easily. The mortar should hold onto the trowel without sticking.

Sand

Sand for bricklaying mortar should be 'well graded', having large, medium and small grains (see Figure 6.1). If all the grains were of even size, this would be termed 'poorly graded' and would require more cement to fill in the voids between each grain. Sand is dug from pits or dredged from the sea and in both cases must be thoroughly washed to remove mud and silt. A way to check for the cleanliness of sand is to carry out a silt test.

The silt test (see page 98) is an easy method to determine the amount of mud and silt that is mixed in with the sand once it arrives on site. It will also show the amount of clay left in the sand, as this will stop the mortar from bonding to the sand particles. The amount of silt and clay should not be more than 10 per cent of the volume of aggregate.

> **Did you know?**
> On cold mornings, brickwork should not be started unless the temperature is 3°C and rising. If the temperature is too cold, the cement will not go off properly

> **Remember**
> In Scotland, mixed mortar is also known as compo

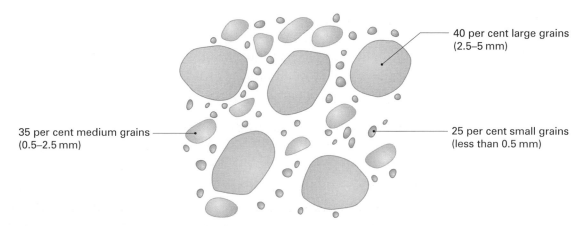

40 per cent large grains (2.5–5 mm)

35 per cent medium grains (0.5–2.5 mm)

25 per cent small grains (less than 0.5 mm)

Figure 6.1 Graded samples of sand

Cement

Cement is made from limestone or chalk and is chemically controlled with added calcium, aluminium, silicon and iron. It takes 1.65 tonnes of raw material to make 1 tonne of cement, with half of the weight of the limestone material being lost through carbon dioxide emissions during the manufacturing process. The materials are then proportioned to form a raw mix and introduced into a kiln.

There are four stages within the kiln:

- evaporation and pre-heating
- calcining
- clinkering
- cooling.

The first stage removes moisture and then raises the temperature of the material to between 800 and 900°C ready for calcining, which breaks down the calcium carbonate into calcium dioxide and carbon dioxide. This process produces a substance known as clinker, which is then ground into a powder and mixed with gypsum to produce the finished cement powder. The gypsum controls the rate of hydration of the cement in the setting process.

Cement is used to bind the grains of sand together. A layer of cement slurry coats the particles of sand, which chemically sets after the addition of water, resulting in a hardened layer holding the bricks in place. The most common cement used is Ordinary Portland Cement (OPC), which is suitable for most general work and, if handled correctly, will produce mortar of a high-quality and strength.

Masonry cement is often used for bricklaying mortar. It is similar to OPC, but has a plasticiser added to the cement powder. As a bag of masonry cement contains 75 per cent cement powder and 25 per cent plasticiser, a higher proportion of cement must be used.

Sulphate-resisting cement is suitable for use below ground, where high levels of sulphate may damage OPC. It is normally used for foundation works and drainage.

The most common type of cement used for concrete is also OPC. Over the years, however, several types of Portland cement have been developed, which can be used for concrete in more specified construction. These include:

- Rapid-Hardening Portland Cement (RHPC), which gives strength more quickly than OPC.

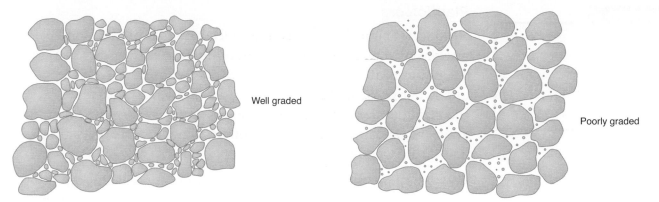

Figure 6.2 Well graded and poorly graded concrete

- Sulphate-Resisting Portland Cement (SRPC), which should be used in ground containing a high level of sulphates (this is because sulphates damage OPC).
- Low Heat Portland Cement (LHPC), which produces less heat during hydration. This makes it more suitable than OPC where large masses are needed that could produce high temperatures, which might lead to the concrete cracking.

Cement is tested by British Standards to ensure that it is suitable for use. It is then given a kite mark and a number to show that it has passed the test. Part of the test specifies the setting time for cement as being not less than 45 minutes before its initial set has started and not more than 10 hours before its final set has taken place. The cement must be used before its initial set has taken place as any remixing or movement will result in the cement mortar not bonding or setting properly.

Working life

Seb is mixing mortar for six bricklayers building the cavity brickwork on the second floor of a block of flats. They are using Ordinary Portland Cement. He suddenly realises that he is down to the last bag. There are eight bags of sulphate-resisting cement in the shed. Should he use these?

Water

Water is used to make the cement paste and to cause the cement to set due to a chemical reaction (**hydration**). This makes the cement 'workable'. Water is also used in the production of concrete to enable the cement to set and also to make the concrete 'workable'. Water must not contain any impurities that might affect the strength of the concrete. The general rule for the quality of water is that it should be drinkable (potable).

Key term

Hydration – the addition of water to cement paste to produce a chemical reaction to set mortar

> **Remember**
>
> Never use plasticiser below ground level because sulphates in the ground will attack and break down the mortar, weakening the joint

Plasticisers

Sand, cement and water make a mortar that is difficult for a bricklayer to use. To make a bricklaying mortar 'workable', a plasticiser must be added. Most plasticisers nowadays come in powder or liquid form and should be added to the water according to the instructions. The plasticiser works by coating the grains of sand with tiny bubbles of air, which allows the sand to flow easily when being spread.

Hydrated lime may be used as a plasticiser, but washing-up liquid, etc. must never be used as the number of air bubbles cannot be controlled and would result in a weak mortar mix as the chemicals and detergents react to the cement, breaking down the hydration.

Colouring agents

Colouring agents are also available in powder or liquid form, but are only really suitable for pointing brickwork as it is almost impossible to keep a consistent colour in a large quantity of mortar using this method. If powder pigments are to be used for pointing, it is recommended to mix enough mortar to point the whole of the work and keep it stored in airtight bags in a dry store.

> **Remember**
>
> When using colouring pigments, always follow the instructions on the packaging

Where large quantities of coloured mortar are required, it is recommended to use a ready-mix mortar, available from mortar suppliers.

Pre-mixed mortars

On most larger sites, mixing mortar is a thing of the past as it is brought in already mixed. There are many advantages to using pre-mixed mortar:

- the mix is always consistent and not affected by the weather
- the mix has better productivity
- there is less site activity transporting materials
- there is less waste and contamination.

There are two main ways that pre-mixed mortars are available, in:

- a mortar silo
- ready-mixed spread tubs.

Mortar silo

A mortar silo is a holding unit for mortar. The silo is delivered to the site and has the advantage of taking up little space and preventing contamination of materials (which means waste).

Double compartment silo

The silo is usually filled before transport to site. The mixing unit inside is split into two separate compartments: one is normally filled with a sand–lime mix to the required mix as specified and the other is filled with cement. The mix ratio is calibrated before delivery so that it is exactly the same for each mix. On site, the silo is connected to a power and water supply.

Liquid admixtures or colour pigment can be added according to the customer's requirements before transportation.

Single compartment silo

This type of silo only has a single compartment, which is filled by the supplier with dried sand, cement and lime (if required), plus admixtures or colour pigment as required. Water is then added for the required consistency.

Ready-mixed spread tubs

Also known as retarded mortar, these are ready-mixed plastic tubs containing the required mix of mortar. They have a life span of approximately two days after delivery. The plastic tubs are returnable and carry enough mortar to lay about 350 bricks. They normally have a plastic cover to stop contamination and to stop the mortar drying out too quickly. They are very versatile as they can be lifted by forklift straight onto a scaffold for use. They also come in a wide range of colours. There is no site mixing and labour costs are reduced.

Choice of mortar mixes

The choice of the mortar to be used for a project depends on:

- cost
- exposure
- weather conditions
- type of brick to be used.

Before starting a concreting project, it must be decided whether to use ready-mix or to self-mix the concrete. Each has advantages over the other.

Advantages of self-mix:

- cost is much lower
- no need to order in advance (if materials are on site)
- project can be postponed without advance notice (e.g. owing to bad weather).

> **Remember**
>
> For ready-mix to be an advantage, the concrete lorry must have good access to the pour area

Advantages of ready-mix:

- no need for storage of materials
- able to provide large batches of materials
- no need to employ labourers to mix the concrete.

A general rule is that the mortar must not be stronger than the bricks to be used. This enables a wall to be simply re-pointed if there are any cracks in the joints due to settlement. If the mortar was stronger than the brick, the settlement crack would go vertically through the brick, resulting in the brickwork having to be rebuilt.

Mortars are usually described as a ratio of materials, for example 1:1:5. The first number is always the proportion of cement, the second is the proportion of lime and the third number is the proportion of sand.

Designation	Type		
	OPC: Lime: Sand	Masonry cement: Sand	OPC: Sand with plasticiser
v	1:3:10–1:3:12	$1:6\frac{1}{2}$–1:7	1:8
iv	1:2:8–1:2:9	$1:5\frac{1}{2}$–$1:6\frac{1}{2}$	1:7–1:8
iii	1:1:5–1:1:6	1:4–1:5	1:5–1:6
ii	$1:\frac{1}{2}:4$–$1:\frac{1}{2}:4\frac{1}{2}$	$1:2$–$1:3\frac{1}{2}$	1:3–1:4
i	$1:0:3$–$1:\frac{1}{4}:3$		

Table 6.1 Mortar mix designations

> **Remember**
>
> Make sure the buckets used to gauge materials are the same size

Many mortar mixes are given a 'designation' number (i, ii, iii, iv, v), as shown in Table 6.1. This allows different batches of mortar to be approximately the same strength. The lower the designation number (i), the stronger and more durable the mortar, while the higher the number (v), the greater the ability of the mortar to allow for movement of the wall.

Tools and equipment

There is a range of tools and equipment you will need to use in order to build solid walling. Some of these tools may already be familiar to you.

Brick trowel

This type of trowel is used to take the mortar off the mortar board, lay it on the wall and spread it to form a uniform bed ready for bricks. Made from solid carbon steel, they are available for left- and right-handed people. Always clean the trowel with water after use, drying it thoroughly and lightly oiling it to prevent rust.

Pointing trowel

This trowel is used for filling in joints and pointing certain types of joint. It is available in different sizes and needs cleaning like the brick trowel.

Club or lump hammer

This type of heavy hammer is used with a bolster chisel to cut bricks by hand. It is also used for knocking holes in walls and for removing joints, using a plugging chisel. Made in forged steel, it comes in a number of different weights.

Hand hawk

The hand hawk is used by the bricklayer in the process of filling joints in pointing and jointing. The mortar is placed on the top of the hawk and used with the pointing trowel to avoid having to repeatedly return to the mortar board. The hawk is usually made of wood or plastic, although some plasterers use steel hawks. Clean it with water after use.

Joint raker

The joint raker often goes under the name 'chariot'. This tool is used for raking out soft mortar joints, whether to give a joint finish on new work or to take out old mortar ready for repointing. Made of steel, it has an adjustable raking pin to change the depth the joint is recessed.

Figure 6.3 Brick trowel

Figure 6.4 Pointing trowel

Figure 6.5 Club/lump hammer

> **Remember**
>
> In Scotland, a club or lump hammer is also known as a mash hammer

Figure 6.6 Hand hawk

Figure 6.7 Joint raker

Jointer

Usually made from steel, this tool is used to form the joint finish after building a wall. This helps to make the joint more waterproof and makes the appearance of the wall more pleasing. Jointers are made from rolled forged carbon steel.

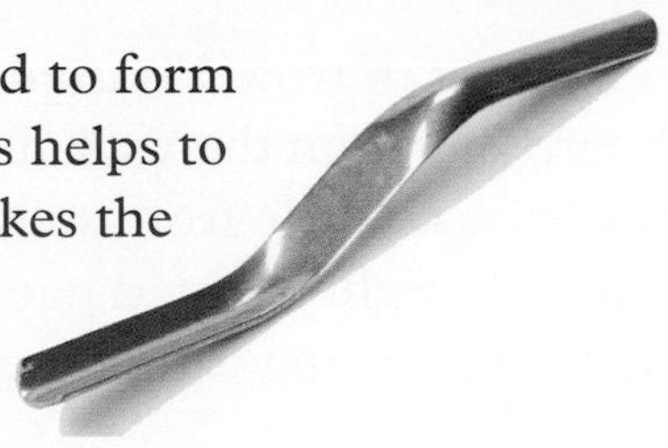

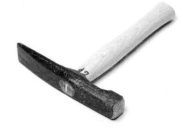

Figure 6.8 Jointer; this type is used to form a half-rounded joint, also referred to as a **bucket-handle finish**

> **Key term**
>
> **Bucket-handle finish** – a shallow, round inward joint

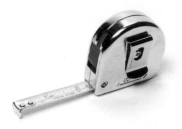

Figure 6.9 Steel tape measure

Tape measure

Tape measures come in many sizes, from 3 m up to 10 m for the pocket type, and from 10 m to 30 m for larger setting out tapes. Some can even go up to 100 m. Most give only metric measures (centimetres and metres), although some also give imperial (inches and feet). They are used for measuring and checking sizes. They are usually made of steel and come in a plastic or steel case.

Always make sure that tapes are wiped clean after use as moisture will result in the steel rusting and dirt will clog up the tape.

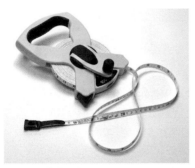

Figure 6.10 A 30 m tape measure

Brick hammer

Brick hammers are used for rough cutting and shaping bricks. They are made from forged steel with a hickory handle. The brick should be held stable, with the hammer held in the appropriate hand. With the square edge of the hammer, you tap the brick at the position you require the cut.

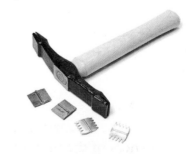

Figure 6.11 Brick hammer

> **Safety tip**
>
> Great care must be taken when using a brick hammer as it is very easy to hit your supporting hand with the hammer

Scutch or comb hammer

This is used to trim bricks or blocks to the correct size or shape. It is made from forged steel with a hickory handle and it can come with a single or double scutch head. Small combs are inserted into the head to give the trimming blade.

Figure 6.12 Scutch or comb hammer

> **Safety tip**
>
> Great care must be taken with a comb hammer as the particles of material being trimmed can fly off. You must also be careful not to hit your hands

Bolster chisel

Used mainly for cutting bricks or blocks to the size shape, a bolster chisel is made from hardened tempered steel in blade sizes from 64 mm to 100 mm.

Spirit levels

Made from aluminium and available in various sizes from 225 mm to 1200 mm, spirit levels are used for levelling things horizontally and for plumbing vertically. Some levels have an adjustable bubble at the bottom for levelling angled work.

Figure 6.13 Bolster chisels

Figure 6.14 Spirit level

Lines and pins

Lines and pins are used for laying bricks and blocks once the corners have been erected to ensure work is in a straight line. The pins are placed into the **perp** joints at each end of the run so that the line runs from the top of the laid brick at each end. Placing the top of the brick to the line also keeps the bricks level between the two points, assuming that the corners are correct.

Figure 6.15 Brick lines and line pins

The pins are normally made from forged steel for light duty work. Some are made from thicker steel for heavier duty work. The line can be made of nylon or cotton. Nylon is more durable but less flexible, whereas cotton is the opposite.

Corner blocks

Corner blocks are used to attach the line to keep the brickwork straight. They are made from wood, plastic or steel and fit onto the corners of the brickwork with the lines pulled tight to hold them in place. They are then raised to complete each course as the brickwork progresses.

The corner block is placed onto one **quoin** with the line pulled tight. The other corner block is then fixed to the line about a quarter brick short of the quoin, depending on the length of the wall to be built. The block is then pulled and fixed to the second quoin. Both blocks are adjusted so the line is level with the course of bricks to be laid.

Remember

Great care must be taken when using levels as they can easily become inaccurate, resulting in work that seems level, but is in fact wrong

Key term

Perp – the vertical joint between two bricks or blocks

Remember

The line comes in different lengths so make sure it is long enough for the work to be undertaken

Remember

Be careful not to over tighten as the line can break or the corner blocks could be pulled out of plumb

Key term

Quoin – the corner of a wall

Remember

Corner blocks can only be used on external corners

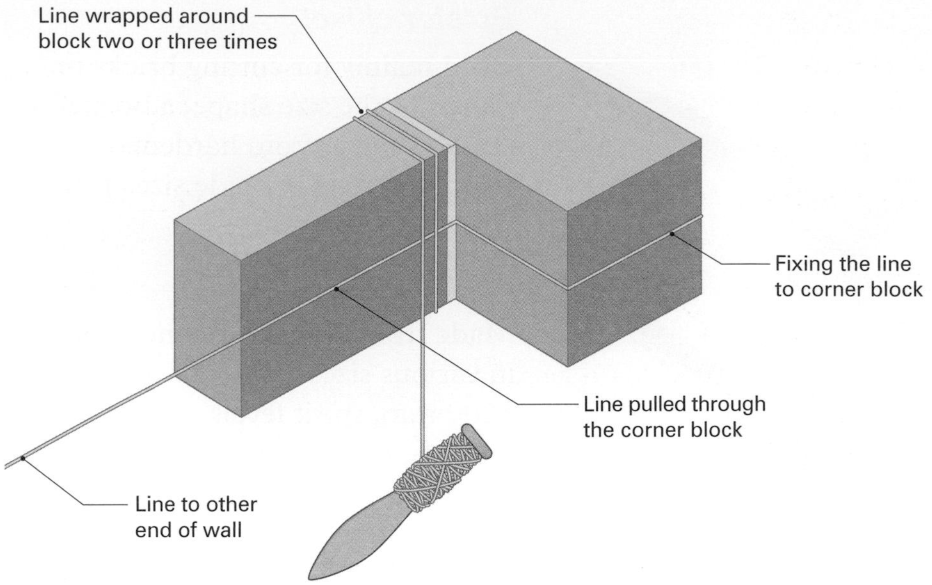

Line wrapped around block two or three times

Fixing the line to corner block

Line pulled through the corner block

Line to other end of wall

Figure 6.16 Corner block

Tingle plate

When building very long courses of brickwork, the line may sag even when pulled tight. A tingle plate is used to hold the line up in the middle of the wall, preventing it and the wall from sagging. If the wall sags in the middle, the work will have to be re-done.

A tingle plate is made of steel sheet. The tingle plate is placed at the centre of the wall on top of a previously lined, levelled and gauged brick. The line is fed under the ends and over the middle prong on the plate so that the line stays at the bottom. A brick is then placed on top of the plate to hold it secure, and the course is then laid to the line in the normal way.

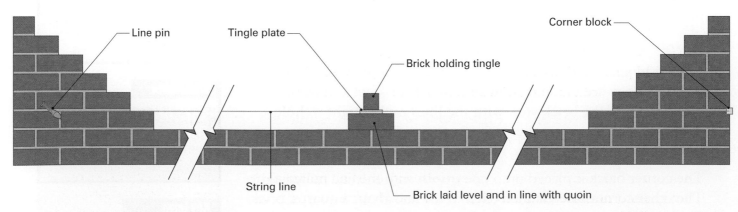

Line pin

Tingle plate

Corner block

Brick holding tingle

String line

Brick laid level and in line with quoin

Figure 6.17 Tingle plate on the line

Concrete mixer

A concrete mixer is a drum-shaped tool that mixes together cement, aggregate (such as sand or gravel) and water to form concrete. The materials are placed in the revolving drum to make the mix.

For smaller volume mixes, a portable drum is used. This means the concrete can be made on site ready for the construction and allows the workers to use the cement before it hardens.

This mixing can also be carried out by hand in a wheelbarrow or with a larger concrete mixer trailer.

Figure 6.18 Concrete mixer

Calculations and formulae required for building solid walls

Brickwork areas are calculated by using the number of bricks per square metre. In the case of a single thickness wall or half brick wall, 60 bricks are required per square metre. In the case of a 1 brick thick wall, 120 bricks are required per square metre.

To work out the number of bricks required for a project, you will need to know all the measurements for the length, height and width (or thickness) of the wall.

The formula for working out an area is: length × height. The answer to the calculation will be in square metres or m². This should then be multiplied by the amount of bricks required for the relevant thickness of the wall.

K2. Erect solid walling to required specification

Preparing to build solid walling

Location of components for use

Once you have a drawing to work to, you will need to look at preparing your working materials in the workshop ready for building your wall, as shown in Figure 6.19.

After working out the number or volume of materials required, you will have to stack them in your area. Each site has different rules for arranging materials. Some smaller sites may position materials close, ready for use. Other sites may hold all materials in a compound until needed and then transport them into position via fork lift as required.

Your supervisor will explain the correct method of setting out the job. All walls must be set out correctly, and the positions checked

Remember

Use the information from the drawings and plans to work out the materials you require and then stack them in your area

Safety tip

Only lift and carry one block at a time, because of the weight. If a new stack of blocks is to be opened, use a Stanley knife on the plastic bands and metal cutters for the metal straps

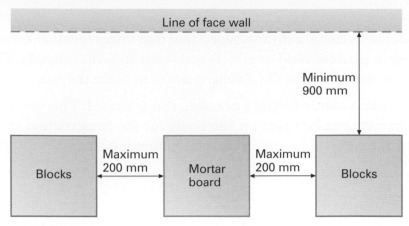

Figure 6.19 Setting out your area

before any excavation or construction work begins. Correcting errors made in setting out can be both time consuming and expensive. The wall must be set out in the right place, level and square.

Types of wall

Half brick walls

Half brick walls are 102 mm thick and are nearly always built in stretcher bond or 'half bond' (see Figure 6.20). Half bricks are used on stopped ends to form the corners. Walls should be set out to use as many stretchers as possible and no cuts should be less than a half bat (102 mm).

This type of wall is mainly used as the face wall on cavity walls or garden walls if piers are incorporated, and as brick or block internal walls to partition rooms.

In the case of face walls, the corner pattern should be the same at both ends but is sometimes reversed to help with bonding. If cuts are required, sometimes it is better to place them under a door or window. This arrangement would normally be determined at the design stage by the architect.

Remember

Half bats and three-quarter bats are used to gain bond

Remember

Reverse bond cannot be used without the permission of the architect

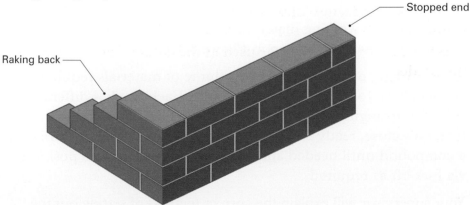

Figure 6.20 Half bond wall

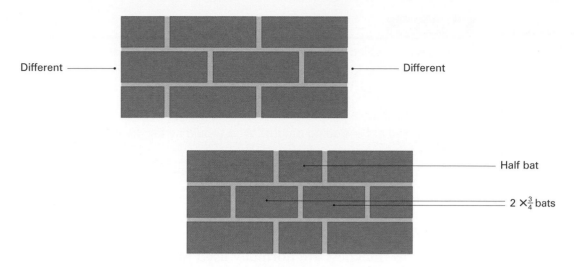

Different ———

——— Different

Half bat

$2 \times \frac{3}{4}$ bats

Result if a reverse bond is not used (broken bond)

Figure 6.21 Reverse bond wall

1 brick walls

1 brick walls are 215 mm thick and enable the bricklayer to place headers across the wall, which make it possible to create several different bonds. This type of wall is used where more strength is required, as with fire walls, garden walls, inspection chambers, areas where steelwork is to sit and for sound proofing. There are four main bonds used:

- English bond
- Flemish bond
- English garden wall bond
- Flemish garden wall bond.

With these bonds, the bricks lap the course below by a quarter brick and a queen closer should always be used at the corner (quoin) next to the header.

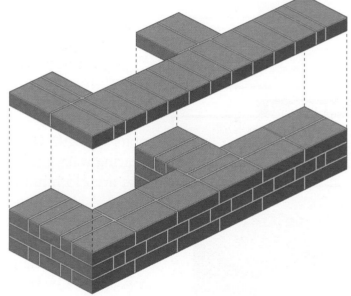

Figure 6.22 1 brick wall

Remember
Make sure the perps are plumb

Remember
In Scotland, a queen closer is also known as a pup or closure

Unit 2047

How to build solid walling, isolated and attached piers

Key term

Retaining walls – walls built to hold back earth or, in some instances, water

Did you know?

In some instances, wall ties may be used to tie the brickwork to the blocks

Working life

John has been asked to build a one brick wall, 30 m long and 1.5 m high in English bond. The foundation concrete has been put in and all materials are on site ready to use.

Are there any problems with what John is planning here? How could he check if what he is doing is right? Who should he talk to about any problems?

When should John think about starting work?

$1\frac{1}{2}$ and 2 brick walls

Walls of this thickness are normally used for **retaining walls**, load-bearing piers or piers to garden walls.

Suitable concrete blocks may be used in conjunction with bricks when constructing retaining walls. The use of bricks alone in walls of this thickness can be costly. However, by using bricks to provide the face finish and blocks to provide the main body of the walling, you can significantly reduce costs. The blocks would be laid flat and tied into the brickwork face every three courses.

Bonding for solid walls

Many different types of bond can be used to construct solid walling, some of which will already be familiar to you. They are all variations on quarter bond, used for solid walling because of its strength. Quarter bond is used for garden walls, load-bearing walls and retaining walls, as well as inspection chambers that are 215 mm thick or thicker.

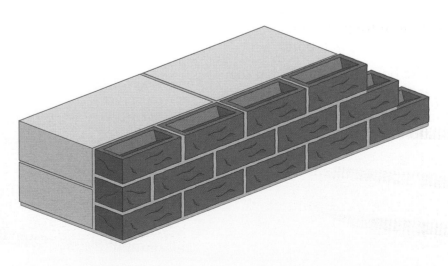

Figure 6.23 Retaining wall using combination of brick and blocks and a $1\frac{1}{2}$ brick pier

The four main bonds regularly used are:

- **English bond** – the strongest of all the bonds with alternate courses of stretchers and headers. It is used for inspection chambers, garden walls, etc.

- **English garden wall bond** – consists of either three, five or seven courses of stretchers to one course of headers. It is not as strong as English bond, as there is a straight joint in the centre of the wall on the three stretcher courses. As downward pressure is not a problem, it is often used for garden wall construction.

- **Flemish bond** – uses alternate stretchers and headers in each course. The header should be positioned in the centre of the stretcher course below and above, making it the most attractive bond used (especially if the headers are carried out in a coloured brick).

- **Flemish garden wall bond** – consists of three stretchers and then one header, alternating in each course. The header is positioned in the centre of the middle stretcher each time. In all cases, the corner header should have a queen closer next to it to form the quarter bond.

Figure 6.24 English bond

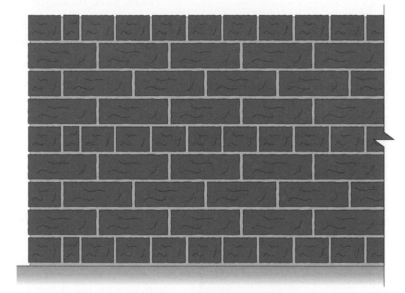

Figure 6.25 English garden wall bond

Figure 6.26 Flemish bond

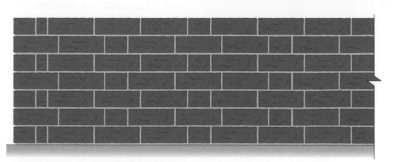

Figure 6.27 Flemish garden wall bond

Basic rules about bonding and building solid walls

- If measurements are given for the length of a wall, set out to avoid unnecessary cutting.
- Avoid broken and reverse bonds if possible.
- Work from the ends to the middle of the wall.
- Keep vertical joints plumb and uniform.
- Avoid wide vertical joints – ideally joints should be 10 mm, although there is a tolerance of 3 mm.
- Queen closers should be 46 mm wide to achieve the correct lap.
- Use two quarter bats instead of a queen closer – it can be easier and prevents waste.
- Take care in English and Flemish bonds to maintain quarter brick overlap, especially in long walls where you can 'lose' or 'gain' ground.
- Use a line on both sides in garden wall bonds, but remember only one side can be plumbed in 1 brick walling.
- Make sure you always lay cut bricks frog up.

Providing foundations to walling

Foundations were covered earlier in Unit 2003. Refer back to that unit on pages 110–112 for more detailed information on the types of foundation used for solid walling.

Strip foundations

The most commonly used strip foundation is the 'narrow strip' foundation, used for small domestic dwellings and low-rise structures. The trench is filled with concrete up to 4–5 courses of ground level damp proof course (DPC). It must be deep enough to prevent the soil being affected by weather.

Wide strip foundation

This type of foundation is similar to the above, but with steel reinforcement placed within the concrete base. This means the depth does not need to be considerably increased to spread a heavier load.

Raft foundations

This type is used where the soil has a poor bearing capacity. It consists of a slab of concrete covering the base of the structure. The depth is greater around the edge of the raft to protect the load-bearing soil underneath from the effects of moisture.

Remember

The design of the foundation will be the decision of the architect and structural design team. The final decision on the suitability and depth of foundation, as well as the thickness of the concrete, will rest with the local authority's building department

Pad foundations

These foundations are used where the main loads of a structure are imposed at certain key points, for example, with brick or steel columns. The simplest form uses individual concrete pads at various points around the structure with concrete ground beams spanning across them. The depth depends on the load.

Piled foundations

There are a number of different types of piled foundation, each with an individual purpose. Short bored piled foundations are the most common. They involve a series of holes being bored around the base of the proposed building. These are spanned with lightweight concrete beams and filled with concrete. This reduces the amount of excavated soil.

Stepped foundations

These are used on sloping ground. The height of each step should not be greater than the thickness of the concrete. Ideally the steps should coincide with the brick course height.

Transferring walling positions onto foundation concrete

It is essential that the correct height is achieved when constructing walling from the base of a trench up to the required DPC level. You can achieve this easily by using a gauge rod and spirit level as shown in Figure 6.28.

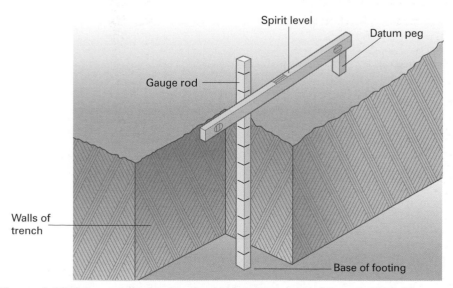

Figure 6.28 Using a gauge rod and spirit level to ensure the correct height

> **Remember**
>
> If a split brick course method is used, the split course must always be laid as the first course and not anywhere else within the height of the wall, otherwise this will cause significant weakness within the construction

Where the depth from DPC level to the concrete below does not work to the normal 75 mm course heights, you may need to lay a thicker bed joint underneath the first course. In instances where there is a difference of half a course, you will need to lay a split brick course.

Before construction of the walling below ground level can commence, you will need to transfer the line of the face of the brickwork, down from the ranging or setting out lines onto the concrete in the base of the trench. This task must be carried out with care and accuracy to ensure that the building elevations remain truly vertical.

The ranging or setting out lines will be attached to wooden profiles. A spirit level is used to transfer this line down onto the concrete. A mortar bed is spread over the area directly below the setting out line, which identifies the face of the wall to be built. When using the spirit level to transfer the face line down onto the concrete it is advisable to use a straight edge to steady the spirit level. This helps to maintain the level's upright position and to obtain accurate positioning of the markings in the mortar bed.

Constructing walls to given datum heights

Figure 6.30 shows a datum with an 'assumed' level of 10.000 m. The floor level is 10.000 m so the floor level is the same as the datum. The bottom of the excavation is 9.000 m, so the excavation is 1.000 m below the datum peg. The top of the foundation concrete is 9.150 m, so the thickness of the foundation concrete is 9.150 − 9.000 = 0.150 m.

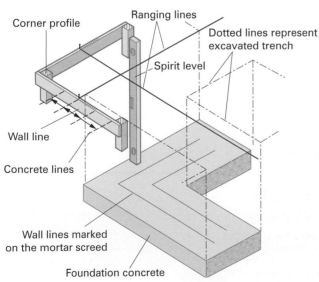

Figure 6.29 Transferring the ranging lines

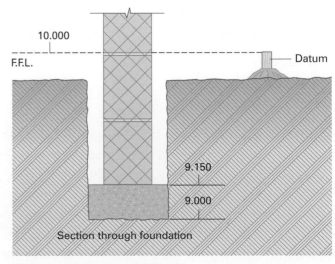

Figure 6.30 Datum with levels

Damp proof barriers

Damp proof barriers is covered in greater detail on pages 87–88. Please refer to this section for more information on the ways in which damp proof barriers can be placed. The main damp proof barriers are:

- flexible DPC
- semi-rigid DPC
- rigid DPC.

Health and safety

As with all materials, great care should be taken with moving, storing and using bricks, blocks and mortar.

Protecting brickwork

Remember to protect work from damage at the end of every day. To prevent damage to walls, cover them with a plythene sheet or taupaulin, held in place by scaffold board or bricks. More information on protecting brickwork can be found on page 167.

Junctions and intersections in solid walling

It may be necessary to alter the direction of a length of solid walling or to connect an adjoining wall to the main solid wall. Where this needs to be done after the main walling is built, provision must be made within the main walling as the work proceeds.

This provision can be made using a number of methods. Described in more detail below, these include:

- toothing
- indents
- proprietary wall connectors.

Sometimes the change in direction of a length of wall or the inclusion of a junction or intersecting wall needs to be incorporated at the same time as the main walling is built. In this case, the correct bonding methods must be used. Figures 6.31 and 6.32 give some examples of the more common bonding arrangements for junction and intersecting walls.

> **Remember**
>
> Rain will cause mortar joints to run over the face of the wall, causing unsightly stains. Cold weather could cause the water in the mortar to freeze, damaging the bonds between blocks and bricks, making the wall weak and possibly causing the wall to be taken down

> **Remember**
>
> Always set out in stretchers no matter what the bond is

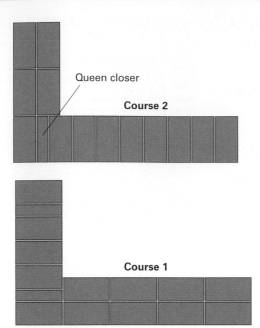

Queen closer

Course 2

Course 1

Figure 6.31 1 brick thick wall in English bond which changes direction

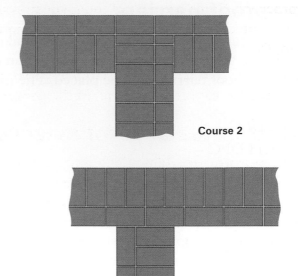

Course 2

Course 1

Figure 6.32 $1\frac{1}{2}$ brick thick intersecting wall in Flemish bond

Toothing

Bricks are left out on alternate courses at the end of a wall so that the new wall can be 'toothed' in at a later date. This method is not recommended as it leaves a weakness within the wall because it is very difficult to make the mortar joints solid.

Indents

Holes are left out in a wall to receive a brick or blockwork junction. Alternate courses can be left out in the case of brickwork. However with blockwork, three courses of brickwork are left out to accommodate the blockwork. These are sometimes referred to as block indents.

Figure 6.34 Wall connector with a metal plate attached with angle brackets

Proprietary wall connectors

Wall connectors provide a method of joining walls without cutting into an existing wall. A metal plate is attached to the existing wall by plugging and screwing.

There are different types of attachment for the new wall. Some have angle brackets that can be attached to the plate by protruding lugs. The brackets are then built into the wall as the

Figure 6.33 End of a wall to be toothed at a later date

work proceeds. Some are part of the main structure and fold out onto the courses, others are slid down the main connector into position, then built in.

This method is quicker and less damaging than the other two, as little vibration is caused to the wall in the connecting process.

Decorative features for masonry walling

The main purpose of adding decorative features to brick walling is to enhance the appearance and aesthetic value of long, flat lengths of walling, rather than its strength. Decorative features can be panels placed within the brickwork or can be created by cutting or laying bricks using particular methods and bonding arrangements.

Decorative work must be of the highest quality of craftsmanship in order to achieve the desired effect. Good planning and setting out is essential as there is very little room for error. Materials should also be carefully selected because flawed, or sub-standard, materials will be even more visible as the feature in which they are used is the main focal point for the untrained eye.

Raking cutting

Raking cutting refers to cutting brickwork at an angle, as at the gable end of a roof, or ramped brickwork in a solid retaining or garden wall.

Raking cutting can be done by hand with the use of a hammer and bolster, or by machine using disc cutters or a table saw.

Figure 6.35 Brickwork with holes for junction

Remember

When using wall connectors, the manufacturer's instructions must be carefully followed

Remember

In Scotland, a gable end is also known as a pein end

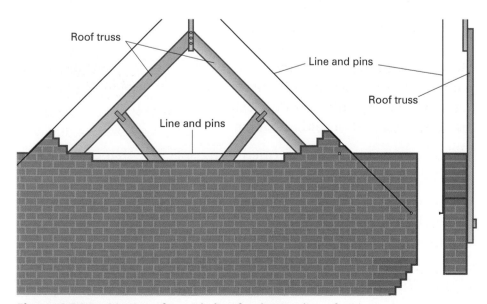

Figure 6.36 Positioning of a guide line for the true line of cut

Roof truss

Line and pins

Roof truss

Line and pins

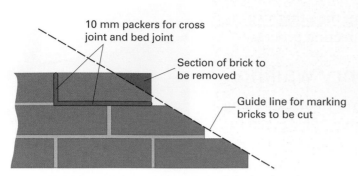

Figure 6.37 Positioning and marking of the brick to be cut

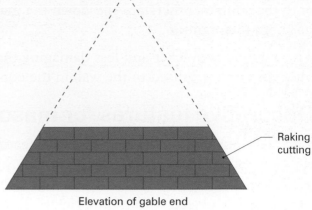

Elevation of gable end

Figure 6.38 Gable end showing raking cutting

Motorised cutting is better where the angle of the cut is very low on the brick or the bricks being cut are very hard or have holes.

Whichever method is used, raking cutting should be neat. A guide line needs to be erected to show the true line of cut and aid accurate marking of the bricks to be cut. The cut bricks should not protrude above the line, as this could interfere with whatever finish is to be applied.

String courses

String courses are normally introduced towards the tops of walls, particularly at the last few courses of large boundary walls, as a decorative feature. String courses can be built in using a variety of bonding arrangements. These include:

* soldier courses
* dog toothing
* dentil courses.

String courses are sometimes used lower down in the face of the wall as a decorative feature. However, these are more commonly known as 'band courses'. The most common arrangement used for band courses is a soldier course.

String courses can also be formed using specially shaped bricks, of which there are numerous types and variations.

Wherever string courses are constructed above normal 'eye-line', the bricks used in these courses must be lined up along their bottom edge as opposed to the top edge. This ensures that on the underside of the feature, the edge that will be seen appears straight and seamless.

Figure 6.39 Soldier courses used as decorative features

Soldier courses

Soldier courses are simply bricks laid on end next to each other. However, unless great care is taken to ensure soldier bricks are laid both plumb and level across the length of the course, the finished article can be unsightly.

When laying soldier courses, a line must be used along the top edge of the soldier course throughout the construction. In addition, a small spirit level (boat level) must be used to ensure that the individual soldiers are kept plumb. Just one brick out of plumb will affect the line and result in a poor finish to the feature.

Remember

In Scotland, a boat level is also known as a pocket level

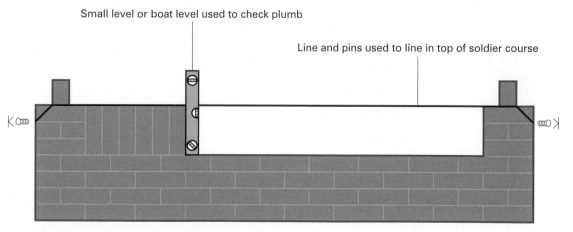

Figure 6.40 Using a brick line and boat level to construct a soldier course

Figure 6.41 Dog toothing

Figure 6.42 A dentil course

> **Did you know?**
>
> Dog toothing can also be used to form decorative panels

> **Did you know?**
>
> Once the first brick has been cut at the correct 45° angle, it can then be used as a template for all the other cuts

Dog toothing

Dog toothing refers to a bonding arrangement in which the bricks are laid at a 45° angle to the main face of the wall. This type of bonding arrangement can either project from the main face or can be built flush with the main face. By building the edge of the angled bricks flush with the main wall, a recessed effect will be produced.

When constructing a course of projecting dog toothing, the projecting bricks must be lined in by fixing a brick line across the face of the bricks. The brick line will maintain even projection along the length of the feature. The use of a spirit level placed against the underside of the projecting course will ensure the 'seen edge' (the underside edge of the feature) remains straight and even to the eye.

Dentil courses

A dentil course refers to a string course where alternate headers in the same course are projected from the face of the wall. When constructing a dentil course, the same principles apply as for dog toothing in that the underside of the bricks must be levelled as the work progresses and the brick line must be fixed across the face of the bricks being laid.

Both dog toothing and dentil courses should always be finished off with a course of bricks above them. These courses can either be laid flush with the feature course or project out past the feature.

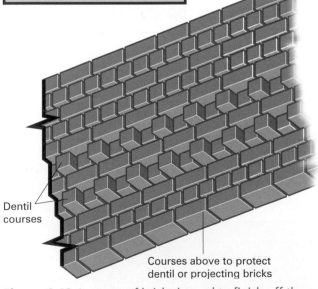

Dentil courses

Courses above to protect dentil or projecting bricks

Figure 6.43 A course of bricks is used to finish off the feature

This additional course is intended to finish off the feature, provide protection from the elements and prevent possible damage to the face and upper edges of the feature bricks.

Diaper work

Diaper bond is quite simply the forming of diamond-shaped patterns within the face of a length of walling. This type of work provides no more than decorative value to a building. The diamond-shaped patterns are formed using contrasting bricks to those of the main walling and incorporated as recessed, projecting or flush to the face.

There are numerous variations to the patterns that
can be formed. Normally patterns are formed using headers, as the use of stretchers makes it more difficult to maintain bond and does not provide the same uniformed diamond effect.

Whenever projecting diaper bond is used, it is important to remember that all projecting bricks must be plumbed to ensure equal projection throughout the pattern. The projections should be plumbed both on the face and side elevations.

When producing a recessed diaper bond pattern, it is advisable to use a depth gauge or template to ensure that the same recess depth is maintained throughout the pattern. These gauges can be made from timber notched to the exact depth required for the recess.

Figure 6.44 Diaper bond

Reinforcement in brickwork

Brickwork is extremely strong in compression (being squashed), but weak in tension (being stretched). If there is any chance of brickwork being subjected to tensile forces (i.e. being stretched), some kind of reinforcement can be built into the wall.

Reinforcing can be done in several ways, but the most common way is to build in a steel mesh called expanding metal. The mesh is built into the bed joints. Various widths can be obtained for different thicknesses of wall. Brickwork can also be reinforced vertically with steel rods and concrete.

Some places where reinforced brickwork could be used are:

- over a large span door or window openings
- where high security is required (such as a bank vault)
- gate pillars
- foundations where there is a possibility of subsidence
- concrete columns.

Providing coping for masonry walling

Weathering a wall

A protective finish can be added to walls that are likely to be exposed to weather such as rain and frost, which can weaken the wall and cause the top brick course to break up. Cavity walls do not require such protection as they are not exposed due to the roof structure covering the top courses. Garden walls, retaining

Figure 6.45 Brickwork reinforced with expanding metal

Remember

Always check the specifications to determine the type and size of reinforcement required

Figure 6.46 Column reinforced vertically with steel rods and concrete

walls and **parapet** walls will require finishing, however. A bricklayer can use one of several methods to weather a wall:

- with a brick finish
- with a concrete finish
- with a stone finish.

Key term

Parapet – a low wall that acts as a barrier where there is a sudden drop (e.g. a balcony wall)

Brick finish

Common bricks can be used to weather the top of a wall. However, it is advisable to use a hard stock brick or engineering type of brick, which are more resistant to water penetration and frost damage. The different finishes that can be achieved will depend on the thickness of the wall. On a half brick wall there are two main ways to finish with bricks.

- The main way to achieve a brick finish is by using a brick on end, more commonly known as a soldier course (see Figure 6.47).
- Half bats can be used in the same way (see Figure 6.48), but they will need to be cut exactly in half (although this does not allow for the difference in brick sizes). In addition, the bricks would have to be cut by machine as cutting by hammer and bolster may not always cut squarely, resulting in variable back joint sizes, which gives a poor appearance to the finish.

Remember

In Scotland, half bats are also known as half bricks

On a 1 brick wall, bricks are laid on edge to protect the top (see Figure 6.49). It is always best to use a hard water-resistant type of brick. Sometimes the wall may have what is called a tile creasing under the brick on edge. This is normally two courses of flat concrete tiles bedded on mortar and half bonded. This helps to stop rainwater penetration as water that would normally run down the face of the bricks is pushed away because the tiles are wider than the wall. A brick-on-edge finish can also be used on walls that are $1\frac{1}{2}$ and 2 bricks wide, as well as a finish to 1, $1\frac{1}{2}$, and 2 brick **piers** (see Figure 6.50).

Key term

Piers – vertical support structures that gives strength to a wall

Figure 6.47 A soldier course brick finish

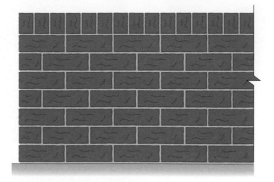

Figure 6.48 A half bat brick finish

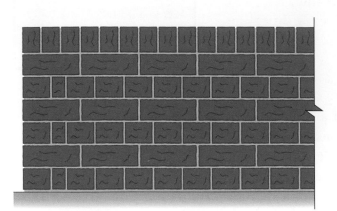

Figure 6.49 A brick on edge finish on a 1 brick wall

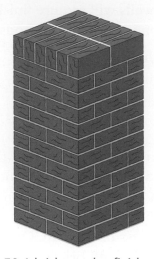

Figure 6.50 A brick on edge finish on a pier

Concrete finish

Concrete can be used to weather a wall in the form of pre-cast sections called copings. These are usually factory manufactured and come in a range of width sizes to suit requirements but are normally 300 mm or 450 mm in length. Two main profile types of coping are normally used: saddleback and feather edged (see Figures 6.51 and 6.52). Copings are made slightly wider than the wall to allow water to drain past the face of the wall.

Stone finish

Natural stone cut to the desired size can be used to weather a wall in the same way as concrete (see Figure 6.53). Stone will give a more rough-looking finish as not all the pieces will be regular sizes. Stone is also a more expensive option for weathering due to the higher cost of the material.

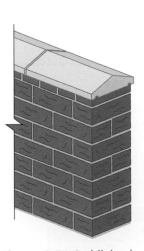

Figure 6.51 Saddleback coping

Figure 6.52 Feather edge coping

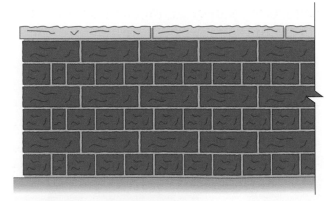

Figure 6.53 A stone finish on a wall

Types of joint finish

Jointing is carried out to make sure that the mortar joint is completely filled and in contact with each brick. This will prevent rainwater penetration and possible damage from frost, which would crumble the joint. Another reason for jointing is to give the overall appearance of the wall a pleasing look to the eye. Once the jointing is completed, rainwater should run down the surface of the wall and not into any gaps left in joints.

On larger sites, before commencement of any brickwork, sample brick panels may be constructed and pointed to show how the finished product will look, giving architectural staff a chance to change the type or colour of pointing required. This is because sometimes coloured mortar may be used for the joints.

One of the most important things to consider is at what time jointing should be carried out. As the brickwork is carried out over the course of the day, lower courses will dry out, but other factors need to be taken into consideration:

- **The type of brick used** – stock or engineering bricks do not absorb moisture as fast as some softer bricks. Therefore the joints will take longer to dry to the required texture for jointing.
- **The moisture content** – the bricks may be damp before use. Therefore moisture absorption will be slow.
- **The weather** – when working in summer the heat will dry out joints faster, due to the warmth of the bricks, than in damper conditions, when moisture stays in the air.

Joints need to be checked by touching to see if they are ready for jointing. If they are too dry, it will be difficult to carry out jointing and if too wet the joint mortar is inclined to 'drag', giving poor adhesion to the bricks and a poor quality appearance. The drying out of mortar has no given time span, so understanding and experience are key to knowing when it is the right time for jointing.

Pointing

Pointing is the process of joint filling to brickwork when the mortar joints have been previously raked out to approximately 12 mm on work that is fresh and to 12–18 mm on older work that has had existing mortar ground out and is to be repointed at a later date. This type of work requires more skill and patience than jointing as it is very time-consuming and great care must be taken not to smear the new mortar onto the face of the brick.

Find out

Who would normally request that sample brick panels be built?

Did you know?

Some bricks can 'swim' with water and may require pointing the next day. To 'swim' means to float on the bed joint due to delayed drying out time

There are different types of joint finishes, which are covered below. Some take longer to carry out than others, hence the cost of pointing varies considerably as some types can take twice as long to complete.

When pointing, remember the following points.

- Always start from the top and work downwards to prevent dropped mortar, or mortar brushed off, can fall onto already completed work.
- Make sure the joints are clean of any loose old mortar.
- Brush the area to be pointed to remove any dust.
- Wet the wall so that the bricks absorb the water to give good adhesion for the new mortar. Some bricks will require more water than others.
- Apply the mortar filling to the perps first so as to keep a continuous bed joint when applied.
- When sufficiently dry, brush off with a fine brush to remove any excess particles of mortar.

Raking out

Joints need to be raked out to a depth of between 15 and 18 mm. This can be carried out in several ways.

- You can use a raking out tool (or chariot) set to the required depth to rake out the joints evenly. This is perfect for very soft joints but may not be for harder or variable joints.
- Use an angle grinder, but great care and expertise is required not to touch and mark the brick faces or damage the **arrises** of the brick as joint depths can be varied. Dust from the cutting can cause problems if working in a built-up area (dust gets on to people's property).
- Rake out using a bolster, chisels or comb chisel, but again great care should be taken not to damage the arrises of the brick and the depth could be varied.

Sometimes a combination of the above may be the best solution. Once raked out, pointing can be carried out.

Key term

Arris – the edge of a brick

Ironed or tooled joint

This type of joint is the most commonly used as it covers up slight impurities in the brick arrises and is the quickest to carry out (see Figure 6.54). There are different sizes so care should be taken to use the same size each time. Smaller sizes give a deeper profile whereas the larger diameters give a shallower, rounded look. The jointing is carried out as work progresses.

Figure 6.54 Tooled joint

Recessed joint

With this type of joint the mortar is dragged out to a maximum depth of 4 mm and then ironed to compress the joint's surface. Great care should be taken to ensure that all of the joint is removed. A recessed joint is better used when the bricks are a harder, more frost-resistant type as water can lie on the edge of the recessed arris on the brick. Care must be taken to ensure all the joints are full before commencing the raking out process. Again, jointing is carried out as the work progresses.

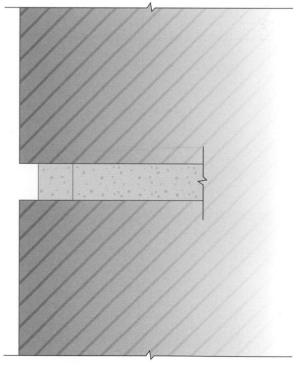

Figure 6.55 Recessed joint

Flush joint

This type of joint gives a simple look but it is quite difficult to keep a complete flush surface finish (see Figure 6.56). If modern type finishes are not required, it gives a **rustic** look, which may be more in keeping with the surroundings. This type of joint is carried out by using a hardwood timber or plastic block to smooth and compact the surface of the mortar into place.

A flush joint is not ideal if the bricks used are not regular in shape as the joints will show any deviation and could look wider than they are. Jointing is always carried out as work progresses.

Key term

Rustic – old and natural looking; traditional

Remember

If on a large site, make sure all bricklayers 'strike' to the same side on the perp joints

Remember

In Scotland, a flush joint finish is also known as a bag rubbed finish

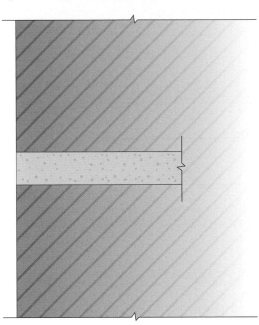

Figure 6.56 Flush joint

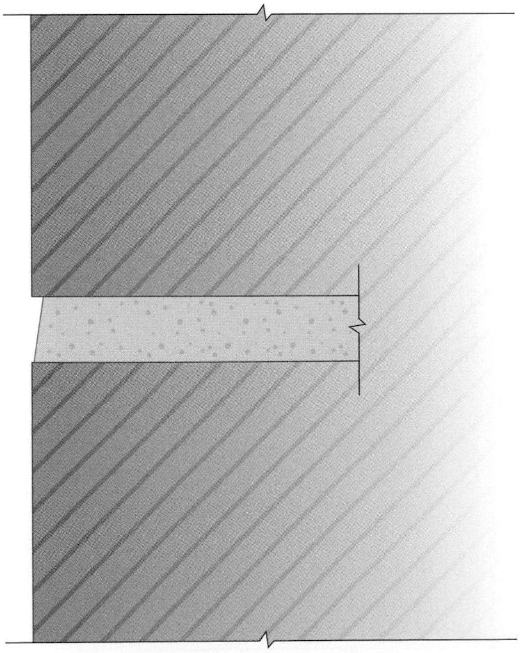

Weather struck joint

This type of joint is slightly sloping to allow rainwater to run down the face of the brick rather than lie at the joint (see Figure 6.57). The mortar is smoothed with a trowel, with the mortar the thickness of the trowel below the top brick and flush with the brick below. The same process is carried out with the perps and the left side of the joint is below the surface.

Figure 6.57 Weather struck joint

Weather struck and cut pointing

This is the most common type of jointing carried out on previously raked out joints (see Figure 6.58). It can cover any irregularities to bricks, creating a straight appearance. This type of pointing is the hardest and most time-consuming to do. The mortar is smoothed flush to the brick at the top of the joint and about a trowel thickness proud of the brick at the bottom. The mortar is then allowed to dry slightly and is then 'cut' in a straight line using a tool called a Frenchman.

The straight edge should be kept off the wall using cork pads, nails or screws, so that the cut excess can drop and not be squashed against the face of the wall. Perps are again angled to the left and finished in the same way as the bed joints, but cut with a pointing trowel. All perps should be completed before the bed joint so as not to mark the beds with the trowel and to keep a continuous joint to the bed. This should then be lightly brushed sideways so as not to drag the edges of the bed joints.

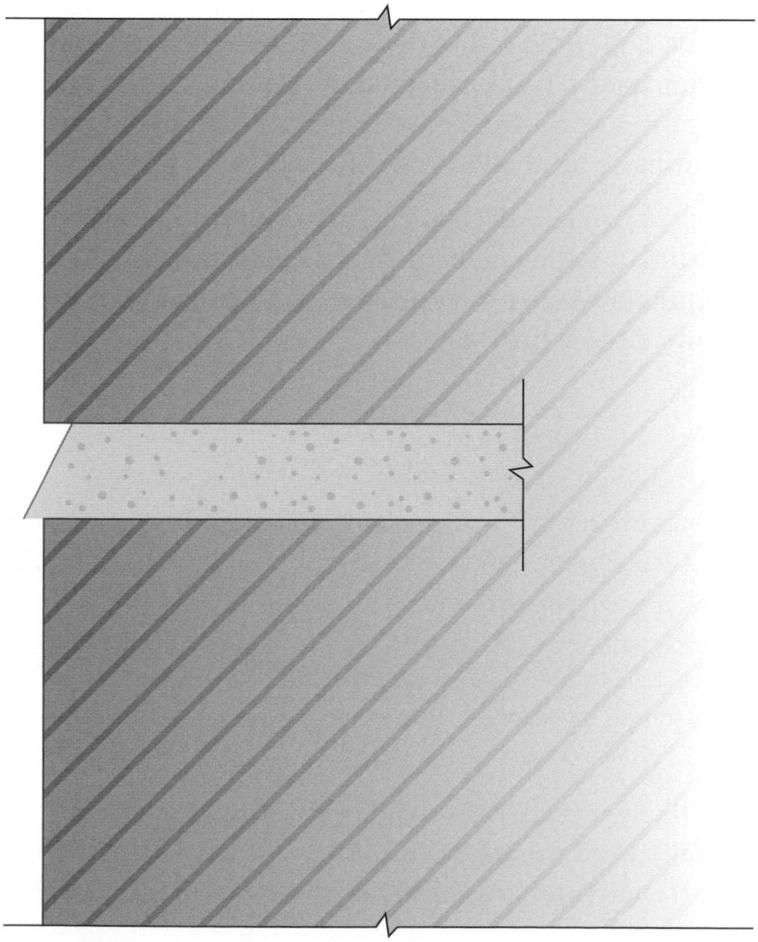

> **Did you know?**
>
> Sometimes a glue (PVA) can be added to the mortar to give a better adhesion to the brick and help bond to the existing mortar

Figure 6.58 Weather struck and cut joint

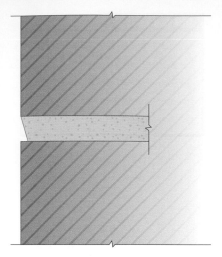

Figure 6.59 Reverse struck joint

Reverse struck joint

This type of finish is normally used for internal walls, giving a smooth finish to work that is not plastered as no shadows appear at the joint area (see Figure 6.59). Care must be taken to ensure the bottom edge is flush to the brick to stop the joint becoming a dust trap when work is complete. The wall would then be given a paint finish.

With all types of pointing, it is essential that the new mortar bonds well to the existing material, otherwise moisture will be trapped between them and, with frost, will break the newer material down, resulting in costly repairs.

Mixes

When mixing mortar for pointing, fine sand should be used to give a smoother finish, especially if the joint is to be cut with a trowel. This is because any edges would break unevenly if coarser sand were used.

If pointing is being carried out to relatively new brickwork, it would be better to use the same mix as for the original works. Sometimes pointing may be done, allowed to dry, raked out and a different coloured mortar used. This is usually done because of the time aspect (i.e. the brickwork could have to be finished, then raked out for future pointing so as to allow the other trades to progress).

Different types of bricks will require different mixes. Engineering bricks will require a strong cement-based mix whereas soft clay bricks will require a weaker mix, possibly with lime incorporated. Table 6.2 shows a basic breakdown.

Group 1	Class A engineering bricks	1:3 or 1:4
Group 2	Class B engineering bricks	$1:\frac{1}{2}:4\frac{1}{2}$
Group 3	Face bricks	1:5 or1:1:5 or 1:1:6

Table 6.2 Mortar mixing ratios for different types of brick

Lime is more likely to be used on older buildings, where the mortar originally used was sand and lime, but with cement added to give extra strength and durability. In most cases, the mix should not be stronger than the original material used.

The mixes shown in Table 6.2 can also be used for jointing mortars.

The importance of remedial work

It is important to understand that if discrepancies or mistakes are found, whether they are on drawings or to do with measurements or just something to do with an actual work situation, your role is limited to making decisions to rectify the problem. There will be some problems that develop on site that you will not have the responsibility or authority to make decisions on. For these problems, you must refer the issue to your manager, who can either make a decision or escalate it. You must remember there is a chain of command on a building site.

Working life

James has built a garden wall to full height. All that is needed to finish the wall is to lay the coping stones on the top. When he goes to the compound in order to get the coping stones, he finds that there are none there. Geoff, another bricklayer, tells him to build a brick on edge to finish the wall.

Should James follow this advice? Is it his decision to make? How important is it to the final build? Although this issue might seem quite small, it could have larger impacts on the whole project and what the client wants.

Who should James talk to before he makes a decision? What else could James do to solve the problem?

Meeting industrial and safety standards

Safety standards

Most of the legislation that affects building on site requires risk assessments to be carried out. The Management of Health and Safety at Work Regulations 1999 require every employer to make suitable and sufficient assessment of:

- the risks to the health and safety of employees to which they are exposed while at work
- the risks to the health and safety of persons not in the employer's employment arising out of or in connection with their work activities.

You must be aware of the dangers or hazards of any task, and know what can be done to prevent or reduce the risk. You will need to make sure that your work reflects this knowledge and keeps both you and your fellow workers safe.

There are five steps in a risk assessment:

- **Step 1** – identify the hazards.
- **Step 2** – identify who will be at risk.
- **Step 3** – calculate the risk from the hazard against the likelihood of an accident taking place.
- **Step 4** – introduce measures to reduce the risk.
- **Step 5** – monitor the risk.

Constantly changing factors mean any risk assessment may have to be modified or even changed completely.

Method statements

A method statement is a key safety document that takes the information about significant risks from the risk assessment and combines them with the job specification, to produce a practical and safe working method for the workers to follow on site.

Method statements should be specific and relevant to the job in hand and should detail what work is to be done, how the work should be done and what safety precautions need to be taken.

These method statements for working on site should always be referred to and worked with.

Industrial standards

For both brickwork and blockwork, industrial standards cover the standards and tolerances allowed on site for the plumbness, level and finish of a wall. They also cover if the wall is to gauge, if the joints run true and plumb as well as the cleanliness of the wall.

The standards the project is to meet are usually set out in the specification or the bill of quantities on site. As well as checking all the measurement requirements throughout the building stages, experience and a good eye will also help you to tell whether a job looks right or not.

Carrying out checks

As with blockwork, periodically carry out checks to ensure the wall is straight, plumb and level. Slight knocks or the movement of a corner can move the wall out of plumb. Make sure bricks are kept dry to avoid moisture from soaking in.

Remember

If there are no specifications for the work, an experienced bricklayer should know that whatever they build needs to be level and plumb with a good appearance. If nothing else, these serve as a good advert for bricklaying skills and help to get future work

K3. Erect isolated and attached piers to required specification

Isolated piers

An isolated pier is a solid pier built independently (not a part of) another structure, for example, for a gate entrance to hang the gate to.

Isolated piers built in $1\frac{1}{2}$ and 2 brick thickness can also be constructed in conjunction with other materials, to provide additional stability and strength. One instance is where isolated piers are required to support garden gates. The hollow formed in the centre of a $1\frac{1}{2}$ brick thick pier is filled with concrete and further strengthened with the use of steel reinforcing rods cast into the concrete.

Isolated piers are sometimes built as solid structures with no vertical hollow at the centre. This requires much more cutting during construction and can be more costly and time-consuming in terms of the number of bricks used.

Remember

Brackets that support garden gates must be built into the pier as work proceeds. If the brickwork has to be cut out after construction to accommodate the brackets, this can seriously damage the stability of the pier

Isolated piers can also incorporate decorative finishes (see page 215–219). Some of these finishes can act as a weathering to give added protection from the elements. Isolated piers can also incorporate larger weathering features, such as copings.

Isolated piers built for garden gates may need to support a lot of weight, in particular wrought iron gates. These types of gates are hung on special support brackets built into the brick pier as the work proceeds. The vertical distance between the brackets is determined by the hinges on the gate.

Pier core filled with concrete   Mild steel reinforcement rods

Figure 6.60 2 brick thick isolated pier with concrete and steel reinforcement

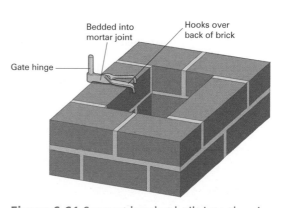

Bedded into mortar joint   Hooks over back of brick

Gate hinge

Figure 6.61 Support bracket built into the pier

Attached piers

These provide lateral support to the main walling, particularly in long lengths of retaining walls. For example, two or three piers might be attached to the back of a main wall to add strength to it. Attached piers are also sometimes used in garage or garden wall construction, when the wall is not built as a solid 1 brick wall, or at one end of a wall to add strength for hanging a gate or door.

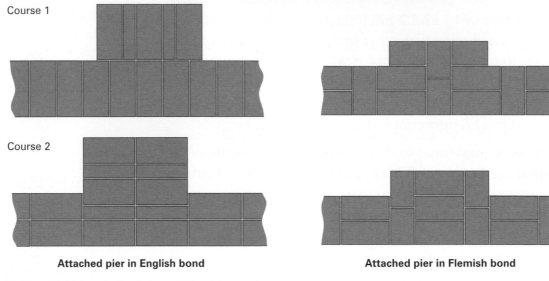

Course 1

Course 2

Attached pier in English bond

Attached pier in Flemish bond

Figure 6.62 Attached piers in English and Flemish bonds

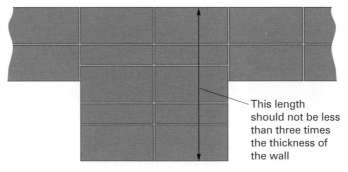

This length should not be less than three times the thickness of the wall

Figure 6.63 Attached piers showing required thickness

When constructing attached piers, the golden rule is to maintain the same bond on the face of the pier as that used on the face of the main wall. In retaining walls, where the majority of the piers may be covered by the soil being retained, there is a tendency to use stretcher bond, which reduces the amount of cutting required. However, this is not recommended as the properties of the pier can be affected and using stretcher bond may result in failure of the pier.

Another important point to remember when constructing attached piers is that the pier itself should have an overall thickness of not less than three times the thickness of the wall.

Capping

We have already looked at some of the ways a pier can be weathered but we will now look specifically at caps. A concrete cap can be bedded to the finished brickwork of a pier in order to protect the top (see Figure 6.64). Caps are factory produced and come in a range of standard sizes to suit most piers. The higher centre point causes water to run off the cap and an overhang means that the water drips away from the brickwork, thus offering further protection.

An alternative to a concrete cap is a flat stone cap (see Figure 6.65). As with stone finishes to walls, this choice of finish gives an irregularly shaped appearance and is more costly than other options.

On some older walls that are two or more bricks wide, tiles can be used to form a small roof-like structure to protect the brick or chalk wall that is exposed to the elements.

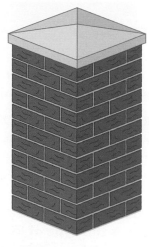

Figure 6.64 Concrete pier cap

Figure 6.65 Flat stone pier cap

FAQ

I've heard that mortar can be made up without cement and just have lime added to it – why is this?

Before Portland cement (OPC) was introduced, mortar was made from sand, slaked lime and water. Mortar made without OPC and just the addition of lime is often used in restoration work. This is because many old buildings were not built with OPC and so mortar made with OPC will be stronger than the bricks it binds.

What is a half-round profile joint (also known as a bucket handle finish)? Why is this type of joint, along with a tooled joint, the most commonly used method when pointing?

A half-round profile is a shallow, round, inwards joint finish so-called because bricklayers used to use a bucket handle to create it. A special tool can now be bought to do this instead. The reason this type of joint, along with a tooled joint, are the most commonly used is simply because they are the quickest and therefore the cheapest to do.

What finish should I use to weather a wall?

You could use a soldier course for a half brick wall or a brick on edge for a 1 brick wall.

Check it out

1. Name the four main bonds used for 1 brick walls and draw a diagram to show each one. Describe why you would use different bonds for different walls.
2. Name three types of material that could be used to finish the top of a wall and state why they are required. What are the differences between the types of material? What might affect your decision for which material to use?
3. Draw a diagram showing a saddleback coping and a feather edge coping. Describe when these are used.
4. Name four areas where reinforcement may be used in brickwork and explain why. Use diagrams to demonstrate the different qualities of these.
5. Draw a diagram to explain how brickwork is built to a gable end. Prepare a method statement to accompany this.
6. Explain what a detached pier is and give two examples of where it could be used. Why might you use a detached pier?
7. Describe three ways to join a new wall to an existing wall and explain each method in full with diagrams where necessary.
8. Given two examples where a retaining wall may be used. What is the purpose of the retaining wall?

Getting ready for assessment

The information contained in this unit, as well as continued practical assignments that you will carry out in your college or training centre, will help you with preparing for both your end of unit test and the diploma multiple-choice test. It will also aid you in preparing for the work that is required for the synoptic practical assignments in building solid walls.

You will need to be familiar with:

- how to identify and calculate the materials and equipment required
- setting up your area
- learning how to set out, level, gauge and plumb bricks for solid walls and piers
- cutting blocks to given sizes.

All these points will be needed for the synoptic test when carrying out the building of the different walls required. This unit has explained the methods used for constructing solid walls and piers. For example, for learning outcome two you have seen the methods used to construct walling to datum heights explained, with the reasons for providing for damp proof barriers and providing foundations clearly explained. You will need to use this information to set out your own solid walling, including positioning ranging lines to construct 1 brick walling in a variety of bonds. You will need to use the information in this unit to select the correct bond for the wall you are planning to build.

Before you start work on the synoptic practical test it is important that you have had sufficient practise and that you feel that you are capable of passing. It is best to have a plan of action and a work method that will help you. You will also need a copy of the required standards, any associated drawings and sufficient tools and materials. It is also wise to check your work at regular intervals. This will help you to be sure that you are working correctly, and help you to avoid problems developing as you work.

Your speed at carrying out these tasks will also help you to prepare for the time limit that the synoptic practical task has. But remember, don't try to rush the job as speed will come with practise and it is important that you get the quality of workmanship right. Check the marking list to ensure your tolerances are correct on the areas of plumbing gauge and levels as you progress. Professionally, you will need to report any problems to an authorised person.

Always make sure that you are working safely throughout the test. Make sure you are working to all the safety requirements given throughout the test and wear all appropriate personal protective equipment. When using tools, make sure you are using them correctly and safely.

Good luck!

Knowledge check

1 Which material is used to band bricks?
   a) Copper
   b) Plastic
   c) Lead
   d) Zinc

2 What is the strongest bond for building a 1-brick wall?
   a) English Bond
   b) Flemish Bond
   c) Flemish Garden Wall Bond
   d) English Garden Wall Bond

3 What type of foundation involves a series of holes bored around the base of a proposed building?
   a) Raft
   b) Strip
   c) Piled
   d) Pad

4 What is normally the maximum thickness of a solid wall?
   a) $\frac{1}{2}$ brick thick
   b) $1\frac{1}{2}$ bricks thick
   c) 2 bricks thick
   d) 1 brick thick

5 What should sand for mortar be made up of?
   a) Mainly small size grains
   b) Mainly large size grains
   c) Well graded grains
   d) Mainly medium size grains

6 What bricks are laid at a 45° angle to the main face line used as a feature?
   a) Brick on Edge
   b) Soldiers
   c) Indents
   d) Dog Toothing

7 Which bond consists of either 3, 5, or 7 courses of stretchers and one course of headers repeated?
   a) Stretcher Bond
   b) English Garden Wall Bond
   c) Flemish Bond
   d) Flemish Garden Wall

8 Which is not a material used to finish the top of a wall?
   a) Block
   b) Brick
   c) Concrete
   d) Stone

9 What is the most common type of cement used for concrete?
   a) RHPC
   b) OPC
   c) SRPC
   d) LHPC

10 Which of these tools may also be known as a 'chariot'?
   a) Jointer
   b) Hand hawk
   c) Joint raker
   d) Pointing trowel

How to build cavity walling forming masonry structures

Cavity walling is mainly used for house building and extension work to existing homes and flats. Cavity walls are two separate walls built with a cavity between them. The two walls are joined together with metal ties. The outer wall is often made with brick, the inner wall with block.

The cavity prevents water penetration into the building. It creates a barrier that prevents moisture from travelling from the outer wall into the inner wall. In places where the walls do not meet, such as doors and windows, a damp proof course (DPC) is used to stop water penetration. The cavity is insulated either partially or fully to make the building warmer and energy efficient.

This unit also supports NVQ Unit VR40 Erect Masonry Structures. This unit contains material that supports TAP Unit 3: Erect Masonry Structures and Unit 4: Provide Details to Masonry Structures.

This unit will cover the following learning outcomes:

- How to plan and select resources for practical tasks
- How to erect cavity walling to required specification
- How to form openings in cavity walling.

Functional skills

There are many different types of documents in Building Information. To use them correctly and understand the information they are giving you, you will be using FE 1.2.1 – 1.2.3 which relate to reading and understanding information. As with the other units, if there are any words or phrases you do not understand, use a dictionary, look them up using the Internet or discuss with your tutor.

K1. Plan and select resources for practical tasks

To carry out the construction of cavity walling, you will need to refer to the project drawings and plans to determine the exact nature of the wall construction you will be carrying out. We covered this material earlier in Unit 2003 and the concepts will be the same for solid walling. Please refer back to this earlier section for more information on:

- type of drawings and conventions commonly used (pages 54–57)
- scales commonly applied to drawing (pages 54–57)
- methods of reading and taking measurements from drawings (page 132–133)
- methods of reporting inaccuracies in information sources (page 133)
- reasons for checking datum points (page 57).

Information sources

The key information sources you will need to use for cavity walling are:

- drawings and specification
- *Building Regulations* (approved documents)
- local authority requirements – this will give the location of the building line
- British Standard specifications/codes of practice
- manufacturers' information (catalogues, data/information sheets)
- Ordnance Survey bench marks (OSBM)
- temporary bench marks (TBM)
- site datum.

Resources required for cavity walling and their working characteristics

The main resources needed for cavity walling are of course bricks and blocks. Both are available in several different types. The type you will need to use depends on the job to be carried out.

There are several factors that need to be taken into account when working with different resources. These are known as working characteristics. The main working characteristics that are likely to be important on most constructions are:

- insulation
- solar gain
- resistance to moisture
- resistance to fire.

Bricks and blocks

Most bricks and blocks have good fire resistance and provide thermal insulation, which is particularly important for cavity walling. Some are also designed to provide good resistance to moisture. The particular qualities of certain bricks and blocks are described below.

Clay bricks

These are the most common type of brick. There are three main types of clay brick.

- **Engineering bricks** – have a high compressive strength and low water absorption rates. They are rated either as class A or B, with A being the strongest. Class B bricks are sometimes known as **semi-engineering bricks**. They are ideal for use below ground level and for damp proof courses.
- **Facing bricks** – are literally the bricks that 'face' the person looking at the building. They give the building a good look and are designed to be to provide an attractive appearance. They are provided in a huge range of colours and sizes.
- **Common bricks** – have lower compressive strength and are lower quality than engineering or facing bricks. They are not decorative as no attempt is made to control their colour or appearance. They should only be used for internal brickwork.

Other types of brick

There are some other types of brick you will encounter.

- **Concrete bricks** – are similar to blocks and are available in several colours and patterns. These bricks deaden exterior noise and provide good fire protection and thermal insulation.
- **Sand lime bricks** – are decorative bricks sometimes used in place of facing bricks.

Blocks

There are two main types of block you will use:

- **Lightweight insulation blocks** – provide good insulation qualities and should be used above the DPC. This is particularly important for cavity walls.
- **Dense concrete blocks** – should be used up to the DPC.

Remember

Information about the storage of bricks can be found in Unit 2001 on page 23

Find out

There are several different types of design and quality of clay bricks available – use the Internet to research this by looking at the websites of leading manufacturers

Safety tip

Blocks have the same storage and potential hazards as bricks – make sure you are storing them safely and correctly, as well as using them correctly

Other resources

The other primary resources you will need for cavity walling are covered below.

- **Damp course** – used to prevent the penetration of damp.
- **Lintels** – placed above openings in brick and block walls to bridge the opening and support brick and block work above. They are made from concrete with a steel reinforcement placed near the bottom for strength.
- **Cavity frame liners** – fitted around openings and used to allow windows and doors to be fitted. They are fitted flush to the wall and covered by an **architrave**.
- **Cavity tray** – a moisture barrier placed above a window or door opening, designed to force moisture to flow away from the inner wall to the outer facing brick. The downward curve of the tray forces the moisture out and away from the interior of the house.
- **Wall ties** – these tie the internal and external walls together for a stronger job, adding stability to the structure.

Tools for cavity walling

The key tools used for cavity walling are:

- trowel
- pointing trowel
- hammer
- bolster
- lines and pins
- corner blocks
- pointing iron or jointer
- tape measure
- level.

K2. Erect cavity walling to required specification

Many of the skills you will need to use to erect cavity walling are identical to those used to construct solid walling. More information on these areas can be found on the following pages:

- identifying the position of bricks, blocks and other components (pages 165–166)
- methods of cutting and preparing components (page 166)

Key term

Architrave – these are decorative mouldings used to hide the gap between the frames and the wall finish. Skirting is a moulding that covers the gap between the floor and base of a wall

---

Remember

All tools need to be carefully maintained and positioned in an easy-to-access place near the job. When tools are not in use they should be locked away in a secure location to prevent theft

---

- methods of providing substructure and walling (pages 205–212)
- methods used to maintain industrial standards when erecting brick and blockwork (page 167)
- methods used for the provision of insulation requirements for cavity walling (page 177)
- methods of providing decorative features to masonry walling (pages 215–219)
- reasons for, and positioning of, vertical movement joints (page 179)
- types, uses and limitations of jointing and pointing (pages 223–228)
- purpose of protecting surrounding areas from damage arising from work activities (pages 167, 213)
- reasons for carrying out checks to confirm work conforms with instructions (pages 229, 230)
- when to carry out remedial work (page 229)
- why work needs to be accurate and meeting standards (pages 229–230).

How to construct cavity walls, including the provision of service entry and damp proof course

Cavity walls mainly consist of a brick outer skin and a blockwork inner skin. There are instances where the outer skin may be made of block and then rendered or covered by tile hanging. The minimum cavity size allowed is 75 mm, but the cavity size is normally governed by the type and thickness of insulation to be used and whether the cavity is to be fully filled or partially filled with insulation.

The thickness of blocks used will also govern the overall size of the cavity wall. On older properties, the internal blocks were always of 100 mm thickness. Nowadays, due to the emphasis on energy conservation and efficiency, blocks are more likely to be 125 mm or more.

In all cases, the cavity size will be set out to the drawing, with overall measurements specified by the architect and to local authority requirements.

Once the **foundations** have been concreted, the **footings** can be constructed, usually using blocks for both walls (see Figure 7.1).

> **Key terms**
>
> **Foundations** – concrete bases supporting walls
>
> **Footings** – brickwork between the foundation concrete and the horizontal damp-proof course (DPC)

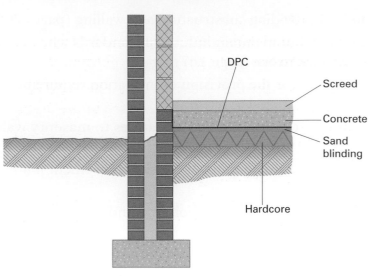

Figure 7.1 Section of footings

DPC

Screed

Concrete

Sand
blinding

Hardcore

Remember

The correct size must be
used for the internal wall,
with the cavity size to suit

Safety tip

One safety hazard that
is often forgotten when
working with cavity walling
is exposed wall ties. If wall
ties are left exposed higher
up on a wall, it is very easy
to catch your head on the
wall tie, cutting or injuring
yourself in the process

Key term

Bridge – where moisture
can be transferred from the
outer wall to the inner leaf
via material touching both
walls

In some situations trench blocks may be used below ground level
and then traditional cavity work constructed up to the damp proof
course (DPC). A horizontal DPC must be inserted at a minimum
height of 150 mm above ground level to both walls. This is to
prevent damp rising, below ground, up through the block and
brickwork to penetrate to the inside. The cavity must also be
filled with weak concrete to ground level to help the footing resist
the pressure of the soil against the external wall and oversite fill
material.

Erecting basic cavity walling

The older, traditional way to build a cavity wall is to build
the brickwork first and then the blockwork. Now, due to the
introduction of insulation into the cavity, the blockwork is
generally built first, especially when the cavity is partially filled
with insulation. This is because the insulation requires holding in
place against the internal block wall, by means of special clips that
are attached to the wall ties. In most cases the clips are made of
plastic so that they do not rust or rot. The reason for clipping the
insulation is to stop it from moving away from the blocks, which
would cause the loss of warmth to the interior of the building, as
well as causing a possible **bridge** of the cavity, which could cause
a damp problem.

The brick courses should be gauged at 75 mm per course but
sometimes course sizes may change slightly to accommodate
window or door heights. In most instances these positions and
measurements are designed to work to the standard gauge size.
This will also allow the blockwork to run level at every third
course of brick.

Providing substructure for service entry

Drainage was covered in detail in Unit 2045 on pages 140–146. Please refer back to this section for more information.

Where a pipe passes through a wall to enter the building, certain precautions are necessary to prevent damage to the drain:

- the wall above the pipe must be adequately supported to prevent any weight of the structure settling on the pipe
- a 50 mm gap should be maintained all around the pipe
- a rigid sheet material should be placed on both sides of the hole to prevent vermin entering the building and backfill entering the 50 mm clearance.

Safe working practices when erecting cavity walling at height and recommended heights of walling

It is recommended in the British Standards (BS 5628) that a single wall should not be raised more than six courses of blocks or 18 courses of bricks without being backed up by the opposite material in cavity wall construction. The health and safety issues related to the positioning of wall ties are the main reason for this. The ties will be set into the first single skin built and will therefore be a hazard while building the other cavity skin, as workers may catch themselves on them.

There is also the risk from the weather. High winds could damage a high wall or even cause it to collapse.

The needs of other trades

It is important when building masonry structures to take other trades into consideration. The measurements used to fit buildings in place need to suit the needs of other trades on site as well. It is also important to remember that it is very difficult indeed for two trades to work on the same part of the site at the same time. They need to work in the correct order, for example, a bricklayer couldn't start working in a kitchen site after the units had been installed. Sites need to be well organised so that trades are in the required places at the right time. Damage to materials used by other trades will have a negative impact on the project as a whole, even if it doesn't affect your work.

Figure 7.2 All trades need to work alongside each other in a clear and cooperative manner

The workers in these trades may be carrying out associated work after your trade has finished. So it is vital that you ensure, for example, that frames and openings positioned in walls are exactly plumb and square, opening heights are correct for fitting linings, wall plates are bedded level and parallel to the correct measurements to take roof trusses, etc. 'That will do' is not good enough!

K3. Form openings in cavity walling

Openings are put into walls in the form of door and window frames to allow entry and give natural light to a property. The frames can be made of wood, metal or uPVC. Whichever type of frame is used, the frame has to be secure to the wall.

Wooden frames

Wooden frames are bedded onto the wall using mortar with the brickwork, then built to the sides. Ties should be used to fix the frame to the brickwork to stop the frame from moving or even falling out. There are many different types of tie that can be used in this process. During construction of the wall, the frame should be held in place normally using timber or scaffold boards to stabilise it until the mortar has set. The back edge of the frame should sit flush with the back edge of the brick to help prevent dampness.

Metal frames

Metal frames usually come in either galvanised steel or aluminium and can either be built into the brickwork in the same way as wooden frames or incorporated into a wooden frame. If they are put in without a wooden frame, the sill is usually made of preformed reinforced concrete. Special ties are used to secure this to the brickwork.

uPVC frames

These are the most popular type used nowadays as very little maintenance is required after fitting. Made of reinforced plastic, this type of frame is fitted into completed brickwork, so the opening left has to be very accurate. The opening is usually formed by using a 'dummy frame', which is timber fixed to make a temporary frame 10 mm bigger than the size required. This allows expansion of the plastic once fitted. The uPVC frame is normally fitted by drilling through it into the finished brickwork and is then secured by means of plugs and screws. The gap left on the outside is then filled with expanding mastic to prevent water penetration, but allow expansion.

Did you know?

The number of frames and their sizes are calculated to meet *Building Regulations* according to the amount of light required for a room

Remember

In Scotland, in traditional construction of brick/block-work, the bricklayer will leave openings for doors and windows to be installed at a later date

Ayesha is building cavity walling for an extension. She has built the wall up to window sill height, but no windows are on-site. She has been told that uPVC windows are to be used.

What information does she need to carry on with the extension? The type of windows will have an impact on how she builds the wall, as she will need to make sure she is leaving the correct space for them, as well as making sure that the wall will be adequately supported.

Where could she get that information? Who should she consult if she has any problems? Ayesha will need to be familiar with the specifications as well as knowing who to talk to on-site.

When faced with a problem on-site, such as this problem with cavity wall construction, you will have the opportunity to practise the interpreting elements of functional skills. This includes FM 1.3.1: Judge whether findings answer the original problem; FM 1.3.2: Communicate solutions to answer practical problems.

Providing brick and proprietary sills

In some instances, openings in walls may have a decorative feature incorporated into them. The feature may blend with existing brickwork or be added to relieve a bland finish. It will also allow water to drain away and not penetrate under the frame sill. This can be achieved by using a brick on edge set at an angle, different types of tiles set at an angle or purpose-made concrete sills.

Whichever is to be used, you must be aware so that allowances can be made for any openings to be left. This is especially so when using dummy frames – you don't want to have to take down brickwork to accommodate the sill.

Bridging openings with steel and concrete lintels

Lintels are components placed above openings in brick and block walls to bridge the opening and support the brick and blockwork above. Lintels made from concrete have a steel reinforcement placed near the bottom for strength, which is why pre-cast lintels have a 'T' or 'Top' etched into the top surface. Pre-cast lintels come in a variety of sizes to suit different opening sizes.

When forming openings for windows and doors, manufacturers of the thin joint system recommend the use of either box type or combination type lintels. However, where a combination type lintel is used, this will need to be supported with props until the outer leaf is constructed to prevent the lintel tipping forward. It is also recommended that lintels be bedded using traditional mortar and joint thickness to allow for any discrepancies in the lintel measurements.

Steel box type lintel

Outer brickwork skin · Inner blockwork skin

Figure 7.3 Box type lintel in-situ

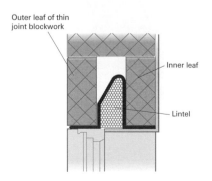

Outer leaf of thin joint blockwork

Inner leaf

Lintel

Figure 7.4 Combination type lintel in-situ

Damp penetration

Where openings are found in cavity walls, much care must be taken to prevent water or dampness from entering the building. The main areas of penetration are shown in Figure 7.5.

Main areas of penetration

A = The threshold of the doorway where rising damp from the floor can be a problem and the door itself can collect rainwater which runs down and collects at this point.

B = The sill of the window, which has to deal with any water that runs off the window itself.

C = The jambs area of the openings, the main problem here being the passage of moisture between the outer and inner skin of the cavity wall.

D = The head of the opening where a structural support is required; any water entering the cavity above the head must be prevented from sitting on top of the head and channelled to the outside.

We will now break down these areas and look at them in more detail.

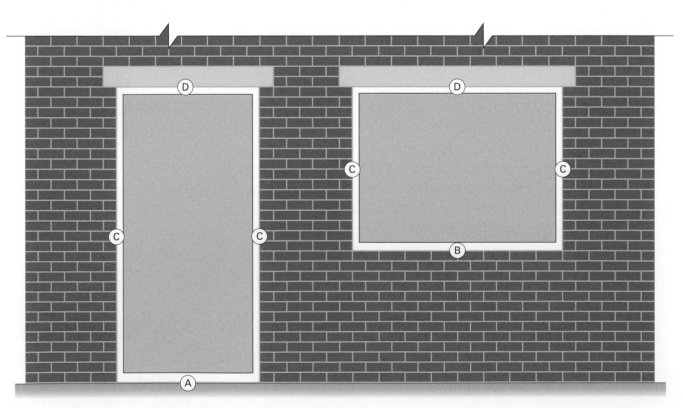

Figure 7.5 Damp penetration areas

At the threshold

The **horizontal DPC** prevents rising damp and the waterproof membrane under the floor prevents dampness rising into the concrete floor. The **cavity fill** slopes outwards to throw water that runs down the cavity towards the outer leaf and the sloping door sill throws water away from the door. All these points help prevent dampness entering the building at the threshold.

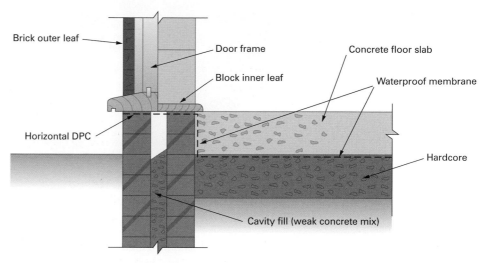

Figure 7.6 Section at threshold

At window sill level

Figure 7.7 shows a groove under the window sill. This is called the throating or drip and prevents water from running across the bottom of the sill. The brick on edge is sloping outwards to throw water outwards. It is bedded on a DPC to prevent the passage of damp or water at this point.

At the jambs

At jambs (the sides of frames), the penetration of damp can be prevented by a number of different methods. One method is the use of a **vertical DPC** (see Figure 7.8), placed at the back of the outer leaf, at the point where the inner leaf is returned to close off the cavity. If a vertical DPC is used, it must have a strip of insulation attached to it to avoid cold bridging.

> **Key terms**
>
> **Horizonal DPC** – a layer of impervious material (water will not pass through) built in a wall 150 mm minimum above ground level
>
> **Cavity fill** – concrete put into a cavity up to ground level
>
> **Vertical DPC** – a layer of impervious material placed up to the sides of openings in cavity walls to prevent the passage of moisture

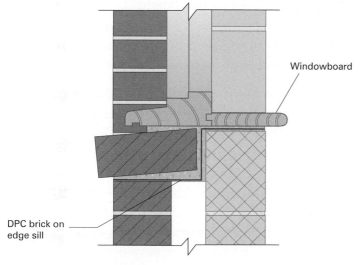

Figure 7.7 Section at sill level

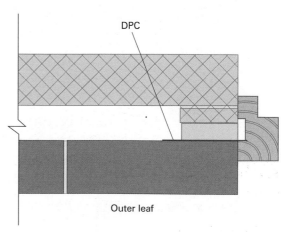

Figure 7.8 Jambs

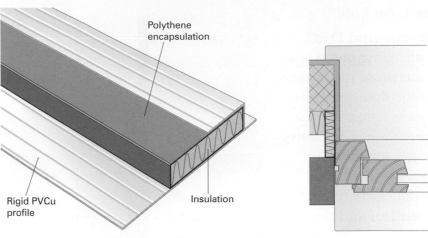

Figure 7.9 Using a PVC cavity closer at reveals

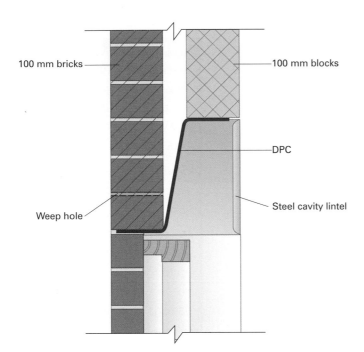

Figure 7.10 Head of frame

Cold bridging can cause condensation and mould growth at points such as window and door reveals. It can also cause heat loss from the building, particularly at these points.

Another common way to close cavity reveals is by using a cavity closer. These are made from PVC and consist of a strip of insulation enclosed by a PVC profile (see Figure 7.9). With this method, there is no need for the inner blockwork leaf to be returned to close the cavity, as this is done with the profile itself.

At head level

The top or 'head' of the frame has to be supported to carry the weight of brick and blockwork above this height. Therefore a lintel has to be positioned. The two main types of lintel used are usually 'Catnic' or 'IG' and in both instances a DPC tray must be used above to prevent water/moisture penetration.

With the 'Catnic', the central frame of the lintel slopes outwards to throw any water towards the outer leaf, where it is discharged through **weep holes** in the outer wall. The ends of the tray must be turned up (enveloped) to prevent the water running off the end and back down into the cavity. Both types of lintel are made of steel and must have a minimum end bearing of 150 mm and be the correct type to accommodate the width of the cavity used as well as the thickness of block. Manufacturers' catalogues show the ranges available with widths and lengths for easy ordering but the drawing specification will usually show the type required.

Key term

Weep holes – vertical joints left out in brickwork for water to run out

Steps to take to prevent damp penetration

- Set out openings carefully to avoid awkward bonds.
- Take care during construction to make sure damp or water does not enter the building.
- Wall ties and DPCs should be carefully positioned.
- Steel cavity lintels should have minimum 150 mm bearings solidly bedded in the correct position.
- Weep holes should be put in at 450 mm centres immediately above the lintel in the outer leaf.

No insulation has been shown in the drawings because they only show one situation. In most cavity wall construction, insulation of one kind or another will have to be incorporated to satisfy current *Building Regulations*.

> **Remember**
>
> You must read the drawings and specifications carefully to see what is required and always fix insulation to the manufacturers' instructions

Fire spread

In addition to the prevention of damp penetration and cold bridging, there is a requirement under the *Building Regulations* that cavities and concealed spaces in a structure or the fabric of a building are sealed by using cavity barriers or fire stopping. This cuts down the hidden spread of smoke or flames in the event of fire breaking out in a building.

Closing at eaves level

Cavity walls have to be 'closed off' at roof level for two main reasons:

- to prevent heat loss and the spread of fire
- to prevent birds or vermin entering and nesting.

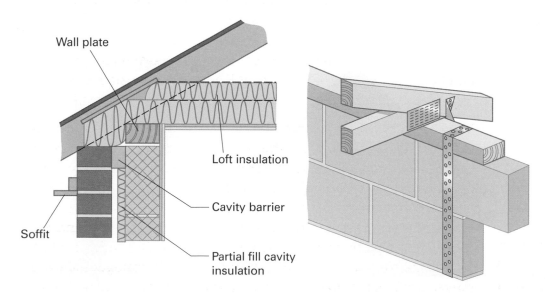

Figure 7.11 Roof section

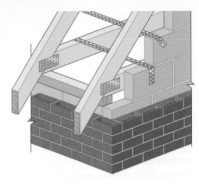

Figure 7.12 Roof section showing gable restraints

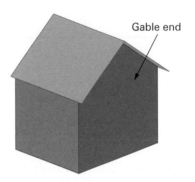

Gable end

Figure 7.13 Roof with gable

Key term

Corbel – several courses of bricks laid in front or behind the normal face line to produce a feature on a gable end

This area of the wall is where the roof is connected by means of a timber wall plate bedded onto the inner leaf. The plate is then secured by means of galvanised 'L' shaped restraint straps screwed to the top of the wall plate and down the blockwork. This holds the roof structure firmly in place and also prevents it from spreading under the weight of the tiles, etc. The straps should be secured at a minimum distance of 1.5 m apart. In some instances they may be connected directly from the roof truss to the wall.

If a gable wall is required, restraint straps should also be used to secure the roof to the end wall (see Figure 7.12).

The external wall can be built to the height of the top of the truss so as not to leave gaps or 'closed off' by building blocks laid flat to cover the cavity above the external soffit line from inside, avoiding damp penetration. In some instances, the cavity may be left open with the cavity insulation used as the seal.

Gable ends

A gable end is where the wall carries on above eaves level to 'fill in' the shape of the roof, usually in the form of a triangle (see Figure 7.13).

When constructing gable ends, there are three main considerations:

- how to start at the eaves
- how to maintain accuracy of the raking cut
- how to maintain plumb.

Starting at the eaves

Gable ends very often start with projected bricks or **corbels**, which fill in the void that is made by the eaves of the roof. Other materials, such as concrete or tiles, can be used at this point.

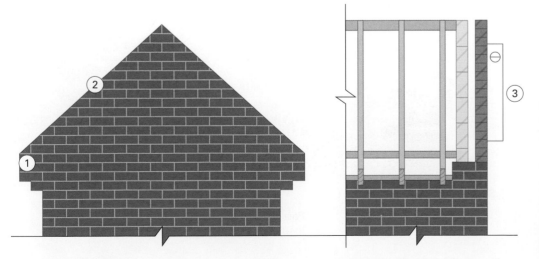

Figure 7.14 Three main considerations when constructing gable ends

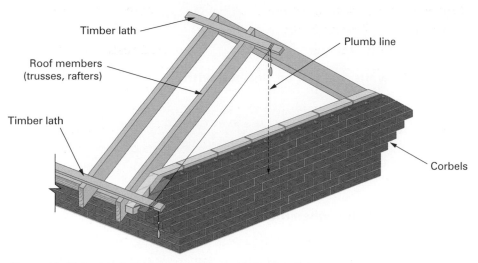

Figure 7.15 A plumb line should be used to maintain accuracy

Maintaining accuracy of the raking cut

Timber laths or battens are fixed to the roof trusses or rafters. The wall is plumbed up and marked on the top lath(s). A string line is then pulled between the laths to maintain the accuracy of the cutting line and maintain plumb.

Maintaining plumb

When constructing raking cuts on gable ends, the plumb point disappears as you progress so temporary plumb points called dead men can be used. These can be formed either by building bricks plumb or by fixing timbers and pulling a string line between them.

Did you know?

The gable may have a timber bargeboard with soffit, so cutting is not so critical as long as it is not above the roof line

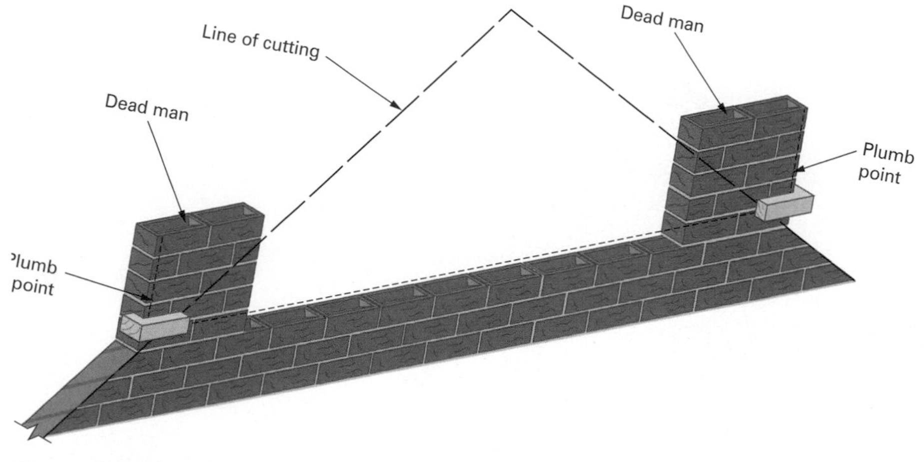

Figure 7.16 Dead men

FAQ

Can Aircrete blocks be used for external walls, but not be finished with render or cladding?

Yes, in certain instances, such as where the external wall is built very close to an existing wall and it is difficult to provide a finish. This new wall will not be too exposed to the elements and will be protected to a high degree by the shelter provided by the existing wall.

Why do I need to put a cavity tray above a lintel, when most trays have a lintel incorporated?

Lintels do not have end stops so any moisture can still run down the cavity causing dampness. A flexible DPC cavity tray placed into position will have the ends turned up to ensure any moisture runs out through the weep holes to the outside. This will prevent the encroachment of moisture.

Check it out

1. Draw a sectional view of a catnic lintel in place.
2. Explain, with the use of a sketch, how restraining straps are used on a gable.
3. Draw a corbel in relation to a gable end.
4. Explain why vertical DPC is used near frames.
5. Sketch a sectional view of a wooden window sill in relation to the surrounding brickwork. Describe what factors you will need to remember when building the brickwork.
6. Write a method statement which explains the process of how to set up a door frame ready for building to.
7. Sketch a diagram of a segmental arch and name all the parts. When are segmental arches used and why?
8. Explain why cavity barriers are used in construction. What benefits do these give to buildings?
9. List eight tools required to build cavity work. What are these tools used for? Describe when you would use them and any health and safety issues connected to these.
10. Explain how an arch centre is set in position. Prepare a method statement, with suitable diagrams, showing how this is assembled.

Getting ready for assessment

The information contained in this unit, as well as continued practical assignments that you will carry out in your college or training centre, will help you with preparing for both your end of unit test and the diploma multiple-choice test. It will also aid you in preparing for the work that is required for the synoptic practical assignments on cavity walls.

You will need to be familiar with:

- how to understand and work to drawings
- how to set out corners using different methods
- why it is important to carry out checks on measurements
- understanding the material and equipment required to build cavity walls
- how to find out and transfer different levels associated with setting out.

All these points will be needed for the synoptic test when carrying out the building of the different walls required. For example, for learning outcome three we have seen the methods used to form openings in cavity walling. This unit has described the methods used to form and bridge openings in masonry walling. You will need to use this knowledge to select the correct method to form openings for doors and windows in your walls, making provision for jambs, lintels and sills. You will need to select the correct arch style for your construction.

Many of the practical skills you will use when building cavity walls are very similar to those used in Unit 2047 to construct solid walls and piers. You will need to refer back to the information you learnt in this unit to complete any work accurately.

Before you start work on the synoptic practical test it is important that you have had sufficient practise and that you feel that you are capable of passing. It is best to have a plan of action and a work method that will help you. You will also need a copy of the required standards, any associated drawings and sufficient tools and materials. It is also wise to check your work at regular intervals. This will help you to be sure that you are working correctly, and help you to avoid problems developing as you work.

Your speed at carrying out these tasks will also help you to prepare for the time limit that the synoptic practical task has. But remember, don't try to rush the job as speed will come with practise and it is important that you get the quality of workmanship right. Check the marking list to ensure your tolerances are correct on the areas of plumbing gauge and levels as you progress. Professionally, you will need to report any problems to an authorised person.

Always make sure that you are working safely throughout the test. Make sure you are working to all the safety requirements given throughout the test and wear all appropriate personal protective equipment. When using tools, make sure you are using them correctly and safely.

Good luck!

Knowledge check

1 As work progresses, what can be used to stop mortar from bridging the cavity?

a) Core holds

b) Cavity tray

c) Insulation

d) Cavity batten

2 What is the maximum distance horizontally that walls ties should be set to?

a) 900 mm

b) 910 mm

c) 450 mm

d) 460 mm

3 Which of these is not a type of damp proof course?

a) Flexible

b) Semi-rigid

c) Semi-flexible

d) Rigid

4 What are the projected courses often used at eaves level or as features, called?

a) Soldiers

b) Gables

c) Corbels

d) Doglegs

5 What is normally used to maintain plumb when building a gable?

a) Level

b) Deadman

c) Straight edge

d) Optical level

6 What should be placed between hardcore and a concrete slab to avoid moisture penetration?

a) Vertical DPC

b) Horizontal DPC

c) Polystyrene

d) Polythene membrane

7 What type of floor uses beams and blocks?

a) Solid floor

b) Wooden floor

c) Concrete floor

d) Suspended concrete floor

8 What are inserted above cavity trays to allow water to discharge from the cavity?

a) Core holes

b) Weep holes

c) Test holes

d) Corbels

9 What is the maximum distance wall ties should be set vertically?

a) 450 mm

b) 460 mm

c) 900 mm

d) 910 mm

10 Which answer is incorrect when describing wall tie requirements?

a) Should be rust proof

b) Able to resist moisture

c) Must be flexible

d) Must be of sufficient strength

Index

Index